China and India

For my sisters: two of life's other great powers

China and India

Asia's Emergent Great Powers

Chris Ogden

polity

First published in 2017 by Polity Press

Polity Press
65 Bridge Street
Cambridge CB2 1UR, UK

Polity Press
350 Main Street
Malden, MA 02148, USA

ISBN-13: 978-0-7456-8986-9
ISBN-13: 978-0-7456-8987-6 (pb)

A catalogue record for this book is available from the British Library.

Library of Congress Cataloging-in-Publication Data

Names: Ogden, Chris (Christopher), author.
Title: China and India : Asia's emergent great powers / Chris Ogden.
Description: 1 | Cambridge, UK ; Malden, MA : Polity, 2017. | Includes
    bibliographical references and index.
Identifiers: LCCN 2016038445 (print) | LCCN 2016059761 (ebook) | ISBN
    9780745689869 (hardback) | ISBN 9780745689876 (paperback) | ISBN
    9780745689890 (Mobi) | ISBN 9780745689906 (Epub)
Subjects: LCSH: China--Foreign relations--21st century. | China--Military
    policy. | Strategic culture--China. | India--Foreign relations--21st
    century. | India--Military policy. | Strategic culture--Inida. | BISAC:
    POLITICAL SCIENCE / Globalization.
Classification: LCC JZ1734 .O44 2017 (print) | LCC JZ1734 (ebook) | DDC
    327.51--dc23
LC record available at https://lccn.loc.gov/2016038445

Typeset in 10.5/12 Sabon by Servis Filmsetting Limited, Stockport, Cheshire
Printed and bound in the United Kingdom by Clays Ltd, St Ives PLC

For further information on Polity, visit our website: politybooks.com

CONTENTS

ABBREVIATIONS

AIIB   Asian Infrastructure Development Bank
ASEAN   Association of Southeast Asian Nations
BJP   Bharatiya Janata Party
BRICS   Brazil–Russia–India–China–South Africa [grouping]
CAFTA   China–ASEAN Free Trade Agreement
CCP   Chinese Communist Party
CMAC   Central Military Affairs Commission (China)
CTBT   Comprehensive Test Ban Treaty
CYLC   Communist Youth League of China
DPRK   Democratic People's Republic of Korea
EEZ   exclusive economic zone
FDI   foreign direct investment
GATT   General Agreement on Tariffs and Trade
GDP   gross domestic product
IAF   Indian Air Force
IBSA   India–Brazil–South Africa Dialogue Forum
IMF   International Monetary Fund
INC   Indian National Congress
IOR   Indian Ocean Region
IR   international relations
LoC   Line of Control
MEA   Ministry of External Affairs (India)
MoFA   Ministry of Foreign Affairs (China)
NAM   Non-Aligned Movement
NDB   New Development Bank
NFU   no first use
NIEO   New International Economic Order
NPT   [Nuclear] Non-Proliferation Treaty

NSA	National Security Adviser (India)
NSC	National Security Council (India)
P5	Permanent Five [UN Security Council Veto Members]
PAP	People's Armed Police (China)
PLA	People's Liberation Army (China)
PLAN	People's Liberation Army Navy (China)
PMO	Prime Minister's Office (India)
PPP	price purchasing parity
PRC	People's Republic of China
RMB	renminbi
SAARC	South Asian Association for Regional Cooperation
SCO	Shanghai Cooperation Organization
SOE	state-owned enterprise
UNPKOs	United Nations Peacekeeping Operations
WTO	World Trade Organization

TABLES

ACKNOWLEDGEMENTS

It has been a pleasure to work again with Louise Knight at Polity on this project, with the capable assistance of Nekane Tanaka Galdos (and her predecessor Pascal Porcheron). I am grateful to Louise for her timely and erudite editorial advice, along with that of the various anonymous reviewers who provided valuable and discerning comments during the book's formative stage. I also wish to thank my postgraduate and undergraduate students in the School of International Relations at the University of St Andrews (variously taking IR3046, IR4528, IR4545 and IR5040), who – via our fervent discussions and arguments over the last five years – helped to critically gestate some of the key ideas present in this book, as well as Jascha Zittel, who carried out the initial literature review underpinning the volume. Finally, thank you to Sally Cummings, who back in 2010 initially planted the idea of comparing China and India as *emergent* great powers.

Edinburgh, September 2016

INTRODUCTION: GREAT POWER AND THE RISE OF CHINA AND INDIA

China and India's contemporary rise to prominence will significantly impact upon geopolitics over the coming decades. Providing a comparative analysis of their shared emergence as great powers within the international system, this book evaluates the impact of Asia's two largest powers upon the definition, delineation and nature of power politics. Focusing upon the factors integral to such a phenomenon (from both historical and theoretical perspectives), and through a wide-ranging analysis of our understanding/definition of great power, we will build up a comprehensive and detailed understanding of these two states' past, contemporary and future global significance. With their world-leading economic prowess, mounting military expenditures and increasingly heard – and sought after – diplomatic voices, both China and India are resolutely on the rise. As a key dimension of present-day international politics, it is the *shared* emergence of these two immense states that is also of particular significance, especially their geographical presence within the same – if highly complex – world region that is Asia. Their simultaneous analysis therefore not only provides us with an appreciation of their similarities and differences as they endeavour to fulfil a common goal, but also helps us to determine what great power represents and symbolizes in the twenty-first century – a century that appears set to be largely Asia-dominated and Asia-centric.

Within traditional Western paradigms, India and China are often expected to rise in much the same way as the current and previous great powers, primarily via the accumulation of traditional material and military measures. This volume strongly contends, however, that domestic political/cultural values and historical identities are central driving forces behind their mutual status ambitions and worldviews. Indicating as it does that both states will necessarily follow their own

1

Table 1   Percentage share of world GDP (1–2008)

	1	1000	1500	1700	1820	1900	1950	1975	2000	2008
China	25.5	22.7	24.9	22.3	32.9	11.1	4.6	4.8	11.8	17.5
Europe	13.7	9.0	17.8	21.8	26.6	34.2	26.2	25.1	20.6	17.1
India	32.0	27.8	24.4	24.5	16.0	8.6	4.2	3.3	5.2	6.7
Japan	1.1	2.6	3.1	4.1	3.0	2.6	3.0	7.6	7.2	5.7
Russia	1.5	2.3	3.4	4.4	5.4	7.8	9.6	9.4	3.5	4.4
US	0.3	0.4	0.5	0.8	1.8	15.8	27.3	21.1	21.9	18.6

Source: Maddison Project, 2013.

unique pathways to achieving great power status, the book argues that how their elites understand – and then attempt to realize – such a vision gains ever greater importance. With the current presence of ardently nationalist leaders in both China and India, in the form of, respectively, Xi Jinping and Narendra Modi, the acquisition of such a status, and the respect and esteem that it brings, is being openly pursued. Through regular exhortations, these leaders (and their many predecessors, if somewhat more reservedly) have declared their states to be in the world's top tier, with a global significance that cannot be ignored, and that they – just as other great powers have done – will shape our world. In turn, as our analysis will show, both India and China envisage a multipolar world order of several great powers, a perspective that differs from the common Western view of a dominant hegemon. At its core, this vision innately threatens the continued global dominance of the United States.

Crucially, as Kissinger notes, China 'does not see itself as a rising, but [as] a returning power, . . . [not] an unnatural challenge to the world order but rather a return to a normal state of affairs' (2012: 546). Much the same is true for India, whose leaders proclaim a willingness to rediscover a glorious past before their subjugation by colonial Britain, when they were also a power of global centrality. Their historical shares of world gross domestic product (GDP) over the long span from AD 1 to 2008 serve to highlight these historically rooted sentiments, as detailed in Table 1.

Common Conceptions of Great Power

Despite the prevalent usage of the term 'great power', there is little consensus within international relations (IR) concerning what elements constitute this status. Reflective of the central understandings of

IR's various theoretical approaches, which place a differing emphasis upon material and/or ideational aspects, the concept of great power – whilst generally assumed – remains inconsistent. As Levy notes, the 'widespread recognition of the importance of the Great Powers is not matched by analytical precision in the use of the concept' (1983: 10). Matching this uncertainty has been a proliferation of terms to describe those elite powers situated at the top of the hierarchy of international states, with great power being used interchangeably with 'major power', 'dominant power' or 'essential actor.'[1] These terms contrast with other labels, such as 'minor powers', 'regional powers' and 'small states', and serve to indicate difference and ordering, as well as relative superiority/inferiority – and exceptionality – among actors. Essential to the international system, and reflective of particular eras, great powers remain, however, the central actors without whom IR would not be what it is.

Whilst such centrality is undeniable, the abundance of terms to describe these top-tier actors has been accompanied by an ever-multiplying spectrum of elements deemed to be essential to their identification. Albeit dependent upon which scholarly perspective is undertaken, determining great power can thus be seen to rest upon an overall synthesis of multiple interconnected variables, criteria and indicators. As discussed below, this mixture encompasses both 'hard' and 'soft' power attributes representative of material (primarily objective) and perceptual (mainly subjective) characteristics. When taken in combination, great power is therefore 'an all-round characteristic with multiple determinants' (Buzan, 2004: 60). Besides capturing tangible and intangible elements, as IR has developed over time its remit has also broadened from solely covering traditional aspects such as war, conquest and trade to include non-traditional indicators like terrorism, environmental degradation and transnational crime. Pointing to mounting complexity, this combination of influences remains dependent upon structural factors – i.e. the nature of the international system and the dominant understandings underpinning these workings, as shaped by its constituent states – that are mutually constraining and co-constitutive.

This proliferation of reference points further underscores the contested nature of great power. Such debates largely oscillate between those scholars concerned with the preponderance of military power (realism in most of its forms) and those concerned with economic and

[1] In this volume, the term 'great power' will be utilized, despite sharing characteristics associated with 'major power'.

3

institutional power, including the provision of responsibility (most strands of liberalism). Other perspectives involve ideational sources of great power, which largely examine identities, norms and perceptions (various kinds of constructivism, along with classical realism). These latter approaches argue that such foundations act as intervening variables between states and their material capabilities, allowing for an approach that emphasizes domestic factors, history and values. An overview of these perspectives is detailed below, from which we identify four key prisms of analysis that will guide the analysis of the book's main chapters. Such elements are critical to our analytical focus on China and India, and will provide for a more state-specific approach towards the two entities. Moreover, this volume contends that our conception of great power is often illustrative of a particular point in time, thus acting as a historically contingent mélange of material and ideational understandings which echoes the distribution of myriad power sources in the international system. Great power is therefore adaptive in terms of its definition, its constituent actors and the global system it seeks to exemplify.

Material Capabilities

The intrinsic quality of a great power is that of being a self-sufficient state that is able to maintain its independence versus any other power, and meet its security needs (and those of allies) via its own capabilities. This self-reliance includes the safeguarding of national military, economic, territorial and ideational interests. For traditional realist conceptions of great power, this autonomy is based upon military power, which for offensive realists can be proactively used 'to put up a serious fight in an all-out conventional war against the most powerful state in the world' (Mearsheimer, 2001: 5). Such power is therefore both comparative and ranked, as a great power possesses a higher level of military capabilities relative to others. The global distribution of material (including economic) power is thus critical to the structural realist outlook. Within this outlook, which is emblematic of periods during which the conduct of war was a central feature, a link persists between great power status and war, and, by extension, varying types of military power. Some accounts hence emphasize land power as the means to conquer and control territory, whilst others stress sea power (especially for access, commerce and trade) and others air power, so as to expand the scope of conflict unrestricted by geography. To these types of military power can be added nuclear weapons as the 'sine qua non for major powers of the modern age'

4

(Danilovic, 2002: 46), although their wider proliferation can also dilute great power authority and increase global instability.

Such predominantly realist conceptions thus collectively rest upon an overall combination of various military power types, with large armies being supported by air and sea power capabilities, and so on. These power means have a spatial element, allowing great powers to project their influence beyond their borders, and to 'think of their interests as continental or global rather than regional' (Levy, 1983: 16). Great powers are heavily interconnected with the various states and regions of the world, and thus their status indicates a relational quality that allows them to influence and change the behaviour of smaller states. To capture this relational quality, several scholars have attempted to quantify (material) great power objectively. Thus, in assessing the great powers of the eighteenth and nineteenth centuries, Rothstein counts a state's infantrymen (1968: 14), while Modelski suggests that a great power holds at least 5 per cent of available military power in the global system (1974: 2). Significantly, these evaluations link to other kinds of power, with scholars stating that it is necessary for a great power to have more than 10 per cent of the system's available capabilities (see Geller & Singer, 1998). Interlocking with other factors, materialist accounts of great power thus recognize how controlling and increasing economic resources (initially coal, iron and steel but now technological production) augments such power. As such, the effective size of a state's military size is dependent upon the conversion of economic capabilities, in terms of its overall wealth, which is enhanced by having a large population that allows higher production.

This critical interconnection of one source of power with another highlights Robert A. Dahl's concept of 'culminative inequalities', whereby 'greater control over one resource, such as wealth, is closely related to greater control over most other resources, such as knowledge, social standing, military prowess and the like' (quoted in Modelski, 1972: 176). Moreover, economic power acts as a uniquely fungible entity that is translatable into other (including non-material) forms of power. Akin to military capabilities, the relative size of a state's economic resources vis-à-vis others can be crucial in determining its international status, particularly concerning its stage of development, and levels of self-sufficiency, innovation and technological capacity. These benefits are exponential, in that the industrial worker can produce more than the non-industrial worker, and capital resources can be subsequently invested to harvest more (economic) power. In an international system dominated by economics (in the current post-Cold War era), such power not only provides a means of diplomatic leverage against other states, but also readily converts into political power, whereby the richest states often have the greatest stake, voice and influence in the system. These states also commonly have high energy consumption rates, which forces them into the international system, both to satisfy their energy security needs and to find the markets/investment by which to pay for them – therefore interconnecting them with more states. In these ways, Paul Kennedy notes a 'causal relationship between the shifts . . . [in] economic and productive balances, and the position occupied by . . . [great] powers in the international system' (1988: xxiv).

Structural Centrality

Beyond delineating their status within the grouping of international states, scholars hence hold great powers to possess 'system determining' (Keohane & Nye, 1977: 295–6) properties. As critical lynchpins, and through their extra-regional presence – especially in the context of globalized trade – great powers have worldwide interests, and thus a central role within the dynamics of the international system, courtesy of their larger material capabilities. From this liberalist position, great powers are, furthermore, able to 'establish and enforce the basic rules and rights that influence their own behavior and that of the lesser states in the system' (Gilpin, 1981: 30), with their material capabilities translating into great power authority and system-ordering. Called upon at key historical junctures, such as at Vienna in 1815, Versailles in 1919 and Potsdam in 1945, or at other times of crisis, great powers use such opportunities to craft the world in their own image, thus shaping 'the parameters of life in the international system' (Bisley, 2012: 5). From this basis, which is context-specific, they have greater responsibilities than most other states concerning upholding international order, maintaining peace and security, and managing the global commons, and their influence is deemed indispensable for any negotiation to be effective and legitimate.

For these reasons, great powers can often be regarded as being 'structural powers' (Strange, 1987: 565–6), as they can determine certain values and understandings upon which the system functions. Such power – both materially (military and economic) and ideationally (values and beliefs, see below) – is 'architectonic' (Modelski, 1972: 152), including the creation of international institutions. By protecting key interests and values, multilateral and regional institutions can also act as a wider form of great power control or 'great power managerialism' (Bisley, 2012: 4–5). Such role-taking and role-making reflect a self-ascribed elite belief among great powers that their state is an actor that is essential to global affairs, and that they have the ability to define the international sphere: for example, using the agency garnered from their material power capabilities to furnish themselves with resultant international influence. This superiority also manifests itself in role-giving by smaller states towards perceived great powers, who recognize and identify them via the granting of special privileges, for instance the allocation of a permanent veto seat on the UN Security Council. Such a process involving multiple actors is collusive through a mutual acquiescence to shared goals, ambitions, visions and ordering, and is legitimized (and often legalized) by the practices of multilateral regimes. Identification in multilateral settings therefore bolsters the social recognition that gives great powers primacy, and crucially conjoins material and perceptual aspects of power. A mutual diplomatic need for partners/allies impacts upon this calculation for minor entities, which is itself dependent upon the wider distribution of material and (to a lesser extent) ideational power.

Values and Identity

A variety of other factors beyond military, economic and structural elements play into the designation and achievement of great power. As noted, a large population (and their relative level of development) has been considered paramount in relation to military and economic capabilities, especially in the modern era. In addition, we can consider a state's geographical position, especially topography (whereby natural barriers and size may aid national defence); climate; number and size of neighbouring states (including land and maritime border lengths); sea access; colonial assets; number of embassies; and access to – and control of – markets and trade routes. Crucially, attitudes towards the active taking of territory have largely shifted from the pre-1945 and colonial era, whilst globalization has deeply diminished the literal meaning of space and territory.

A state's dynamics are also critical in harnessing national power to its maximum potential, with internal cohesion and bureaucratic capabilities being intrinsic to great powerdom. Thus, political capacity, organization and development all depend upon the 'penetration of the national society by central governmental elites to control as many subjects/citizens as possible within the political jurisdiction of the state; and the capability of the government to extract resources from its society' (Organski & Kugler, 1980: 72). Internal stability and administrative effectiveness complement such capacities, and enhance the functioning of domestic infrastructures – civilian, military, intelligence and economic – for external purposes. As Morgenthau notes, 'the quality of a nation's diplomacy combines those different factors into an integrated whole' (1973: 146), while notions of strategic culture and grand strategy vitally inform such perspectives (see Chapter 2).

These understandings are largely antithetical to structural realists, who contend that international politics is determined by external not internal factors. Yet, as is more appreciated by classical realists and wholly embraced by constructivists, values, principles and national morale are inherently crucial measures of what a great power is. Central to such an assertion is that 'power is the production, in and through social relations, of effects that shape the capacities of actors to determine their circumstances and fate' (Barnett & Duvall, 2005: 42). Self-image is critical here, such that the aspiration to be a great power denotes a certain attitude, including a state's proactive demand for rights, acceptance of responsibilities and self-perception as a manager of the international system. Moreover, this self-asserted role-taking/role-making desire – among elites and their populations – rests upon an established worldview of gaining prestige and superior ranking vis-à-vis others, something that is very much evident within China and India. These contentions indicate a need for some essence of ego through which a state's status is proactively presumed, whereupon material capabilities intertwine with a perception of its self-importance.

Being a great power can therefore be regarded as an understanding – an ideational construct premised upon a selection of criteria that are often self-reflecting and self-validating, whereby 'to be a great power is to act like a great power' (Domke, 1989: 161). Thus, how the status of great power is *manifested* reflects inherently how the term is *conceived* and accepted by the comity of states. This conception then becomes embedded through consequent practices, international interactions and resultant (social/institutional/structural) understandings. As great powers have the most invested in the system, they have the largest stake in its overall interests, and hence they shape – and are integral to – the values upon which that system rests. However, just as the role-giving element essential to gaining pre-eminence in international regimes must come from others, so too must the social recognition of being a great power. This process highlights the role of perception and – notably for our analysis of China and India – expectations of future performance. Consequently, being a great power is 'a social category . . . [determined] by your peers in the club' (Hurrell, 2006: 4). Such recognition and acceptance act as a form of socialization for emergent great powers, confirming the efficacy of our constructivist analysis. Most critically, existing great powers have the 'capacity to extend or withhold legitimacy' (Singer & Small, 1972: 21) to would-be, aspirant or potential great powers, and such contender states may also often purposely play 'recognition games' (Ringmar, 2002) in order to gain the approval of others by conforming to their values.

To reiterate, great powers are thus 'differentiated from other states by others' images and perceptions of them' (Levy, 1983: 17). Whilst great power status is based upon either actual or imagined (present or future) material capabilities, it is the values, principles, norms and perceptions of the state under question – and the history that helps shape these – that is of significance. These values help form a great power's self-conception, its understanding of what it is to be a great power, the significance it places on particular attributes, and – by extension – the very nature of institutions that it may form. They also influence its outlook concerning the essence of the international system, and overall the system reflects the dominant values *within* that system. Such an emphasis on values – in conjunction with social recognition and their role in making international regimes – leads us to a further (great) power type, that of soft power. Typically defined as 'the ability to get what you want through attraction rather than coercion or payments . . . [via] a country's culture, political ideals, and policies' (Nye, 2004: x), soft power is non-material and ideational in content. The acceptance by others of a projected worldview, and its incumbent values, hence acts as a further form of international legitimacy, which great powers can use to significantly shape the behaviour of others – both diplomatically and popularly, if it gains global credence. Some scholars note, however, that soft power's efficacy is limited if seen in isolation, since principles and norms 'can be extremely effective [but only] if translated into blood and iron' (A.J.P. Taylor, 1952: 44). Such remarks verify how power capabilities are vigorously interconnected when defining/making great power.

Evaluating China and India

From this appraisal, our consideration of China and India as emergent great powers rests upon the understanding that 'while the great power function may appear to be a "natural" feature of international

9

relations, it is in fact the product of specific historical, material and ideational processes, and as such is always subject to change' (Bisley, 2012: 10). Whilst recognizing that power has material and ideational aspects, this volume deploys a largely constructivist outlook that focuses upon state-specific (and primarily domestically derived) values, norms and identities as essential intervening variables between a state and its hard power /material capabilities. On this basis it is argued that power cannot be reduced solely to its material elements, and that the state itself must be acknowledged as a key factor concerning what we mean by, and what constitutes, great power. This volume's initial focus on domestic determinants and strategic cultures underlines this centrality. Acknowledging that great power is inherently difficult to measure empirically, we thus utilize a 'very broad understanding of power, . . . rather than the narrow understanding of politics that realism stands accused of adopting' (Williams, 2005: 109), so as to show its core complexities.

Our approach also seeks to be multi-dimensional, multi-relational and interlinked, as previously shown by the grouping of factors together by other scholars. In this regard, Danilovic notes 'Three Dimensions': material capabilities, spatial scope and formal/informal status (2002: 28). Domke also has three factors: that a state will not concede to others; has global interests; and will 'pick on small powers when expedient' (1989: 161–2). In turn, Levy focuses on 'Five Elements': military capabilities; global not regional interests; behaving like a great power; being perceived by others as being great; and being recognized in international institutions (1983: 16–18). Waltz, meanwhile, has 'Five Criteria'; 'size of population and territory, resources endowment, economic capability, military strength, political stability and competence' (1979: 131). Finally, Nayar and Paul's 'Ten Virtues' provide the fullest set of measures: four 'hard' – military, economics, technology and demographics – and six 'soft' – norms, culture, leadership of international forums, state capacity, strategy and diplomacy, and national leadership (2003: 32). These best mirror IR's gradual genesis to include material, institutional and ideational sympathies, which this book's chapters collectively reflect.

Our analysis of China and India further embraces the historical particularism associated with the identification, prevalence and nature of great powers. Crucially, Paul Kennedy's observation that 'economic shifts heralded the rise of new Great Powers' (1988: xxii) points to the current importance of the rise of India and China (see Chapter 4). It also underscores the significance of relative/relational power distributions, whereby a change in economic rank changes the overall international hierarchy. These assertions are supported by the growth, decline and shifting of global power centres over time: from Ming China, the Ottoman Empire (and its Muslim offshoot in India, the Mughals), Muscovy, Imperial Japan and European states in 1500; to a Eurocentric focus upon France, Britain, Russia, Austria and Prussia from 1660 to 1815; then to the vast land powers of the twentieth century – the United States and the Soviet Union – and rising challengers Germany (pre-1945), Japan, China and the European Union. This process crucially involves a 'lag time' between when economic strength is gained and when it is converted into great power (P. Kennedy, 1988: xxv). Such shifts also reflect diverse trade and manufacturing foci: from the Mediterranean to northwest Europe and the Atlantic from the 1500s onwards; from Europe to the world in the 1880s; from developed to developing states in the 1980s and 1990s; to China and India from the 2000s onwards.

Prisms of Analysis

From this foundation, this book deploys four key analytical prisms with which to study China and India's contemporary rise as Asia's emergent great powers in the early twenty-first century. Importantly, they allow our study to encompass structural, behavioural and evolutionary axes *at the same time*, so as to produce an exact appreciation of these states' key temporal dynamics.

Interconnection

Collectively highlighting tangible, structural and subjective quotients, the myriad variables central to great power are seen as being intimately interconnected. Such a synergy highlights a key constructivist assertion that the international system and its component states interact in a co-constitutive manner, and hence mutually influence each other. This focus also shows how both India and China's internal/external – and domestic/international – spheres are in a constant interplay with each other, across their relative material, institutional and ideational tenets.

Perception

Since various factors – as well as states and the international system – are intertwined, how they interact with each other is also critical. Here the role of perception, especially in terms of social peer recognition and legitimacy, is paramount and occurs across the self/other dyad in an oppositional, dialectical and shared fashion. Simultaneously indicating similarity *and* difference, it importantly indicates how China and India view the international system (as well as their place within it) and other (great) powers, as well as how these understandings foster commonality and disparity.

Evolution

Developing across different historical periods and various structural environments, great power – as a definition, behaviour and prevailing condition – is constantly evolving. History is central to this process, as states interact with each other via experience, learning and understanding – all of which are core constructivist premises. This focus allows for the analysis of the key values central to a state's security policy, as well as confirming how they change over time – along with the rules/practices of the international system, and our very definition/the nature of great power itself.

Commonality

The (often surprisingly similar) experiences, outlooks, desires and values of China and India, which have risen within close proximity of each other, are instructive concerning the past, contemporary and future delineation of great power. As two post-imperial Asian great powers, how these states behave – and, more critically, how they are perceived by others – will inherently impact the functioning and essence of the international system as the twenty-first century progresses. If seen through either a lens that is traditional (Western) lens, new (Asian) view or a selective hybrid, in whose image will they emerge? And what will be the resultant global/regional consequences?

Structure

After this assessment of differing orientating concepts/approaches from IR, the volume evaluates key domestic political determinants (Chapter 1), before considering strategic thinking in China and India (Chapter 2), and the military and nuclear dimensions for each state (Chapter 3). It then analyses how the rise of the two states has been driven by their contemporary economic prowess (Chapter 4), before moving on to investigate their respective peripheral relations and regional statuses across South Asia (India) and East Asia (China) (Chapter 5). Interactions with international society and multilateral institutions (Chapter 6) and with the current international system's most significant actor – the United States (Chapter 7) – are then detailed. Lastly, in the Conclusions, each chapter's findings are synthesized to produce an evaluation of China and India's current and future international positioning, as well as their impact upon the essence and definition of great power. At all stages, the reader is informed, in a clear and direct manner, of relevant empirical/theoretical perspectives regarding how best to conceptualize the foreign and security policies of both states, as well as how their behaviour/interaction resonates with, complements and enhances current debates on great power within IR.

1

DOMESTIC DETERMINANTS

Here, we focus upon how, where and by whom foreign policy is constructed in China and India. Our initial focus upon domestic factors, structures and understandings should not obscure their centrality to ideational great power accounts concerning how states conceive, make and deliver foreign policy. Such an importance also interlinks the domestic and international spheres, indicating how foreign policy is specific to states and institutions, and represents 'the substance of a nation's efforts to promote interests vis-à-vis other nations' (Christopher Hill quoted in Gupta & Shukla, 2009: 2). Rather than overlooking domestic factors, as materialist and realist accounts predominantly do, the interplay between different elites – either as individuals or as groups – and the nature of the international system are underscored. This approach echoes Modelski's definition of foreign policy as 'the system of activities evolved by communities for changing the behavior of other states and for adjusting their own activities to the international environment' (1972: 6).

Comprising assemblages of internal values, central understandings and policy precedents that are reflective of a particular state's international interaction, foreign policy is thus conditioned, regulated and even restricted by its domestic context. Historically contingent, a state's self-conception is transmitted from generation to generation of political elites and leaders, further underlining how critical it is that a state's domestic political features are examined. On this basis, 'shared meanings and intersubjective structures can be as important in shaping international outcomes as material interests' (Nicholas Onuf quoted in Fierke, 2007: 3). The domestic also retains a critical significance for the maintenance of any leader's legitimacy, position and political centrality. With regard to our two subject states, which are

14

developing, modernizing, post-colonial states that desire to be great powers, such a dynamic is of particular contemporary significance.

The chapter begins with an exposition of how Beijing and New Delhi's political systems function, and outlines their key governing structures (both legislative and executive). Here, an analysis of the decision-making process and its generational evolution – in democratic India and authoritarian China – is included. We discuss the viewpoints of major political parties in both states concerning foreign policy, and their various ideological biases, before considering the role of each entity's bureaucrats. The chapter then evaluates the growing and diversifying non-governmental influences upon foreign policy-making, in particular from expanding indigenous security communities, as well as expanding discussion via mass media. It concludes with some deliberation concerning nationalism as a foreign policy issue that links together China and India's relative internal and international spheres.

Core Political Dimensions

Domestic institutional political capabilities are the means by which states implement their political agendas internally and, through specific foreign policy-making regimes, externally. Setting themselves apart from lower-tier states, and in order to lay claim to being a great power, they must have the 'willingness and ability to promote [their] interests further abroad' (Lanteigne, 2013: 21), which requires a combination of high institutional capabilities and political volition. A better understanding of a state's central political dimensions also underpins the key constructivist notion that 'identities are at the basis of interests' (He, 2009: 117). This greater appreciation of intangible factors – such as ideology – also acknowledges not only that Western ideologies and concepts are irrevocably coupled with (most) current notions of what constitutes a great power (Suzuki, 2008: 51), but also that, as India and China emerge to prominence, their specific values (in isolation and perhaps collectively) will gradually challenge this preponderance.

There is a 'negligible separation' in China's authoritarian political system 'between the apparatus of government and the structure of the CCP' (Lanteigne, 2013: 24), the Chinese Communist Party, which is the country's paramount political actor. In an essentially one-party state that is highly centralized, hierarchical and subservient, the CCP controls all major institutional appointments via a *nomenklatura* system based upon fixed vertical transition, which runs in tandem with the governance structure. The CCP therefore sees itself as providing the 'political leadership of the country' (Brown, 2013: 6–7) – a central position it has enjoyed since the consecration of the People's Republic of China (PRC) in 1949. Enshrining such a position has resulted in the strong state-led (and hence CCP-led) nature of modern Chinese politics, economics, foreign affairs and societal issues as a whole. The CCP has also sought periodically to consolidate its political supremacy, most notably during the Cultural Revolution of the late 1960s, when its founding leader, Mao Zedong, first demolished, and then rebuilt, most state and party apparatuses.

Born out of the aftermath of the rebellions, ethnic tensions, myriad instabilities and economic crises of the 1800s that culminated in the nationalist revolution of 1911, the CCP came into being in the 1920s. This period was also punctuated by China's crushing defeats by Britain in the Opium Wars of 1839–42 and 1856–60, and by Japan in the 1894–5 Sino-Japanese War (and later its full invasion of China in 1937), as well as unfair trade concessions given to the United States, France and Germany. China's international stature was consequently seen by the CCP to be debased, as personified by its negative treatment under the Treaty of Versailles of June 1919, which transferred German-occupied portions of Shandong to Japanese control. It was protests against the Treaty that led to the anti-imperialist 1919 May Fourth Movement, and inspired the 1921 formation of the CCP. Collectively these events constituted a 'Century of Humiliation' (*bainian guochi*) for China, and spurred Mao to urge it to 'stand up' again in the international system (D. Scott, 2007). The CCP would base its legitimacy to rule upon defeating Japan in 1945, and winning the subsequent civil war against the nationalist Kuomintang that ended in 1949, which led to a generation of war-hardened leaders who would influence the party until the 1990s.

China's past helped shape the bedrock upon which the CCP's foreign policy and self-image would be based. Indicating that power relations and perceptions of threat dictate policy, Mao stated his aim to have his 'poor country . . . changed into a rich country, [and from] a country denied her rights into a country enjoying her rights' (quoted in Lewis, 1963: 261). The CCP's long revolutionary history was also instructive in forming its central organizational tenets. Based upon Leninist principles, and thus having a structure akin to that of the Soviet Communist Party, its organization was underpinned by three critical notions: democratic centralism (whereby binding decisions, which must be implemented, are made by a small number of

16

leaders); minority protection (through which views can be held and voiced, and all decisions are based upon consensus); and, in the post-Mao era, collective leadership (to avoid over-concentrating power in one individual). Additionally informed by a traditional Chinese worldview, these approaches synthesized, leading to a China-specific 'Sinification of Marxism' (Nathan & Ross, 1997: 33).

With over 85 million members (*Xinhua*, 2013), the CCP is the world's longest ruling political party and, overall, the world's second largest political party (the first being India's Bharatiya Janata Party, BJP). There are also currently over 86 million members in the Communist Youth League of China (CYLC), and competition to join the party remains high, with the CCP accepting only 14 per cent of the 21 million applications made to it in 2010 (BBC, 2011). CCP membership thus provides representation and core benefits to over 6.2 per cent of the population (and to an additional 6.3 per cent if CYLC members are included) – benefits that permeate to family members and relatives. CCP members dominate positions within public institutions, as realized by the concurrent nature of the CCP and the Chinese government in a party-state model, resulting in a necessary, mutual and complementary dynamic through which a proportion of the population has a vested interest in continued CCP governance. The position of 'princelings' (*gaogan zidi* – the offspring of senior CCP leaders, including Xi Jinping) also underlines the continuance of CCP rule from one generation to the next. In recent years, the CCP has diversified its membership based upon myriad different backgrounds, ages, geographical foci, (foreign) education and interpersonal connections (*guanxi*). The party has also accepted capitalists since 2001, reflecting China's fiscal liberalization since 1978 and the centrality of economic growth to its current legitimacy (see Chapter 4). This diversification indicates a crucial need for political consensus-building, so as to avoid 'the same fate as communist parties further west' (Susan Shirk quoted in Breslin, 2009: 821).

Modern India's political system, make-up and core attitudes are also heavily influenced by its colonial experiences prior to gaining independence in 1947, and India is, in many ways, a state based upon promoting a post-colonial identity. Many of its key initial leaders – such as Mahatma Gandhi and India's first Prime Minister, Jawaharlal Nehru – were veterans of the struggle to end three centuries of imperial domination under the British East India Company and then the British Raj. India's largest contemporary political parties – the Indian National Congress (INC) and the above-mentioned BJP – both date from the pre-1947 period, with the former formed in 1885 and the latter's Hindu nationalist roots also taking hold around the same time. Both parties played major roles in the political emancipation struggle from the British – experiences that would impact upon their foreign policy approaches and attitudes concerning achieving political independence and self-determination against external threats (see Ogden, 2014a: 21–74).

The British Empire left a range of legacies for modern India. Domestically, India's political and judicial systems both bear the hallmarks of British imperial rule, especially in terms of the workings of India's multi-party democracy, which is based upon first-past-the-post elections and has upper and lower houses (the Rayja Sabha and Lok Sabha, with 245 and 545 members, respectively). The general election of 2014 was the world's largest democratic exercise to date, with an overall turnout of 66.3 per cent of India's 834 million eligible voters (ECI, 2015). In addition, India is a sovereign republic with a President as head of state but executive power resting with the Prime Minister and cabinet, and it has a non-monarchical federal parliamentary form of governance, as well as an independent judiciary, a single electorate and ostensibly guaranteed social and political rights. The INC's last Prime Minister, Manmohan Singh (2004–14), saw Indian's long-standing Asian democracy as 'an international public good' (quoted in Zakaria, 2009) that enhanced his state's global standing. Perhaps more negatively, other British legacies include intractable territorial conflict with Pakistan concerning Kashmir, and India's perceived dominance over its smaller neighbours and the wider Indian Ocean Region (as all detailed in Chapter 5).

The sustention of domestic legitimacy has also motivated generations of post-1947 Indian leaders. Within 'a political culture which privilege[s] the concept of national autonomy' (Ganguly & Pardesi, 2009: 5), successive Prime Ministers have sought to protect, foster and enhance India's domestic and international standing. A range of key principles have underpinned this approach, serving to embody certain characteristics in India's political system which are frequently reflective of past interaction. These include striving for an anti-majoritarian and secular (meaning universal and inclusive) body politic, based upon equality, tolerance and liberalism, whereby a 'dream of unity has occupied the mind of India since the dawn of civilization' (Nehru, 1946: 55), notwithstanding its highly varied ethnic and religious make-up. Directly related to anti-colonial and anti-imperial stances, and affording India a particular global uniqueness, Manmohan Singh has further noted that 'nowhere else will you find a country of India's diversity, of India's complexity, one billion people

18

trying to seek their social and economic salvation in the framework of democracy' (quoted in Rose, 2006).

Although now essentially resembling a fully matured political entity, for the majority of the post-independence period the INC dominated India's democratic process, resulting in a distinctive Nehruvian legacy. Winning all elections except one between 1947 and 1996, overall the party was victorious in eleven of India's sixteen general elections up until 2014. The 1998–2002 National Democratic Alliance led by the BJP was the first full-term government not led by an INC Prime Minister, and it was only with Narendra Modi's overwhelming triumph for the BJP in 2014 that India saw, for the first time, an alternative political entity gain an absolute parliamentary majority. The BJP itself slowly rose to prominence in the 1980s in the midst of a general proliferation of political actors and organizations across India, including the emergence of a host of smaller regional, state and caste-based parties, along with the persistent presence of several communist groups. In March 2015, BJP membership reached 88 million, making it, as noted, the world's largest political party, although doubts persist about the rigourousness of its application process and assessment, particularly in comparison with the CCP (Balachandran & Dutta, 2015). In contrast, in March 2015, the INC had 40 million members (Phukan, 2015), which equates to 3.2 per cent of India's total population versus the 7.0 per cent now represented by the BJP.

Generational Evolution

Whilst both states have displayed a relative consistency through one-party rule in China and multi-party democracy in India, the style in which their foreign policies have been conceived and delivered has evolved over time. Reflective of the role of leaders in delineating policy attributes, often in conjunction with key pre-independence experiences, such a focus emphasizes how 'the most directly relevant [factor] to a decision maker's perception of international relations is international history' (Jervis, 1969: 470). Further accentuating our concentration upon how ideational sources develop, change, shift and progress, this approach underscores how culture and identity are 'important causal factors that help define the interests and constitute the actors that shape national security policies and global insecurities' (Katzenstein, 1996: 537). Again, this emphasis highlights the interconnection between domestic and international spheres, and how they mutually constitute and influence each other within the sphere of foreign policy.

Driven by an overt, explicit and idealistic strain of internationalism, India's first Prime Minister and primary architect of Indian foreign policy, Jawaharlal Nehru, envisaged a world order based on peace, harmony, cooperation, development and equality. Also acting as India's first External Affairs Minister, Nehru governed in an era of big personality politics, with Edward Shils noting that 'few men so intellectual by disposition occupy comparable positions in any countr[y]' (quoted in Power, 1964: 261). Unswervingly informed by India's colonial subjugation under the British, along with a desire to increase its national prestige, Nehru stated: 'I want neither Western nor Eastern domination . . . if we have no weapons we will fight with sticks, but will not submit to being bullied by anybody' (quoted in Ralhan, 1983: 232). This enlightened national self-interest encapsulated a broader policy of *purna swaraj* – complete independence and self-rule – which directly informed anti-colonial, anti-imperial and pro-democracy principles.

India's new elites also emphasized core principles of non-violence (*ahimsa*), economic self-reliance (*swadeshi*) and positive neutralism away from great power politics. This latter value would inform a policy of non-alignment (see Chapter 6). Designed to ensure that India's voice be heard, rather than being neutral or removed from international affairs, non-alignment was an attempt to position India apart from the bipolar dynamics of the Cold War period. Simultaneously protecting yet projecting India's core values, these perspectives critically informed its foreign policy, and – especially in terms of building up military capabilities – restrained more materially constituted power quotients. Such initial values were also to be held up as an example for others, as its elites regarded India as 'the only stable and progressive nation in the whole of Asia, and as such . . . the natural leader of Asian countries . . . the potential power of India is well realized by the world' (Nehru quoted in Wolpert, 1996: 446). In these ways, India's key foreign policy tenets not only informed its conduct in the decades immediately after independence but also were intended 'to create implicitly the scope and space for a major-power role, if not now, at least in the future, when capabilities matched the ambition' (Nayar & Paul, 2003: 127). Democracy added a further dimension, although not in a necessarily forceful or proactive manner, whereby instead 'the Indian experiment gains meaning and significance in its relevance to two-thirds of humanity, for whom the virtues of freedom and of the rule of law have yet to be proven and tested' (Indira Gandhi quoted in Government of India, 1973: 468). After India's humiliating defeat in a border war with China in 1962 and Nehru's death in 1964, Indian foreign policy, however, became less idealistic and more based upon *realpolitik*, as personified by his daughter, Indira Gandhi (Prime Minister, 1966–77 and 1980–4), and subsequent generations.

Although remaining as a 'free agent that will carefully shepherd its autonomy without entering into security or diplomatic agreements that might curtail its freedom of action' (Narang & Staniland, 2012: 90), India's diplomatic engagement became less passive and more proactive during the 1980s under Indira Gandhi and her son Rajiv. By the 1990s, with the structural constraints of the Cold War having been removed, and India slowly embracing liberalist economic principles after decades of inward-looking autarkic socialism, pragmatic realism via multi-pronged diplomacy typified Indian foreign policy. Although not entirely replacing Nehruvian idealism and its core associated principles, which were downplayed rather than obviated, there was 'a new India . . . ready to question these shibboleths and take decisions on the basis of national interest' (Brajesh Mishra quoted in Mohan 2004: 14). India also became more appreciative of the benefits of diplomacy in a globalized age and less wary of the international system. As a result, New Delhi sought enhanced trade and energy security ties to fuel economic growth, *en route* to developing/modernizing the state, cultivating defence and multilateral capabilities, and ultimately restoring India's great power status within the international system. The Hindu nationalist BJP especially subscribed to this last aim, with Narendra Modi stating to his supporters; 'I assure you that this country has a destiny' (quoted in *Indian Express*, 2014).

Elements of continuity and evolution culminating can also be seen in different generations of CCP leadership under Mao Zedong, Deng Xiaoping, Jiang Zemin, Hu Jintao and Xi Jinping. Marked by both pride in China's great civilizational past *and* humiliation at the hands of external powers, a focus upon ensuring stability and control typified successive leaders, guided by the perception of a 'traditional sovereign-centric, autonomous major power identity' (Johnston & Evans, 1999: 252). Moreover, as Mao remarked in the early 1950s, 'we decided to make self-reliance our major policy and striving for foreign aid our secondary aim' (1998: 155). Propagating images of China as being a victim of foreign aggression, a socialist country and an opponent of hegemony underscored this position, along with a defiance of the dichotomous bipolar Cold War conflict between the system's two superpowers (the United States and the Soviet Union).

Through these actions, a foreign policy 'identity emerge[d] in how the policy making elite perceive[d] and articulate[d] the image of China in its relationship with the outside world' (Whiting, 1995: 296).

Additionally reflecting their struggle of the preceding twenty-five years, the foreign policy of the PRC under its earlier leaders was highly activist in nature. Dominated as China was by charismatic revolutionary leaders, most prominently in the form of Mao but also his eventual successor Deng, there was a major initial ideological basis to foreign policy-making, which mirrored the totalitarian nature of its domestic politics until the early 1980s. Bolstered by anti-imperial and anti-colonial sentiments, as well as its own domestic political success, Beijing actively exported its revolution by supporting various radical movements, which became a central foreign policy goal to increase its political influence across Asia, Africa and Latin America. The 'Five Principles of Peaceful Coexistence', as elucidated by Zhou Enlai in 1954, accompanied these actions. Espousing respect for territorial integrity and sovereignty; non-aggression; non-interference in another state's internal affairs; equality and cooperation for mutual benefit; and peaceful coexistence, they would influence Chinese foreign policy for at least the next sixty years.

Pursuing such ideological dogmatism meant that Beijing was met with 'exclusion, discrimination, and distrust by the US and its allies' (Yong, 2008: 36), leading China to be highly isolationist and have restricted relations with only pro-communist states. Recognizing the limits of such an approach, which left the PRC disadvantaged internationally and had culminated internally in the chaotic years of the Cultural Revolution, after Mao's death in September 1976 Deng initiated a focus on liberal economic growth (see Chapter 4). Designed to create national prosperity so as to enhance internal stability, re-legitimize the CCP's political power and augment China's global standing, his reforms prompted the state to lose its ideological 'straitjacket' (Shirk, 2007: 15). Such an emphasis was also seen as the key means to overcome the weaknesses of the Century of Humiliation. As China gradually integrated itself into the global economy so as to pursue trade, market and investment opportunities, its foreign policy became less revolutionary, and more pragmatic, conservative and impartial, leading to the 'evolution of status quo interests in ... the post-Mao drive for economic modernization' (Johnston & Evans, 1999: 237).

On this basis, subsequent generations of leaders consolidated their focus on gaining economic growth, not only to foster internal prosperity and legitimacy but also to sustain a stable periphery across

East Asia (see Chapter 5). Jiang and Hu were also regarded as being more technocratic, bureaucratic and consensus-orientated than the 'personalistic and top-down pattern of decision-making' (Glaser & Saunders, 2012: 598) of the Maoist and Dengist eras, which had not emphasized ministerial and bureaucratic consultation. Similar to the downplaying of Nehruvian idealism in India, the influence of ideology thus transformed 'from a manual to something more like a catalogue from which the leadership can "order" those items which suit its purposes' (Robinson & Shambaugh, 2004: 45). As such, Chinese foreign policy came to display deep-seated elements of pragmatism. Furthermore, the leader of the fifth generation of the CCP, Xi, appeared to inject a much more assertive strand into China's foreign policy principles, especially concerning his visions of a 'China Dream' and of a 'China Renaissance', both of which are premised upon a return to being a great power through the attainment of economic (and military) strength.

Key Sources of Foreign Policy-making

Regardless of greater consultation under the post-Dengist leadership generations, and despite foreign policy no longer being solely 'formed by centralized rule by fiat' (M. Morrison, 2012: 78), the ongoing essence of the contemporary economic reform period has been that of continued CCP control. The Chinese state thus maintains a highly proscriptive attitude towards any group that deviates from the CCP's political, national or ideological monopoly, as typified (for example) by potential separatists in Tibet or Xinjiang (who threaten its territorial control), as well as any alternative political, social or religious groupings, such as the China Democracy Party (which threatens its ideological control). Increased censorship, internet controls and general surveillance are also symptomatic of the CCP's desire for control and its fear of instability, and of the implications that this would have for its own legitimacy and power. These considerations have ensured that the CCP's domination of Chinese politics has continued, which translates into its preponderance in the field of foreign policy-making process. Jiang Zemin's 'socialist legality', which is seen to institute rule *by* law rather than rule *of* law, additionally makes economic, social and legal reforms all extensions of state (and thus *de facto* CCP) control.

The CCP's organizational structure rests upon a hierarchical frame resembling a vast pyramid, with the presence of fewer and fewer members in key roles as one rises up its ranks. At the higher echelons of this organizational pyramid is the National Party Congress, which serves 'the key functions of evaluating the work of the CCP, . . . selecting a new Politburo and setting out the key objectives for the coming five years' (Brown, 2013: 10). With around 2,200 members, the Congress meets every five years and functions in a symbolic manner by ratifying policies agreed higher up the structure, most ostensibly from the smaller Central Committee, which is made up of around 200 members, meets annually and announces important policy changes. In turn, the Central Committee is regarded as a rubber stamp for the twenty- to twenty-five-member Politburo, which meets monthly, and whose Standing Committee is the most powerful body in the CCP. With seven members in 2016 (always an odd number so as to attain consensus, as per the notion of democratic centralism) and meeting weekly, the Standing Committee represents 'the purest expression of th[e] attempt to create consensus' (Brown, 2013: 6). As an inner cabinet, it contains the most senior leaders of the CCP and various government institutions, and takes information and advice on foreign policy from the Ministry of Foreign Affairs (MoFA), the Ministry of Commerce and the People's Liberation Army (PLA), among others.

Within the legislative structure, the MoFA is the most significant bureaucratic actor, robustly interpreting and substantiating foreign policy decisions and policies made by the Politburo Standing Committee in order to aid their implementation and enactment. In turn, it oversees more routine/lower-level policies and practices, especially for Beijing's relations with smaller states, and has been significantly professionalizing from the Jiang era onwards (particularly concerning graduate training and seeking external expert opinion). With international trade retaining its centrality within China's foreign policy calculus, liaison with the Ministry of Commerce (the body responsible for foreign trade, investment and negotiating bilateral and multilateral trade agreements) has also increased, especially as Beijing's appreciation of the benefits of globalization has improved. Other important influences upon the Politburo Standing Committee include: the Chinese People's Political Consultative Conference, which liaises with additional political groups beyond the CCP and acts as a forum for discussion and change; the State Council, which, as 'the executive organ of state power' (Bo, 2013: 19), implements national (including foreign) policy directives to localities and oversees the government machine; and the CCP's related small policy groups (*xitong*), which permeate the entire system.

The PLA has a major influence on foreign policy that reflects the key historical role of the military throughout the CCP's existence. Dating from the 1920s Red Army, the PLA played critical stabilizing roles at the time of the Cultural Revolution (1966–76) and the 1989 Tiananmen Square protests, and takes a central position in the contemporary protection of China's border, maritime, trade and territorial interests. The PLA's mainstream influence has, though, become 'less pervasive . . . than [it was] in the past' (Lampton, 2001: 61), as it has become gradually separated from the CCP, less political and more akin to a professional modern military. However, it remains loyal and subordinate to the CCP, following Mao's dictum that '"political power grows out of the barrel of a gun" . . . our principle is that the Party commands the gun, and the gun must never be allowed to command the Party' (quoted in Blasko, 2013: 28). As the Ministry of Defence under the State Council is only a nominal institution, the Central Military Affairs Commission (CMAC) sets national defence policy. With one on the government side and one on the party side, the CMACs are led by civilian party leaders and chaired by the CCP General Secretary – in 2016, Xi Jinping – who is the commander-in-chief of China's armed forces. Since 1997, no uniformed member of the PLA has sat on the Politburo Standing Committee.

The nature of India's political system also deems that those in power – in either a ruling majority or a coalition government – have a high degree of control over the foreign policy-making process. As observers note, such a structural importance results in a 'disproportionately large role played by central authority in national security affairs' (S.P. Cohen, 2002: 95), which is highly Prime Minister-centric (itself a legacy of Nehru's omnipotence in the decades after independence, and a dominance replicated by virtually all his successors). In practice, a small group made up of the Prime Minister and some key individuals – primarily the External Affairs Minister, the Home Minister and the Finance Minister – form the fulcrum of foreign policy-making through the Prime Minister's Office (PMO). As such, Indira Gandhi's 'Kitchen Cabinet' allowed her 'almost total control over the formation and implementation of foreign policy' (Saksena, 1996: 398), whilst the 1998 decision to test nuclear weapons (see Chapter 3) was made by a handful of individuals under the auspices of Prime Minister Atal Vajpayee. Even though India is governed through a Cabinet-based system, the dominance of the Prime Minister is so significant that he/she need not automatically consult Parliament on any decision, including the signing of treaties or the conduct of war. Within such a context, foreign policy decisions are often critically regarded as being more indicative of the outlooks of certain high-ranking elites than on-the-ground realities.

From this basis, Indian foreign policy-making 'tends to be highly centralized, informal, elitist, ad hoc and reactive' (Hardgrave & Kochanek, 2008: 477). Some analysts regard this over-dominance by a small set of elites as also leading to 'a reactive and defensive approach, devoid of any assessment of how India's unique position . . . [can] be harnessed to further Indian interests' (Pant, 2009a: 95). Intrinsically, and at its worst, foreign policy-making in such a limited domain and on a day-to-day basis lacks a clear, all-inclusive framework. However, and as noted below, consultation has improved since the Nehru era, with leaders now seeing the Indian bureaucracy as 'a partner rather than a servant' (Benner, 1984: 204). Beyond the immediate sphere of those occupying government office, India's major national parties – such as the INC, the BJP and the communist entities – also all have longstanding dedicated foreign policy cells usually staffed by ex-Ministry of External Affairs (MEA) officials and diplomats, and which can influence the direction of foreign policy. Most smaller regional parties do not have an explicit foreign policy remit but may have a cross-border/ethnic focus depending upon their geographical position, and will lobby the central government accordingly. There remains a degree of parliamentary debate and consultation on major issues – most recently concerning the 2008 Indo-US nuclear deal.

Across time, the foreign policy predilections of the inner circle of officials in the PMO 'have been socialised and transmitted within the institutions of the bureaucracy' (Narang & Staniland, 2012: 80), resulting in an established institutional memory that perpetuates the core assumptions central to Indian foreign policy. Within these dynamics, the major bureaucratic seat of influence is the MEA, which is responsible for the implementation of foreign policy after it has been formulated by the PMO, and additionally carries out speech-making functions, conducts research and provides policy alternatives for India's elites. The personal charisma of the Minister of External Affairs is of importance, such that if he/she 'has the skills to command the respect of the [diplomatic] officers, he [or she] will make policy and implement it, . . . otherwise . . . the civil servants . . . make the policy and the minister is simply the figurehead' (Jaswant Singh quoted in Miller, 2013: 14). Bureaucratic inertia can play a role in these dynamics, as was evident after the end of the Cold War when India's foreign policy bureaucracy was slow to adapt to new global realities. Although showing evidence of some policy innovations, the MEA is an efficient yet highly under-developed body and (while expanding) currently has only half as many active diplomats as China and around a twentieth of US capabilities (Markey, 2009: 83–4).

Beyond the MEA, there are a range of other pertinent influences upon the PMO. Outside the ring of the Commerce, Finance, External Affairs, Home Affairs and Defence Ministries, India's internal (the Intelligence Bureau) and external (the Research and Analysis Wing) intelligence agencies provide some inputs through the Ministry of Home Affairs and the Cabinet Secretariat, respectively. Of all of the inner and outer groupings, it is the National Security Council (NSC) that acts as the 'apex national security body' (Ogden, 2014b: 22), and encapsulates the key members of the PMO along with a Strategic Policy Group (which undertakes periodic defence reviews), a Secretariat (which analyses all intelligence data) and an Advisory Board, plus a National Security Adviser (NSA – a post normally held a very highly renowned career diplomat). Contemporarily, 'interactions between the NSA/NSCs, the PMO, and the MEA take place regularly and in both structured and unstructured settings' (Ramachandran, 2013: 3). In turn, the military plays a minimal role and is somewhat marginalized concerning policy; indeed, 'probably no military of equivalent importance or size has less influence' (S.P. Cohen, 2002: 114). Historical factors relating to colonialism and an elite fear of military coups have influenced this position. However, as the 2010s progress, more higher-level interactions are taking place, especially concerning the military's budget, modernization and expanding international role (see Chapter 3). Although the Indian President is the nominal commander-in-chief of India's armed forces, the Prime Minister ultimately fulfils such a position.

Some critical caveats must be noted concerning the relationship between China and India's political elites and the bureaucratic/institutional structures particular to their states. In China, this issue centres upon the over-concentration of power at the top of the political system, bolstered by the informal nature of politics (*guanxi*) built upon patron–client relations, factionalism and legacy protection. Because the mechanism for transferring leadership across generations is not institutionalized, such in-built insecurities lead to political uncertainty, as underscored most recently by the Bo Xilai affair, which accompanied Xi Jinping's ascent to the leadership in 2012 (Xiang, 2012). They additionally reveal difficulties concerning predicting the make-up of any future Politburo Standing Committee, as well as the policies to be pursued by any new leader. In India, there are issues around the 'ascriptive and hereditary criteria in Indian society ... [, which] encourage a hierarchical, stratified and nepotistic system

27

based up kinship and inherited positions of influence' (Ogden, 2014b: 18). Such entrenched structural factors encourage a host of inter-generational political dynasties (most notably the Nehru–Gandhis – four generations of whom have led the INC) via widespread 'political inheritance' and evidence of 'vote-banks' (a loyal bloc of voters from a single community). High levels of criminality among serving – yet inviolable – politicians also reduce the legitimacy and stability of Indian politics, and inject elements of doubt, inefficiency and opaqueness concerning India's foreign policy-making process.

Additional Influences and the Role of Nationalism

As the scale and scope of China and India's foreign policy interactions have increased over the past decades, so too has the number of agents influencing the formulation of that policy in both states. Such an augmentation of inputs has been further strengthened by the less ideologically driven nature of how foreign policy is made, which has become increasingly mutually pragmatic in its delineation. The diversification of actors involved within the policy process further highlights the degree to which evolving domestic conditions and public opinion, as well as structural change in the wider global system, notably impact upon the foreign policy prerogatives and calculations of Asia's two emergent great powers. Such an assertion is ever more valid in light of Beijing and New Delhi's shared aims of achieving internal modernization and development via liberal economic growth and the general ascent of globalization, as well as particular norms and values associated with multilateral institutions (see Chapter 6).

Whilst the CCP maintains its paramount political role, 'the perception of China's international relations being decided by a very centralized and cloistered elite in Beijing is no longer as valid as it used to be' (Lanteigne, 2013: 19). Such a change can be partially attributed to the fact that leaders of the post-Deng generations originate from scientific and technocratic – rather than solely revolutionary – backgrounds. There has also been a notable shift from vertical to horizontal authoritarianism, whereby the number and strength of those shaping the making of foreign policy have increased, resulting in a process that is less monolithic and more collective. In conjunction with some of China's larger provinces having a louder voice in terms of foreign economic relations, these factors mean that the majority of decisions at the international level are reached via bureaucratic consultation. Foreign policy is also now much more openly discussed within

28

Chinese society, courtesy of a rise in visual and print media from the 1990s onwards, links to tourism and overseas study, and rising (if highly monitored) internet usage (numbering 649 million people in 2015 – McKirdy, 2015). Such a range of dynamics underscores 'the growing impact of public discourse on leaders when choosing between competing policy options' (Glaser & Medeiros, 2007: 302).

As a result, there are now more varied sources of information used by the Politburo Standing Committee and the MoFA, which primarily stem from myriad non-governmental actors in the form of academics, consultants and think-tanks – many of whom often have established links abroad. In particular, think-tanks were revived under Deng, and the most powerful example of the impact of such groups is the rhetoric of 'peaceful rise' and 'peaceful development', which was formulated by a CCP-associated research unit called the China Reform Forum. It should be noted, however, that because of the domestic structure within which think-tanks operate, a considerable level of 'stove-piping' can occur, leading to the production of redundant or incomplete research (Lanteigne, 2013: 24). The CCP also continues to appoint senior officials within all of these organizations, which acts to significantly inhibit the independence of their input.

Following a similar trajectory to that set out in China, the range of foreign policy inputs in India has also been significantly broadened over the last couple of decades. Largely symptomatic of New Delhi's programme of gradual economic liberalization and – again – within the context of a globalizing world, Indian foreign policy making has witnessed a growing influence from a range of domestic factors. Indicating a commensurate increase in complexity, there now exists a 'push and pull tension between executive decision making and domestic demands' (R. Chaudhuri, 2012: 104). India's democratic basis is an important factor within this dynamic, as 'fierce electoral competition has meant that marginal voters matter more for electoral success . . . and while foreign policy . . . may not enjoy issue salience with the median voter, if it matters for the marginal voter, then . . . [it] become[s] more potent' (Kapur, 2009: 290). The fracturing of domestic politics away from the monopoly of the INC via the rise of the BJP, along with a host of narrowly focused regional and caste-based parties, has also increased the importance of public opinion within political discourse.

For this reason, various domestic constituencies – be they the public, the media, business, academia or the wider Indian diaspora – have all gained greater agency within foreign policy debates. Such an intrinsic structural interplay means that many foreign policy decisions are 'increasingly linked to and conditioned by domestic crises and events' (J. Chaudhuri, 1993: 469). Heightening discussion of foreign policy in India's print, visual and digital media from the 1990s onwards has significantly contributed to this phenomenon, while the widespread use of English within these media further connects the Indian population to global news and opinion sources. The presence of several major think-tanks facilitates these discussions, most notably the Institute of Defence Studies and Analyses, which is linked to the Ministry of Defence, along with a wider security community. In September 2014, India had 812 million mobile telephone users (TRAI, 2014), whilst the number of internet users was predicted to rise from an expected 354 million in 2015 to 503 million in 2017 (M. Srivastava, 2015). Overall, such factors challenge India's traditional foreign policy inertia but also aid 'Indian policy-makers[, who] are looking to portray New Delhi as the largest, wealthiest and most diverse non-western democracy' (I. Taylor, 2012: 789). It is also of note that India's internet is subject to heavy state surveillance (see Ogden, 2014b: 69).

For both India and China, nationalism needs to be included as a further variable that impacts upon foreign policy-making, and is particularly salient within the context of their mutual great power rise. Reinforcing notions of historical exceptionalism, the linkage between nationalism and historical memory is an essential means for elites to mobilize their populations. Such a process is inherently selective, with Ernest Renan remarking that 'to forget [and to] . . . get one's history wrong are essential factors in the making of a nation' (quoted in Farnham, 2004: 445). For this reason, and building upon the specific principles that can be highlighted when analysing a state's foreign policy proclivities (as discussed above), nationalism can be regarded as a construction, involving 'artefact, invention and social engineering [in] . . . the making of nations' (Hobsbawm, 1991: 10). Following in the constructivist vein intrinsic to this volume, Benedict Anderson further notes how history, identity and myth realize 'imagined communities . . . [that] produce particular solidarities' (1991: 21) – observations that pertinently apply to China and India as two post-colonial identity projects created through their respective emancipation and independence struggles.

Emphasizing particular political and territorial self-conceptions, bolstered by social, cultural and historical influences, the idea of what – currently and expectantly – constitutes either India or China has a significant bearing upon the nature, consistency and focus of each state's foreign policy. For China's various leaders, nationalism has used the guiding rhetoric of the Century of Humiliation to augment the CCP's role in 'saving' the PRC from longstanding outside aggression, which points to 'the never-forgotten historical dimensions of Chinese nationalism' (S. Shen, 2004: 124). Frequently this account has focused on an image of victimhood vis-à-vis the international system, and essentially sustains core CCP policies to restore national esteem and status *en route* to China (re)becoming a great power. Within these narratives, Japan, the United States and the international system have been the primary foci, whilst ensuring China's territorial integrity (by regaining Taiwan and other areas – see Chapter 5) has been a central tenet. Moreover, the CCP projects itself as the sole guarantor of national safety and prosperity as the PRC's only legitimate governing force. Thus Xi Jinping, in his inaugural leader's speech to the National Party Congress in late 2012, spoke of 'accepting the baton of history and continuing to work for realising the great revival of the Chinese nation, in order to let the Chinese nation stand more firmly and powerfully among all nations around the world' (quoted in BBC, 2012a).

Many observers see China as currently having a form of pragmatic nationalism, which veers away from the overt negativity of the Century of Humiliation and 'relies less on ideology, and more on loyalty to the state and the need for stability to promote prosperity' (Lanteigne, 2013: 34). There is also a 'growing national pride in the destined rise of China and a more nationalist pursuit of geopolitical interests . . . [which] transcends the boundaries between the domestic and the international sphere' (Barabantseva, 2012: 154, 163). The 'advanced culture' element of Jiang's 'Three Represents' (*san ge dabiao*), as well as notions of restoration (*fuxing*) as exemplified by the hosting of the 2008 Olympics and the 2010 World Expo, sustains such contentions. However, such highly populist domestic nationalism can also represent a volatile entity for China's elites, especially when linked to current CCP legitimacy as garnered through continued (and high rates of) economic growth. The failure of the authorities to control nationalist protests in 2010 against Japan and over the Diaoyu/Senkaku Islands dispute highlights this unpredictability. Nationalism is thus a double-edged sword, challenging elites' balancing of peaceful economic and social progress with wider calls for international assertiveness and virulent national ambitions.

Partially originating through a focus on national self-realization versus external oppression, in India nationalism has largely been more of a contested domestic issue, typified by high levels of communal violence between different religious groupings. Observers note how such

31

'volatility adds an element of uncertainty within the political process, impacting upon policy making and its implementation' (Ogden, 2014b: 19). Most virulently shown by the Hindu–Muslim violence that accompanied the Partition of British India into modern-day India and Pakistan in 1947, such strains have continued regularly to flare up. Notable instances were in December 1992 when ethno-religious mobilizations by the BJP at Ayodhya led to Hindu–Muslim riots that left at least 1,200 dead, and in 2002 when the BJP (while governing the state of Gujarat) was complicit in violence that resulted in around 2,000 deaths. Extreme acts of political violence also demonstrate how nationalism can impact upon national security and foreign policy. This contention is supported by Indira Gandhi's assassination by her Sikh bodyguards on 31 October 1984 after she ordered troops to storm the Golden Temple in Amritsar to expel Sikh militants desiring self-rule. Her son, Rajiv Gandhi, also suffered a similar fate when a suicide bomber assassinated him on 21 May 1991 after he attempted to balance Tamil and Sinhalese demands concerning Sri Lanka. Mass communal violence accompanied both cases (often aided by the connivance of elites from the ruling INC).

The rise of the Hindu nationalist BJP in the 1990s was firmly positioned in the context of globalization, and provided comfort to those confronted by an India that was beginning to open up to the world through an embrace of liberal, market-led economics. In this way, the BJP exemplified how nationalism is a 'particularly relevant organizing principle at a time when modern society is making increasing demands on individuals' (Kinnvall, 2002: 79), and underlined how values and identities emerge as specific responses to certain domestic and structural factors. The BJP's nationalism has also been projected outwards, most notably during the 1998 nuclear tests, which were seen to 'have given India *shakti*, they have given India strength, they have given India self-confidence' (MEA quoted in Ogden, 2014a: 125). Upon gaining office in 2014, the BJP's Narendra Modi furthermore declared that the twenty-first century was to be 'India's century' (quoted in Gowen & Lakshmi, 2014). Ongoing efforts to restore India's territorial integrity (largely vis-à-vis land disputes with Pakistan and China – see Chapter 5) further inform nationalist concerns regarding the physical self-realization of their state by New Delhi's elites. Indian nationalism also contains an anti-corporate strain stemming from its experience of colonialism. Traditionally anti-Western and anti-US in nature, this current sees these external influences as threatening India's indigenous values and culture – sentiments growing with its economic rise (see Chapter 4).

Identity, Specificity and Complexity

Within both China and India, the foreign policy-making process rests upon a number of influences. These range from the historical experiences/precedents of their earliest leaders, and their political values and principles, to the relative nature and structure of their political systems, and a shared contemporary broadening of inputs and influences. This diversifying process has been largely actor-specific and leadership-driven, resulting in different policy stances that have themselves been influenced by the underlying structural nature of geopolitics across time. As both states' foreign policy dynamics have become more interwoven with the international system, these influences have become more consensual and non-governmental, including business, academic and media dimensions. Counter to this trend, within both states a very small number of political elites remain as the paramount foreign policy actors (in China, the Politburo Standing Committee; in India, the PMO and the NSC), although for both New Delhi and Beijing, public opinion remains a key factor underpinning their legitimacy to govern their respective populations. In turn, whilst we can highlight the foreign policy-making process in China and India as being now more proactive than ever and involving a greater number of agents, the formulation of such policy remains generally impenetrable, and information on agents and structures can be incomplete or misleading.

Through an initial focus upon domestic determinants, a state's identity – as formed via interaction, precedent and history – appears to be a key factor concerning the national values, principles and behaviour orientating the foreign policy basis of a state and its governing elites and institutions. As such factors are not wholly shared by all states, an element of specificity is apparent whereby the particular policy of a particular state rests upon its own particular experiences and precedents. By its very nature, this specificity between states implies that qualitatively different outlooks are necessary in relation to different states (here China and India) concerning how we understand great power. Suggesting that internal – as well as external structural – factors are of importance, it has often been the perception of the international system by India and China's leaders that has influenced their great power predilections, pointing to an interplay and dependency between the two sides. This insight not only underscores the co-constitutive nature of international affairs, but it also further highlights the centrality of internal factors to our understanding of the definition, nature and realization of what we can mean by great power (as per Nayar and Paul's focus on norms, culture and national leadership, and Waltz's vis-à-vis political stability and competence, in the Introduction).

As shown by the development of foreign policy principles across different political generations, as well as the general expansion of foreign policy actors and inputs, how foreign policy is perceived, formulated and realized by both Beijing and New Delhi is inherently evolving. In this sense, the underlying aims within each state have remained relatively constant, but the means to achieve them have historically gestated. For the CCP, this notion has been encapsulated by a necessary and continual recalibration of the basis of its legitimacy, and how to maintain its governing centrality. Displaying balance and equilibrium (*ping heng*), it seeks to maintain its paramount position as the ultimate arbiter of power, development and security for the Chinese population. This adaptability has allowed the CCP to remain in power by discovering new (economic) fonts of legitimacy, even if they are far from its ideological roots. In India, while not aiming at keeping a single party in power, the primary political actors in its democracy (the INC and the BJP) have also displayed elements of adaptation via a similarly shared long-term continuity, whereby 'India's power capabilities are a guarantee of the freedom and security of its people, . . . a means of advancing the[ir] welfare, . . . and a tool for preserving and consolidating the autonomy of our foreign and domestic policy' (Yashwant Sinha quoted in Ciorciari, 2011: 63). Critically, though, a 'state can never ignore history, because to forget it might lead to losing control of the past' (Lary, 2007: 134).

2

STRATEGIC CULTURES AND IDENTITIES

Notions of strategic culture are juxtaposed with static structural realist accounts, which view states as being unitary actors, and disregard any consideration of state-specific identities and their construction. Instead of accepting international relations as being conducted in a manner that is 'culture-free, preconception-free' (Snyder, 1977: v), ideational explanations celebrate the primacy of state-specific values, principles and behaviours. By building upon the domestic focus of Chapter 1, analysing strategic culture further inter-weaves the domestic and international spheres by emphasizing the influence of norms, principles, ideas and other ideational factors upon the demarcation of a state's foreign and domestic policy. As Gray further relates via his lens of 'national style', strategic culture thus represents 'the socially constructed and transmitted assumptions, habits of mind, traditions, and preferred methods of operation – that is, behavior – that are more or less specific to a particular geographi-cally based security-community' (1999: 51). Such historically derived, interaction-dependent and state-specific identities serve to encapsu-late the various cognitive biases that impact upon ruling elites from generation to generation. Performed across time as engrained through history, these sets of assumptions are state-led, and rely upon interac-tion, whereby 'we *make* the world what it is ... by doing what we do with each other and saying what we say to each other' (Onuf, 1998: 59), so as to produce (inter)national security practices.

On this basis, we consider whether or not India and China have a strategic culture/identity that significantly impacts upon the conduct of their foreign policies. By highlighting the major attitudes, geo-political interactions and historical experiences central to the formu-lation of the core strategic outlooks/practices in both states, we first evaluate their foreign policy aims and interests. In particular, a shared self-perception of enhanced status and recognition (*en route* to being great powers) is evident, and such narratives are driving both states towards more prominent international behaviour. Our analysis then investigates how strategic thinking has adapted and evolved in both states, especially in terms of these shared aspirations. We also consider whether or not China and India's main foreign policy ambitions are being pursued in a coherent, joined-up and proactive manner (via a grand strategy or a coherent underlying set of principles), and to what degree they have been informed and influenced by the interplay of their historical experiences with the orientating and evolving dynamics of the international system.

Analytical Perspectives

As Waltz notes, a 'state becomes a great power not by military or economic capability alone but by combining political, social, economic, military, and geographic assets in more effective ways than other states can' (1981: 3). A state's strategic culture (and, for others, 'security identity', see below) enables this interconnection, which acts as an intervening variable between ideational and material aspects of state power. Notions of grand strategy sum up this amalgamation, which rest upon the ability of a state's elites to effectively pool together key military and non-military components so as to better achieve their national interests. Such a strategy is regarded as *grand* as it does not function purely on the operational level but refers to 'the guiding logic or overarching vision . . . [used] to pursue international goals' (Goldstein, 2005: 17). Such a proactive visualization produces a high level of inter-state/structural agency, and can further allow the realization of a state's great power status by enabling an ability to actively shape the international system to its will.

In these ways, Krishna Menon, one of India's earliest foreign policy architects, observed that external affairs are 'only a projection of internal or national policy in the field of international relations' (quoted in Brecher, 1968: 4). Recognizing this relationship – and mirroring Chapter 1's focus upon historical particularities, national beliefs and other domestic depositories –, scholars have endeavoured to unearth the roots of India's contemporary strategic behaviour. Harking back the furthest are those concerning Kautilya's *Arthashastra*, an ancient treatise on statecraft, economics and military strategy, dating from around 350 BC. Classified by Boesche as the 'first great political realist' (2002: 31), Kautilya uses this work to detail his *shadgunya* policy, which varies depending on a state's power relative to others. The work also alludes to a 'mandala' concept, whereby relations are based upon a concentric circle of states – a position seemingly taken by Nehru concerning territorial consolidation, India's regional pre-eminence and New Delhi's zero-sum negotiating style (see Chapters 5 and 6). Despite the text's efficacious observation that 'statecraft is timeless' (Gautam, 2013: 21), we must, however, be cautious when inferring too many links between ancient texts and current policy, particularly in light of ever-evolving domestic and structural constraints.

Focusing primarily on the modern period, many observers have sought to elucidate an Indian strategic culture. With regard to nuclear weapons (see Chapter 3), strategic culture shapes a state's security strategy through its functioning 'as an *intermediate structure* that moulds the responses of the state to both external and internal stimuli' (Basrur, 2001: 185). Elsewhere, analysts see it as tied to primal philo-sophical and cultural values based upon various philosophical and mythical bases; these include goals not being time-bound, India's status being a given, and a belief in a hierarchical world order (R. Jones, 2006: 5). For Tanham, geography, India's previous civiliza-tional standing and British colonial legacies are all seen as critical influences, which have led to a self-conception of India as a singular cultural and strategic unit (1992: 132). Others have highlighted a particular security style, seen as being broadly 'firm, conciliatory and didactic' (S.P. Cohen, 2002: 58–65), and representing a 'cognitive map or 'operational code' (Bajpai, 1998: 162).

Apart from a militaristic focus, strategic culture accounts have been criticized for being tautological, whereby a certain culture informs certain behaviour that – when repeated over time – forms that culture, meaning that its formation has no defined starting point. In response, there has been a focus upon 'security practice' and an emphasis on self and other, through which no definition of the self can be asserted 'without suppositions about the other' (Campbell, 1992: 70). Underscoring key parts of the ideational analysis of inter-national relations – such as learning, experience, history and domestic factors –, the deployment of self/other perspectives critically recog-nizes an interrelational exchange. In the Indian context, scholars have sought to emphasize ideational factors (primarily identities and their composite values, principles and norms) so as to provide a superior understanding of Indian security as formed via a state-level 'security identity'. Within this paradigm – and by highlighting the impact of cyclical and temporal factors, and successfully linking together domestic ideology with foreign policy –, 'security identity transmits domestic and foreign policy precedents formulated through interaction, history, culture and memory' (Ogden, 2013: 244). Focusing upon multiple norms across multiple dimensions, accounts highlight composite sets of core norms concerning India's domestic politics, physical security and international outlook that evolve across different political generations (Ogden, 2014a).

With regard to China, several analyses have followed a similar formulation and trajectory by electing for the strategic culture approach. Chinese strategic culture has been defined as a 'system of symbols . . . which acts to establish pervasive and long-lasting strategic preferences' (Johnston, 1995: 46). Deploying a long-term perspective, Johnston purports to have uncovered within Chinese strategic thinking a Confucian–Mencian mix, which emphasizes accommodationist grand strategies before violent defensive or offensive approaches in a ranking of strategic choice. Notions of *parabellum* – 'a preference for offensive uses of force, mediated by a keen sensitivity to relative capabilities' (Johnston, 1996: 217) – critically inform this combination of realist and liberalist perspectives. In turn, others have adopted approaches that focus upon the attitudinal basis of different leaders in Beijing and their ability to shape the beliefs underpinning foreign policy behaviour. Here, individual agency (as we will note below) is seen to interact with any established strategic culture, underscoring its dynamic, specific and evolving nature, thus pointing towards the presence of a unique strategic culture, which innately differs from Western-derived understandings and realities. Central to this basis is the persistence of Confucian thought, which is based upon the self-cultivation and virtue of China's leaders in order to preserve peace and status, rather than using force to invade other states to acquire more wealth, territory or power.

Notions of security identity have also influenced recent work concerning distilling the guiding norms in Chinese foreign policy. As per analyses on India, such approaches are rooted in the experiential and ideational priorities that influence/have influenced China's elites, and emphasize how 'historical and cultural precedents . . . have constructed a "security identity" that has become normalized and conditioned by events in China's foreign and domestic relations' (Ogden, 2013: 243–4). As a result, identity is regarded as 'the lens of a long-standing self-image and a set of established behavioral principles' (Legro, 2009: 51). Such a security identity is argued to have been largely shared by all those who have been socialized into the CCP structure, and therefore 'there is an implicit consensus on broad goals and the means to achieve them, but debates and conflicts will continually arise along the way over priorities and thresholds of risk' (Lampton, 2008: 25). For this reason, China's security practice is constantly evolving, a standpoint that recognizes the growing fluidity and increasing complexity of its foreign policy, the ongoing paramount presence of the CCP and the criticality of ideational great power approaches.

Various norms are seen as evident in such an identity, including a need for centralized control, achieving territorial restoration and (re)-becoming a great power in the international system (Ogden, 2013). Both composite and collective, authoritarian rule through a strong, centralized and hierarchical bureaucracy thus historically binds together the period of Confucian emperors and the current CCP one-party state. Through such a lens, efforts to regain Taiwan and myriad entities in the South China Sea (see Chapter 5) therefore effectively link back to the experience/remembrance of the Century of Humiliation. Notions of self/other embolden such analytical findings, and also point to 'a cultural tradition of "great national unity" (*da yi tong*), which holds that unity is better than division and that division is temporary and abnormal, whereas unity is permanent' (X. Wu, 1998: 149). Such perspectives further confirm how policy-makers' perceptions are manipulated by their experiences, and their interaction, with the international system. In sum, these differing norms underpinning Chinese foreign policy are 'regarded as embodying China's creation, preservation and evolution, acting as transmitting vehicles that are present across political ideologies and through a large span of Chinese history' (Ogden, 2013: 262).

Self-Perception

As will be apparent from our analysis thus far, ruling elites in both China and India regard their states as great powers – past, present and/or future. As a result, they 'share a belief in their entitlement to a more influential role in world affairs; ... [and] the cultivation of such a purpose can both galvanize national support and cohesion at home, and serve as a power resource in its own right' (Hurrell, 2006: 2). Critically informing nationalist tendencies in both states (see Chapter 1), as well as providing shared narratives of restoring past glories and fulfilling future expectations, as Morgenthau notes, in both domestic and international politics 'the desire for social recognition is a potent dynamic force determining social relations and creating social institutions' (1973: 69–70). For constructivists, the realization of such outlooks is enacted within a co-constitutive international sphere manufactured from experience, history and norms, whereby because 'each actor's conception of self (its interests and identity) is a product of the others' diplomatic gestures, states can reshape structure by process' (Copeland, 2006: 1). Therefore, self-perception acts as the crucial element that binds together apparent insight, awareness and understanding with a state's action, behaviour and interaction.

Although China was unified in 221 BC, its history has been punctuated by periodic invasions, such as those of the Khitans and Jurchens in the twelfth century, the Mongols in the thirteenth century and the Manchus in the seventeenth century. This vulnerability sharpened threat perceptions amongst Chinese leaders of invasion by outsiders, and triggered the construction of the Great Wall (initially as a series of non-connected defensive structures) from AD 589 to 1643. Interwoven with these threats was a sense of Chinese pre-eminence such that China did not see itself as equal to other states, but regarded itself as a civilized beacon amidst uncivilized barbarians. Through the conduct and experience of traditional tributary relations with Central Asian states via the Silk Road, and with Southeast Asia and the Middle East via sea trade, China's elites regarded their state as the self-sufficient/non-expansionist centre (*zhong*) of the global order. This pre-eminent position was widely recognized and respected by others, and thus seemingly confirmed (at least perceptually) the self-ascribed superiority of the Chinese civilization both morally and culturally versus others, leading to a largely undisturbed Sinocentric view of the world until the 1900s.

China was thus self-perceived as the Middle Kingdom (*zhongguo*), a great power with an inherent manifest cultural and civilizational supremacy. This positioning furthermore encapsulated the innate differentiation inherent in the self/other dyad that is so critical to how identities are created, realized and sustained within (mainly) non-realist accounts in IR. Such a guiding mindset led Chinese elites to believe in a naturally existing hierarchy within the global system 'with China at the apex' (Mahnken, 2011: 11). Sustained over many centuries, it was both through its repetition as a form of behaviour and its acceptance by others that such a mindset became a regularized – and hence normalized – benchmark central to the guidance of China's strategic policy. Furthermore, it provided different generations of emperors with a coalesced, shared and established sense of what role their state was deemed to fulfil, in both an idealized (continuous) and literal (present) manner. Notably, both Confucius (551–476 BC) and Sun Tzu (544–496 BC) also cautioned against the offensive use of force, which was seen as being too costly and unharmonious (Mahnken, 2011: 16–17), thus threatening this equilibrium.

It is for these reasons that the Century of Humiliation was such a significantly traumatic event. China's sense of superiority was deeply affected by the interference of colonial powers, as 'the two crucial bases of the Chinese world order – claim to higher culture and universal kingship – were substantially undermined by the non-acceptance by the Western powers of the cultural superiority of China' (Alagappa, 1998b: 81). Reversing the structural tropes of the preceding millennia, China's paramount regional (and, to a degree, global) position was significantly degraded via the increased involvement of external forces in its internal affairs, interventions that included the violation of her territorial, political and cultural sovereignty. This involvement subverted China's acquired sense of superiority, and overturned the very basis of the worldview of its elites, as the foreign policy behaviour of the once castigated barbarians – expressed by Japanese and Western imperialism – now gained pre-eminence. After a long period of conquest, consolidation and relative peace, the latter years of the Qing Dynasty (1644–1911) during the Century of Humiliation would thus come to be characterized by chaos, uncertainty and instability – the very misfortunes most historically feared and avoided by generations of Chinese leaders.

As was shown in Chapter 1, it is the aim of the eventual successor political system – the one-party state of the CCP in the modern PRC – to overcome this period (and its negative legacies) in order to reassert China's 'natural' standing within the international system. Hence, there has been an explicit emphasis upon self-reliance and maintaining absolute sovereignty in foreign affairs, whereby China must follow the advice of Mao and 'keep the initiative in one's own hands' (quoted in Lieberthal, 2004: 89). By reforming the basis of the power integral to such self-reliance through the economic liberalization policy initiated since the late 1970s (see Chapter 4), China has additionally endeavoured to markedly increase its comprehensive national power. This drawing together of different power repositories shows the interconnection of material and ideational power within the narrative of great power, and is typified by observers who (for example) state that 'China rightly belongs to the great power club by virtue of its vast size, population, civilization, history, and growing wealth' (Yunling & Shiping, 2005: 49). Critically, the Century of Humiliation is deployed as an inspirational touchstone by the CCP through exhortations such as 'never forget national humiliation, strengthen our national defense' (quoted in Callahan, 2006: 180–2), which intimately connect a negative past with a positive future. Thus, only when China has completed its great power rise will its legitimate Middle Kingdom status be restored.

The past also has a critical influence upon the self-perception of India from the viewpoint of its elites. The roots of this image rest upon India's past as an ancient civilization, most notably the Mughal Empire (from the mid-sixteenth to mid-nineteenth centuries), which at its height was five times the size of the Ottoman Empire. As with imperial China, foreign influences were 'accommodated and assimilated ... [via] cultural fusion' (Malone, 2012: 19–20), resulting in unified diversity and religious tolerance, and by 1700 India constituted nearly one-quarter of global economic output (Maddison, 2003: 239). Consequently, India was regarded as being 'a world in itself, a culture and a civilization which gave shape to all things ... [in which] foreign influences poured in, often influenced that culture and were absorbed' (Nehru, 1946: 62). This past significance and gravitas within global affairs, married with a perception of the state's long-term and longstanding existence, underscored the commonly held belief among generations of elites that India's 'strategic role and power potential are indeed of both regional and global import' (Tanham, 1992: 129). For these reasons, India's aspiration to become a great power is firmly rooted in the perceived importance and status of previous Indian empires, its sustained interaction with the outside world (including with both conquerors and colonizers) and its strategic centrality in South Asia.

India's interaction with colonial powers would reach its nadir under the British Raj, which formally dated from 1847 after the previous two centuries of mercantile exploitation by the British East India Company, and represents a period that has had an undeniable effect on Indian foreign policy. For Britain, India was the 'Jewel of the Raj' – the essential centre of its empire and the critical pivot of its global power, which held a crucial geo-strategic position bridging East Asia and the Middle East. The sub-continent also provided geographical access northwards into Central Asia and Afghanistan, and dominated the Indian Ocean – an area crucial for ensuring Britain's trade security. This centrality, owing to which India was desired, needed and valued by other states, would bolster future conceptions of its ascribed great power status, and was summed up by Lord Curzon as follows: 'while we hold on to India, we are a first-rate power ... if we lose India, we will decline to a third-rate power ... this is the value of

India' (quoted in Wulbers, 2011: 21). Furthermore, India would be a critical bulwark during the Second World War against the westward advance of imperial Japanese forces and as a key means for supplying nationalist forces in China.

Courtesy of this history that pertains to a glorious past when its status was of the highest rank in the international system, India was regarded by its post-independence leaders as a (historically) great civilization due special recognition, duties and rights. Such assertions serve to endorse the view of constructivists that foreign policy (and the threats/aspirations inherent in it) is culturally constructed, not pre-ordained, and based upon intersubjectively held beliefs, values, memories and practices. Reflecting this perspective, Nehru noted in 1947 that India had 'a tryst with destiny, . . . [as] India discovers herself again . . . a new star rises, . . . [and] a vision long cherished materialises' (2007), and he would further proclaim that 'fate has marked us [India] for big things' (quoted in Ogden, 2014b: 37). Symptomatic of core notions of social recognition such as destiny, due and restoration (of the past), there would remain 'a classic, underlying and timeless core in Indian foreign policy bequeathed by Nehru, which not even an instinctively anti-Nehruvian political phenomenon like the BJP . . . [would] disregard' (Chaulia, 2002: 221).

The negative associations of the colonial period would also inform a suspicion of the global system among India's new leaders, who were instinctively fearful of power politics of any kind. Imperial occupation would thus result in longstanding anti-Western sentiments, as well as a strategic approach whose basis rested upon defence rather than expansion. The founding aim of achieving strategic autonomy informed this basis, acting as 'the *sine qua non* for great power status' (Brewster, 2011: 831) via key policies such as non-alignment, economic self-reliance (*swadeshi*) and non-violence (*ahimsa*). The poorly demarcated Curzon and McMahon lines along India's new northern borders, which would negatively influence border issues and territorial disputes with China and Pakistan (see Chapter 5), further augmented this understanding of what kind of great power India would be. Reflecting the absorptive and co-constitutive nature of India's historical state-to-state interaction, many of its leaders saw themselves as the British Raj's natural successors.

The aspiration to be a great power is therefore a central part of Indian foreign policy and is a fundamental aim present across all political parties, leading it to being the fulcrum aim of its elites. A consistent interest and an inevitable calling, this belief was confirmed by India's leaders in their statement that 'no power on earth can stop an idea whose time has come' (M. Singh, 1991: 31). In turn, the latest scion of the INC, Rahul Gandhi, would declare in 2008 that we need to 'stop being scared about how the world will impact us, and step out and worry about how we will impact the world' (quoted in Giridharadas, 2008). Within the BJP, there is an accompanying resolve to resurrect India's past status, whereby 'India will be in a position to join the great power oligarchy at the top of international order . . . . [Its] claims will be based not simply on its power but also on its civilizational greatness and cultural contributions to the world' (Golwalkar, 2000: 23). In line with this perspective, the BJP sees India as a Hindu civilization that is destined to lead the world.

Adaptive Strategic Thinking

The logic of a state's grand strategy concerns 'how it can most sensibly serve the nation's interests (goals) in light of the country's capabilities (means) and the international constraints it faces' (Goldstein, 2005: 19). Within this mélange of competences, perceptions of self (as detailed above) and other (the international system as a whole or any combination of one or many of the states within it) have a critical influence upon a state's strategic culture/security identity. Given claims by constructivists concerning the co-constitutive essence of the international system and its composite states, whereby they inform – to a degree – each other's guiding essence, we must also note how 'structural conditions . . . strongly *influence* the strategic options that states face, but [that] these structural conditions do not *determine* the choices that states make' (Ollapally & Rajagopalan, 2013: 74). Furthermore, security as a concept has also become more multifaceted, moving from a traditional basis centred on borders, invasion and conquest to something more non-traditional encompassing terrorism, trade and energy security and transnational crime. Resulting in a political-economic rather than a political-military focus, from the 1990s onwards – after the end of the Cold War – there has thus been a greater concentration on engagement and multilateralism.

Along with the evolution of political leadership in both states from the 1940s onwards (as shown in Chapter 1), we are thus able to determine how *strategic thinking* has adapted across this period – a progression dependent upon the interplay between the substantial agency of China and India's various leaders and the international system in which they have functioned. In the earliest decades of Indian foreign policy, it was Nehru, 'more than any one other person, [who] had foreseen, had helped to shape and form, and had led, the trend of the times' (Appadorai, 1981: 216). Driven by a strong sense of idealism and a suspicion of system, Nehru sought a path of differentiation – buoyed by anti-imperialist sentiments – to preserve India's strategic autonomy, and was openly critical of US policy during the 1950–3 Korean War, as well as the involvement of Western powers during the 1956 Suez Crisis, as it pursued a pathway of self-reliance away from the rigours of Cold War bipolarity. Such criticism was based upon a distinct foreign policy 'where morality played a more prominent role than did the use of force . . . [promoting] non-alignment, peaceful coexistence [and] disarmament' (Uz Zaman, 2006: 241).

A disastrous conflict with China in 1962 marked a significant point of change concerning the development of modern Indian foreign policy. For India, which had shunned the use of force and neglected taking defensive measures, the 1962 defeat revealed how 'the pursuit of a major power role in the absence of hard power or military capabilities was a chimera' (Nayar & Paul, 2003: 19). Effectively serving to then 'socialize' India into system dynamics, the loss helped to redefine Indian strategic thinking, shifting it away from a singular focus upon Nehruvian idealism towards a more realist outlook. This step-change appeared to be quickly apparent in the *realpolitik* bias of Indira Gandhi – Nehru's daughter – when in power, including a close strategic alliance with the Soviet Union prior to the 1971 war that transformed East Pakistan into Bangladesh, and conducting a Peaceful Nuclear Explosion in 1974 (see Chapter 3). Moreover, her Indira Doctrine stated that 'India will not tolerate external intervention in a conflict situation in any South Asian country if the intervention has any implicit or explicit anti-Indian implications' (Devotta, 2003: 367), a belief that led her to interfere militarily in the region in the 1980s.

Marking this evolution – but critically not an outright rejection of Nehruvian principles –, Indira Gandhi asserted that India must conduct its foreign policy 'not merely by idealism, not merely by sentimentalism but by very clear thinking and hard-headed analysis of the situation' (Malone, 2012: 9–10). Thus, as a means to maximize New Delhi's status, the use of force was now a valid option among its leaders' strategic repertoire and marked a more compound use of state capabilities that typifies a grand strategy. Also of importance, though, were India's specific circumstances – historically, territorially and perceptually – which meant that 'Gandhi's strategic perceptions were shaped by her intrinsic sense of hard realism rooted in India's geopolitical compulsions as well as by her ideological preferences and proclivities' (Jain, 2009: 24). Further indicating elements of continuity and change within the development of a state's strategic outlook, despite the Soviet tilt and using military means, India remained non-aligned and had thus solely altered the means to maximize its power but not its inherent guiding aim to be a great power.

Evidence of India's changing systemic relationship became more prolific with the end of the Cold War and New Delhi's necessary introduction of economic liberalization after the 1991 balance of payments crisis (see Chapter 4). Not only did its foreign policy display amplified levels of interaction with an increasing number of states within a plethora of diverse regional trade (primarily via the 'Look East' policy) and security relationships, but the nature of the post-Cold War world also signified new realities for India's ruling elites. Most notably, with the concurrent decline of the Soviet Union as a strategic mainstay and the growing obsolescence of the Non-Aligned Movement (NAM), Indian foreign policy-makers were forced to look for alternative sources of power as the structural underpinnings of the international system also shifted, developed and evolved. The end of the Cold War thus led India to lose some of its 'ideological baggage' (Gilboy & Heginbotham, 2012: 62): in particular, socialism. The foreign policy sphere also became more complex, summed up by the idea of comprehensive security, which 'implies that security goes beyond (but does not exclude) the military to embrace political, economic, and sociocultural dimensions' (Alagappa, 1998a: 624), such as the environment, food and water access, and people and drug smuggling.

As the 1990s progressed, India's strategic thinking became more pragmatic and single-minded in its orientation, especially under governments led by the BJP. Symptomatic of this change were the 1998 nuclear tests (see Chapter 3), by means of which New Delhi declared it was willing 'to take on the world establishment if necessary to protect its national security interests' (ex-Indian Ambassador quoted in Ogden, 2014a: 128). Seemingly running contrary to principles of non-violence, the 1998 tests marked India's 'self-redefinition as a major power' (Nayar & Paul, 2003: 231). From the late 1990s, Indian foreign policy also became based upon 'omni-directional cooperation' that encompassed the joined-up pursuit and attainment of power in all guises – be it hard/soft or material/ideational, with the relationship between different kinds of power being regarded in a more interdependent manner. India further benefited from military capabilities now being primarily used to combat terrorism and piracy (rather than only for war), and from multilateralism becoming the core form of state-to-state engagement (see Chapter 6). Such developments – heightened via the context of globalization – produced an atmosphere that was conducive to India's rise.

Elements of adaptive strategic thinking are also evident in the Chinese domain, and in some ways mimic a similar trajectory to India through their transition via post-independence, Cold War and post-Cold War phases. With China importantly regarded as an entity that is evolutionary rather than static in nature, observers posit that, as its 'modernization progresses and it becomes a stronger power with a greater vested interest in international stability, its security thinking and behavior will undergo further change' (X. Wu, 1998: 143). This understanding is also highly relational and includes an appreciation of security and, by extension, great power that is derived from an inherent interplay between material and other sources of strength. Critically, this relational interchange additionally takes place between China and the international system – and their inter-perceptions – whereby, as China increases its global interests, it leaders also heighten their 'sensitivity to the social and structural dynamics of the fear of a China threat' (X. Wu, 1998: 140). As in the case of India, past interaction (either positive or negative) and its recollection structure such exchanges.

Reflecting the actively revolutionary basis of the CCP and the decades of civil war prior to the creation of the PRC, Mao was an adherent of military power. As such, he cited a belief in 'people's war' (renmin zhanzheng), which 'emphasized the role of man over weapons, support of the population and use of guerrilla tactics until enough combat power could be accumulated for a transition to conventional operations' (Blasko, 2012: 15). This approach was further envisaged as a proactive means by which the communist revolution could be exported to other states. Global in scope, Mao's strategic thought also subscribed to the idea of 'total war' and preparing for 'a great power conflict involving all of China's resources, as well as the inevitability of a nuclear conflict' (Lanteigne, 2013: 86) – initially against the United States as the primary (imperialist) adversary and principal existential threat to the party-state. Military means also linked to China's national rejuvenation after the Century of Humiliation, and its leader's ongoing search for autonomy and self-reliance, as well as the long-term protection of these aims.

During the reform period from the late 1970s onwards, Beijing's elites decided to 'actively participate in the established international economic order, manipulating it to China's maximal benefit while filtering out anti-socialist influences' (Garver, 1992: 180) (see Chapters 4 and 6). In such circumstances, maintaining regional stability necessitated a switch in strategic thinking towards 'limited war' (now with the Soviet Union as the primary enemy) and 'local war'. With ambitions that were less global in scope and non-nuclear, and with forces that were smaller – yet more professionalized (red [loyal communists] *and* expert, rather than Mao's red *over* expert), China had national and international interests whose frontiers were becoming progressively indistinct. Further consistently displayed elements of continuity – in terms of achieving Beijing's desired status and the legitimacy of the CCP – showed, however, that the essential elements of China's grand strategy were comparatively unaffected. Under Jiang and Hu, the focus on border defence and asset protection (namely trade and energy security routes) intensified, evolving Deng's strategy and becoming 'local war under modern high-technology conditions'.

With the ending of the Cold War, international structural conditions changed, and laid the basis for China's deepening economic and multilateral development. As the risk of direct state-to-state conflict declined, and produced a 'peace dividend' through which some border disputes were either resolved (Russia, Vietnam) or demoted (India), forceful ideological promotion also became less necessary in the absence of any direct great power adversary. Via China's burgeoning economic clout, globalization also became 'a major source of "new thinking" in Chinese foreign policy' (Deng, 2008: 62) and, as it was accepted by Beijing, made policy more multifaceted via 'all-directional cooperation'. Firmly based upon a comprehensive security (*quanmianhua*) outlook – as needed to protect its national interests – China's 'rapidly proliferating global interests . . . [served to alter the] external and internal context for its foreign policy-making' (Glaser & Medeiros, 2007: 291).

Responding to the technological advancements experienced across the world in the 1990s and 2000s, China's strategic thinking further developed to focus upon 'building informationized armed forces and being capable of winning informationalized wars' (China's National Defense, 2010: Section III). Such means emphasized the role of cyber warfare and asymmetric warfare, such as developing offensive capabilities concerning domain name service attacks and anti-satellite programmes. Imitating contemporary security concerns in the wider international system, President Xi focused upon combating terrorism, separatism and extremism (mainly inside China), with the threat perceptions of CCP elites equating with wider structural realities. Again, this self-aware broadening of security concerns – via an interfacing between learned elite agency and structural evolution – continued to facilitate the ongoing rise of China to great power status.

Evidence of Grand Strategy

Having such a level of purposeful and proactive agency is a key part of being a great power (a state that influences the very essence of the international system) and is a characteristic shared by states possessing a grand strategy. Thus demanding self-awareness in terms of linking goals with the means to achieve them, Wang Jisi notes that 'any country's grand strategy must answer three questions: what are the nation's core interests? What external forces threaten them? And what can the leadership do to safeguard them?' (2011: 68). Additionally dependent upon the role of external perceptions towards their state's international behaviour, the realization of a grand strategy relies upon the interaction of a state's self-image with those of others towards it. Deliberative in their focus towards a central vision/aim, elites must furthermore have a clear understanding of their specific circumstances and capabilities, so as 'to realize their nation's interests given the constraints imposed by their own resources and the international context in which they must operate' (Goldstein, 2005: 14). Of further importance, for both China and India, is their contemporary quest to amass 'comprehensive national strength' through the combination and coalescence of multiple power sources simultaneously (as detailed throughout this volume).

Multifarious in its nature, China's grand strategy endeavours 'to secure and shape a security, economic, and political environment conducive to China concentrating on its economic, social, and political development' (Yunling & Shiping, 2005: 48). Simultaneously aiming to augment China's internal modernization, international standing and the prominence/political control of the CCP, in the post-Cold War period any grand strategy pursued by Beijing has been inextricably linked to, and is reflective of, key elements within its strategic culture/security identity. As such, analysts have highlighted four key axioms: avoiding conflict; building comprehensive national power; advancing incrementally; and maintaining stability and sovereignty whilst achieving international pre-eminence and parity (see Friedburg, 2006). Concerning the latter point, ego, status and a degree of exceptionalism further inform such perspectives, via the assertion that 'it is the privilege of great powers to have grand strategies – not Papua New Guinea' (Chinese analyst quoted in Lampton, 2008: 25).

Geographical realities also influence such a strategy (see Chapter 5), whereby China's physical characteristics – a combined land/sea border of over 36,500 kilometres with fourteen neighbours (including other actual/contender great powers such as Japan, Russia and India, and to which we can also add the United States as a major regional security influence/threat) – necessitate the underlying logic of a non-expansive approach. Beijing's military interventions in Korea (1950–3), India (1962) and Vietnam (1979) add sustenance to a perceived need to regulate its periphery.

Self-awareness is further evident concerning the perceived trajectory of China's contemporary ascent in the international system. Especially relating to China's rapid acquisition of economic – and increasingly military – power (see Chapters 3 and 4), combined with a large population, its elites seek to conduct a dual policy of power attainment and modernization whilst minimizing the growth of threats from potential rivals. Seen to thus possess 'calculative' aspects, this policy is described by analysts as 'a pragmatic approach that emphasizes the primacy of internal economic growth and stability, the nurturing of amicable international relations, the relative restraint of the use of force combined with increasing efforts to create a more modern military, and the continued search for asymmetric gains internationally' (Swaine & Tellis, 2000: 97–8). Interlocking multiple dimensions of power, this multi-pronged approach personifies the adaptive strategic thinking evidenced through generations of CCP rule. It also rests upon increased market access; a slow military build-up backed by economic expansion to reduce vulnerabilities, whilst increasing diplomatic and political leverage; a good neighbour policy via the avoidance of force to settle territorial disputes; and the warding off of all threats (both internal and external). Regaining Taiwan – so as to achieve a unified modern China – informs this latter dimension, and is seen not as revisionist but as a conservative attempt to regain land lost as a result of historic foreign (Japanese) intervention (Fravel, 2008: 127) – a logic that also applies to South China Sea disputes (see Chapter 5).

Crucially for China, its strategic priorities and aims are enshrined in policy documents that declare a grand strategy, and hence display congruence with the behaviour of other great powers (most notably the United States). In the mid-1990s, Beijing announced its 'new security concept' (*xin anquan guandian*), explicating that 'it is imperative to abandon the Cold War mentality, cultivate a new security concept and seek a new way to safeguard peace' (China's National Defense, 2004). Zhou's 'Five Principles of Peaceful Coexistence' from the

1950s (see Chapter 1) are at the core of such a policy, and display the clear continuity of strategic aims concerning territorial integrity, non-aggression, non-interference, equality and mutual benefit. The new security concept also seeks to reform and improve existing international economic and financial organizations for common prosperity via reciprocity, to uphold anti-proliferation regimes and to focus on security communities (including the United Nations) not alliances. These elements are informed by a central tenet that 'as proven by history, force cannot fundamentally resolve disputes and conflicts, and the security concept and regime based on the use of force and the threat to use force can hardly bring about lasting peace' (FMPRC, 1996). Linking together ideational and material repositories, the concept is 'tantamount to the country's framework for . . . [its] subsequent international behaviour' (Goldstein, 2001: 835), is periodically reiterated by its elites, and was even recrafted to become the 'Asian Security Concept' in 2015.

Further evidence of a Chinese grand strategy can be located in the number of National Defense White Papers that are regularly published by the PRC. The central provisos of these White Papers pertain to 'safeguarding state sovereignty, . . . unity, . . . maintaining social harmony and stability, . . . and unremittingly enhancing the overall national strength' (China's National Defense, 2010) both nationally and internationally, and are the mainstays of Chinese nationalism. Achieving the complete reunification of the PRC, ensuring internal stability and attaining enhanced defence capabilities further underpin these perspectives. Such thinking interconnects domestic and external spheres by 'linking the development of China with that of the rest of the world . . . [through the pursuit of] harmony and development internally, while pursuing peace and development externally" ('Peaceful Development Road' quoted in China Gov, 2005). A national security bluebook released in May 2014 compounds these perspectives by highlighting terrorism, extremism and separatism as paramount national domestic security concerns, as well as environmental and great power politics, and China's maritime/territorial rights (M. Chen, 2014). Overall, Beijing's stated dominant aim is peaceful development, through which 'China does not seek hegemony or predominance in world affairs' (Zheng, 2004: 24). Critics note, however, that such a grand strategy may be time-limited to the current era of US primacy (Goldstein, 2005: 38), raising questions as to whether such a policy is transparent, deliberative or genuinely status quo.

Despite India having a set of clear interests and priorities (as detailed above), along with the strong suggestion of the presence of a group of norms associated with the making and delivery of foreign policy (as elucidated concerning security identity/strategic culture), there is – some contrary efforts notwithstanding – a broad consensus that it lacks a grand strategy (Khilnani et al., 2012). As such, India does not have a pre-ordained strategic outlook that is explicitly designed to articulate its various power sources towards a coherent goal, nor is such a process announced, amended and developed through official White Papers. Thus, while India's overarching goal of becoming a great power has been a strategic aim sustained and maintained across the gamut of its modern democratic existence, the *means* by which this can be achieved remain somewhat ad hoc and non-cohesive in designation, indicating perhaps some missing degree of maturity and even sophistication in its foreign policy-making process.

Scholars attribute this lack of a grand strategy to a number of different factors. Some argue that the deficiency stems from Hindu cultural patterns, whose fatalistic viewpoint prevents the formulation of an active strategy in India (Tanham, 1992: 134). Another perspective contends that as India has only truly been a sovereign state since 1947, its grand strategy has not had sufficient time to blossom fully. Implying a degree of uncertainty with respect to the existence of India, observers also highlight that 'India is a country where not only the future but even the past is unpredictable' (Doniger, 2009: 688), a statement that reminds us of how history can be variously experienced, written and used. Others state that the domestic governmental structure, and its in-built estrangement of the military, inhibits an effective grand strategy (Gilboy & Heginbotham, 2012: 63). New Delhi's foreign policy-making structures have therefore not institutionalized strategic thinking, preventing both strategic elites from being mobilized and India's national resources from being deployed optimally. At their most vehement, critics observe that, 'if there is any continuity in India's approach to foreign policy and national security, it is the inability and unwillingness of policymakers across political ideologies to give a strategic vision to their nation's foreign policy priorities' (Pant, 2011b: 20). Others recall scathing external criticism in this regard, namely Charles de Gaulle's observation that 'India had great potential and always would' (quoted in Uz Zaman, 2006: 231).

Contrary to these arguments, and as discussed throughout this chapter, we can, however, see that India's foreign policy is evolving, as shown by the switch from a largely reactive stance concerning system dynamics during the Cold War, to a more proactive and deliberative foreign policy orientation in the post-Cold War period. Importantly, we can also recall how 'strategic culture provides strategic action with meaning' (Gray, 1999: 52), which adds a clear degree of coherence to a state's foreign policy behaviour and would ultimately underpin any guiding grand strategy. As a result, courtesy of India having a core set of longstanding and engrained strategic norms, we can point to evidence of deep continuities in its foreign policy. Under the umbrella of (re)-becoming a great power, these would include being pro-peace, anti-hegemony and pro-multipolarity; desiring an equitable international system; heightening its global trade to achieve internal development and to enrich its international status; increasing defence spending to ensure its trade/energy security needs; and developing a stable neighbourhood to amalgamate the pursuit of these goals collectively (Ogden, 2014b: 39).

Added to this embryonic sense of India's strategic norms and principles slowly fusing are a wealth of existing military doctrines in all three armed services. In addition to the nuclear doctrine, which was realized in full in 2003 (see Chapter 3), the most prominent of these doctrines is the army's 'Cold Start', aimed at giving it the ability to 'launch decisive offensive strikes from a standing start with little or no mobilization period . . . [including] pre-emptive attacks on enemy forces' (Gilboy & Heginbotham, 2012: 149). In addition, a host of Indian Prime Ministers have formulated (albeit rather narrow/specific) doctrines relating to regional security, such as the Indira Doctrine and the Gujral Doctrine (see Chapter 5) and the (Manmohan) Singh Doctrine interlinking economic power and India's relative status. For these reasons, some would argue that India is slowly developing 'an active grand strategy . . . [as required] to preserve the ability to make independent choices and to leverage the international situation to benefit India' (Menon & Kumar, 2010: 174). As India continues to rise, the articulation of its strategic identity, vision and ambitions will become ever more pressing, and may potentially mirror the path taken by Beijing in the last decade. Of final note is the role played by perceptions concerning the nature of great powers, their inherent behaviour and – most crucially – their recognition by others. Thus, observers state that 'a country that hopes to play a major power role in global affairs cannot be so bereft of ideas to guide its foreign policy' (Ganguly, 2010: 11) and that India thus lacks one of the devices seemingly essential to the tool-box of an archetypal great power. Conversely, and suggesting something unique about the Indian case, another argument states that Indian foreign policy has traditionally deviated from the *normative behaviour* of other great powers that have engaged in power politics, and thus India differs from the classic trajectory used to attain great power status.

Principles, Adaptation and Strategic Vision

As highlighted throughout this chapter, 'strategic thought is always formed on the basis of certain historical and national cultural traditions, . . . [whilst] strategists are always controlled and driven by certain cultural ideology[ies] and historical cultural complex[es]' (Peng & Yao, 2005: 31). Binding together the co-constitutive interplay between their domestic and external spheres, as based upon interaction and experience, states thus formulate ideational precedents, patterns and expectations, which influence their foreign policy behaviour. Showing that the social-psychological milieu impacts upon conceptions of threat, interest and status within inter-state relations, notions of self/other (and any resulting congruence or dissonance) underscore how perceptions inform how states regard and understand each other. Furthermore, this man-engendered, man-constituted, identity-based form of foreign policy analysis directly relates to Wendt's (1992) social constructivist assertion that 'anarchy is what states make it'. Of equal importance, if such perceptions are negative (which they variously can be towards both China and India), 'distrust and suspicion are corrosive, producing attitudes and actions that themselves contribute to greater distrust' (Lieberthal & Wang, 2012: vi). Henceforth, the type of role that emergent great powers are given will depend not only upon their own self-awareness and self-conception but also on how others construe and respond to their rise and emergence, an understanding which confirms the interconnected and self-referential nature of great power.

Our discussion of strategic culture, security identity and grand strategy has sought to overcome the assumption of structural realists that the international system of states has no normative content. It has also showed how the acquisition of great power (particularly in terms of status) goes beyond solely any 'variation in the distribution of objective material power capabilities' (Legro & Moravcsik, 1999: 34) and has a clear ideational edge, which conjoins the performance of a state's past, present and future foreign policy goals, ambitions and capabilities. With regard to India, while its grand strategy appears to be somewhat nascent, uncertain and opaque, a set of India-specific principles have adapted over time to solidify into a clear set of strategic aims. The resultant strategic vision is still evolving, as are the means to pursue it in a coherent manner, and further evidences elements of learning, self-awareness and agency from Indian elites. Vis-à-vis China, a more established grand strategy is in place that is modernizing, flexible and in flux, and whose evolution has equally been dependent upon generational leadership, as well as international/systemic changes. Pulling together national capabilities within a clear framework through which to achieve its external policy ambitions, Beijing more readily possesses a degree of sophistication commonly associated with great powers. However, New Delhi appears to be not so far behind.

There is also the important observation that different principles structuring each state's specific foreign policy proclivities are themselves interdependent. Thus, for instance for China, threats concerning Taiwan and its border regions reveal not only issues concerning restoring territorial integrity (as per Chapter 5) but also perceived threats to China's internal stability and its international status. The very same argument is present for India concerning Kashmir and its assigned territorial, political and ideational meaning. These wide-ranging interconnections confirm the complexity associated with a more ideationally situated account of international relations, as well as great power, but also how it ties together different domains of a state's foreign policy remit. This inherent binding produces a clear state-centric analysis and also underlines the impact of the ideational realm upon the material, and the interplay between the two. An identity-laden approach henceforth enables such specific analysis, which we now apply to traditional material power bases, firstly in Chapter 3 in the form of military capabilities and the possession of nuclear weapons.

3

MILITARY CAPABILITIES
AND NUCLEAR AFFAIRS

Among more traditional expressions of IR, developing military capabilities is regarded as highly integral to becoming a great power, with neo-realists who believe in the primacy of the international system remarking that 'a state's effective power is ultimately a function of its military forces' (Mearsheimer, 2001: 55). This willingness to use force against an enemy further entails a willingness to accept the casualties associated with such actions. Such an understanding links together hard material capabilities with a desire for innate superiority and control, combined with the desire to proactively influence the behaviour of others, as 'great powers are in the business of threatening, rather than being threatened' (Luttwak, 1996: 26). Apart from confirming the importance of material capabilities concerning the enactment and realization of great power status, realist accounts also point to the importance of power being something relational and hierarchical between states. This being the case, power shifts between states can generate instability and conflict as they radically alter the relative distribution of power in the system.

In turn, by analysing the *perception* of military security, in terms not only of status and ambition but also of fears and threats, these contentions indicate an inherently ideational dimension concerning the very *meaning* given to a state's military capacities. Harking back to the previous chapter's emphasis upon strategic cultures/security identities, accounts that focus upon hard military power potentially underscore its importance to those states that have experienced and conducted war, whereby 'once regimes are established, they may feedback on the basic causal variables that gave rise to them in the first place' (Krasner, 1992: 38). Having such a mindset will therefore influence how a state views the international system and its constituents, in that 'when one's favorite tool is a hammer, every problem may look like a nail' (Li, 2013: 392).

This chapter considers the attitude of foreign policy-makers in China and India towards their military capabilities, the use of force and the role of nuclear weapons in international relations. With regard to nuclear weapons, analysis is given as to how they are frequently regarded as a sign of mutual autonomy and self-sufficiency, as well as reflecting technological advancement and status. The current modernization of each state's armed forces is also increasingly being regarded as a sign of shared enhanced influence, despite India eschewing military growth in the 1950s and China focusing upon mass mobilization during the same period. Furthermore, both states regularly utilized their military prowess across their peripheries during the Cold War. With those same capabilities being substantially enhanced in the current era, we examine their potential future use as a hard great power tool, as well as how they are deployed to control significant mutual internal security issues. The chapter also investigates how both countries share a critical and growing contemporary concern for using their military assets to secure key energy and trade security routes.

The Role of the Military

As Levy pertinently notes, 'the priority of military security derives from the perception of a high-threat environment, which in turn derives primarily from the anarchic structure of the international system' (1983: 9). In line with the ideational inclination of this volume, such a mindset would be learnt by states through the interpretation of their interaction and experience, which is informed by their underlying strategic culture or security identity/values (see Chapters 1 and 2). Thus, in a co-constitutive world where the actions of the dominant states make the international structure what it is, if great powers believe in the efficacy of military power and use it as a 'socializing means' versus others, then it will become (among a hierarchical menu of alternative power sources) the lingua franca of that system – its *modus operandi*. In addition, some observers argue that great powers are more prone to experience international conflicts (Braumoeller & Carson, 2011), which would compound this normalcy by engraining – offensively and defensively – the use of military means in their actions. Furthermore, the very meaning given to military power – in terms of its purpose and intended consequences – is crucial, as 'it is not possible to [solely] equate the balance of tangible assets to outcomes' (Mearsheimer, 2001: 58), because non-material factors can also serve to facilitate victory by materially weaker forces.

Moreover, context is of importance, with the relationship between military power and the wider functioning of the international system shifting from the 'dog-eat-dog balance-of-power politics' (Braumoeller, 2012: 70) of the eighteenth century, dominated by frequent (if low-intensity) conflict, to the severe and protracted world wars of the twentieth century, to the current rise of non-traditional threats and non-state actors involving international terrorism, higher degrees of civil war and nuclear proliferation. Socio-political structural change thus re-orders the emphasis given to the military, which in the current era also encompasses trade and energy security. Such developments have further altered the perceived responsibilities of great powers, who have far more active foreign policy agendas than do smaller states. Thus, as new histories are created through the passage of time, and as new great powers emerge – in the guise of China and India – new understandings regarding the utility of military force may also come into being, particularly in the context of competing perceptions towards China and India, and their 'image management'.

For China's elites, military force has been a culturally important dimension in their outlook concerning international affairs, and was a key mediating influence upon the CCP's attitude towards military power. Building upon a mentality crafted through the civil and international wars of the preceding decades, the CCP 'overestimated the prospects for war and the threats to its security, and clung to the use of force as an essential foreign policy instrument; . . . [pointing to]) strong evidence that China's resort to force . . . was driven primarily by ideational, rather than material, forces' (Li, 2013: 404). Through such a zero-sum perspective, China's basic strategy during this period was to endeavour for peace but to prepare for war. Here the primary emphasis was upon self-reliance, territorial integrity and sovereignty versus imperialist and colonial forces rather than more economic, environmental or technological aspects of power. Within these dynamics, revolutionary China was also perceived to be 'the primary enemy of international reactionary forces and faced a very threatening security situation' (Li, 2013: 393).

Central to this marriage of perception and self-conception was the active role of the PLA. Founded in 1946 as the successor to Red Army, the PLA played a key part in the Maoist 'people's war' remit, and gained a strong position via the Korean War (1950–3) and border conflicts with India (1962) and the Soviet Union (1969). Such experience grew out of pre-1949 revolutionary struggles, bolstering their importance, and was buoyed by a mission to protect the borders of the motherland. From 1975, the PLA was 'ordered "back to the barracks" and to withdraw from its political functions' (Blasko, 2013: 27), and then reformed under one of Deng's 'Four Modernizations' (of agriculture; industry; national defence; and science and technology), with the Chinese leader accusing it of 'bloating, laxity, conceit, extravagance and inertia' (quoted in Lampton, 2008: 39). This reform saw all three armed forces reduced by around 20 per cent, which led to the demobilization of over one million personnel – efforts spurred on by China's fruitless performance in the 1979 Vietnam war.

Wider system dynamics also led to the evolution of CCP perspectives concerning the role of the military, especially the relative advancement/superiority of other states' capabilities. In the post-Cold War era, Chinese leaders were struck by the impact of the United States' overwhelming preponderance during the 1991 Gulf War, which displayed the role of high technology and 'action at a distance' to China's elites. Similarly, the appearance of two US carrier groups in the waters around Taiwan in 1996, the Kosovo war in 1999 and the Afghanistan/Iraq campaigns from 2003 onwards all revealed the extent of Washington's power capabilities at sea, in the air and on the ground, as well as a focus on C4I (command, control, communications, computers and intelligence). These events collectively served to formulate, influence and periodically embolden China's contemporary 'revolution in military affairs', which aimed 'to integrate new weapons systems to elevate its overall combat capabilities; [and] to implement reforms in organization, training and personnel' (Yuan, 2013: 101).

Conversely, China's international interests also increased in scope from the 1990s onwards, including an ongoing search for energy and resources (and hence the need to protect economic assets and routes), as well as greater contributions to international peace-keeping and anti-piracy operations. All of these areas deployed China's military capabilities in a more non-traditional manner, which focused less on state-to-state war and more on cooperation concerning shared transnational security problems – such as organized crime, illegal migration, piracy, terrorism, drug-trafficking and environmental pollution. This context (along with the PRC's greater integration into the international system) essentially evolved the outlook of China's leaders and recast their previous militarized worldview. The diversification of its security concerns such that it faced external threats together with other states widened the role of its military, specifically the development of MOOTW (military operations other than war), which allows Chinese military forces to move beyond a more traditional function, including providing domestic disaster relief.

For these reasons, Beijing increased its contemporary focus on modernizing its armed forces, which was linked to the domestic sphere, with 'the state tak[ing] economic development and national defense building into simultaneous consideration' (2010 Defense White Paper quoted in Blasko, 2013: 28) so as to expand its national comprehensive strength. Increasing by between 9 and 17 per cent per annum since the 1990s, China's budget rose from $18.3 billion in 1988 to $40.0 billion in 2000 and to $214.8 billion in 2015 (SIPRI, 2016b). Spending as a proportion of GDP fluctuated from 2.5 to 1.9 to 2.1 per cent over the same period, and as a proportion of government spending it accounted for 13.7, 11.3 and 6.3 per cent in 1988, 2000 and 2015, respectively (SIPRI, 2016b).

A widening sphere of interests, inflation, rising living costs, more pronounced nationalism and efforts to placate a PLA banned from participating in businesses since 1998 can also all explain this mounting expenditure. Now that Beijing has the world's second largest declared military budget, there are continued suspicions among many Western analysts that it 'might be under-reporting its military budget by a factor of two or even three' (Lanteigne, 2013: 83). In addition, some note that China has become more assertive in its international behaviour, especially concerning territorial disputes and regional affairs (see Chapter 5). Drawing together elements related to nationalism, domestic factors and the need for legitimacy and recognition, the PRC continues to celebrate past military achievements, as shown by the seventieth anniversary celebrations of its 1945 victory over Japan in 2015, designed variously to 'solidify the growing idea of Chinese national identity' (Phillips, 2015), augment national pride and (regional) status and showcase its modernization efforts.

In contrast to the militarized worldview of the CCP in the earliest years of the PRC, for India's new elites in 1947 the aggressive use of hard force was anathema. Instead, the military had a minimal influence on the political process, bolstered by key values relating to anti-imperialism and anti-colonialism seen through the prism of non-violence. In accordance with a central belief stemming from key leaders such as Mahatma Gandhi and Nehru that 'power-seeking provokes power-seeking, force begets force' (Bajpai, 1998: 195), military means were largely eschewed in India's foreign policy outlook. Such an approach contradicted the raison d'être of a state's military to such a degree that Gandhi stated to a major of the Indian Army: 'You have asked me to tell you in a tangible and concrete form how you can put over to the troops under your command the need for non-violence. I am still groping in the dark for an answer' (quoted in Basrur, 2001: 188). Critically, although this approach came in part from India's material weakness, it also proactively sought to gain New Delhi some degree of moral/ideational strength, so as to enhance its national autonomy. Thus, Nehru declared: 'Let us not be frightened too much of the military might of this or that group, . . . I want to tell it to the world on behalf of this country [India] that we are not frightened of the military might of this power or that, . . . our policy is not a passive . . . or negative policy' (1961: 30).

Military opinion was further detached from India's elites through a pre-eminent belief in civilian power. With the humbling defeat against China in 1962, however, measures were taken to develop India's military capabilities appropriately. As Nehru publicly stated in 1963: 'We will now clearly have to give considerably more attention to strengthening our armed forces and to the production within the country, to the extent possible, of all weapons and equipment needed by them' (1963: 459). In effect, the experience of 1962 spurred on the first of many (periodic) modernization drives – efforts that would accelerate as India's strategic thinking became more pragmatic in nature (see Chapter 2). Within this paradigm, the acquisition (and sometimes even use) of military power was re-crafted to further encompass Nehruvian notions of self-reliance and self-sufficiency. Continuing to avoid military alliances, Indira Gandhi thus asserted that 'borrowed strength [is not] real strength' (1975: 136–7). Far more insistent on the need for military strength than most earlier leaders in the INC (although not the opposition BJP, which had a much more strident worldview – see Ogden, 2014a: 49–74), she injected elements of hard power into India's foreign policy arsenal, and conducted a programme of substantial military modernization.

Rather than completely avoiding military power in any circumstances, even in the earliest throes of independence the Indian government allowed the military to play a regular – indeed increasing – role in New Delhi's foreign policy calculus. The Indian army has fought on multiple occasions with Pakistan over the status of the disputed Jammu and Kashmir region in India's northwest (in 1947–48, 1965 and 1999); helped to 'liberate' East Pakistan in 1971 *en route* to it becoming Bangladesh; and figured heavily in a mass military standoff in 2002 (Operation Parakram). Regionally, apart from their less than auspicious involvement in the 1962 war with China, India's military have also been involved in peacekeeping operations in Nepal (in 1950), Sri Lanka (in 1971 and 1987–90) and the Maldives (1988). Internally, they also contributed to India's territorial consolidation by helping with the absorption of Junagadh, Hyderabad and Goa in 1947, 1948 and 1961, respectively. Furthermore, the military are involved in some longstanding anti-insurgency and anti-separatist operations across India's northeast, as well as in Kashmir since 1989, and they combated the *Khalistan* liberation movement active in Punjab in the 1970s and 1980s. On this basis, and notwithstanding long-held pacifist tendencies, the Indian military are highly experienced.

Similarly to Beijing, the span of New Delhi's security interests has also significantly expanded in recent decades to cover remits associated with trade and energy security, as well as more non-traditional elements relating to transnational threats such as terrorism, piracy, smuggling, migration and the environment. The switch to an economy closely interwoven with (Western neo-)liberal capitalism from the early 1990s (see Chapter 4) further reinforced this broadening spectrum of involvement. Again, these newer dimensions have been morphed into the remit of self-reliance, and the corresponding necessity of securing India greater national autonomy, as well as accompanying higher levels of international status and recognition. Widening power projection capabilities (see below) personify this broader involvement in international affairs, and embolden New Delhi's own revolution in military affairs, the cornerstones of which are reconnaissance, precision-strike and command and control capabilities. India's spending on defence doubled in real terms since 1997 at an average rate of 6.3 per cent per annum, and for 2015–16 it rose by 11 per cent under Narendra Modi's BJP government (Ladwig, 2015: 2).

India's overall military budget rose from $18.2 billion in 1988 to $27.6 billion in 2000 and to $51.3 billion in 2015 (SIPRI, 2016b). Spending as a percentage of GDP declined from 3.7 to 3.1 to 2.3 per cent over the same period, and as a proportion of government spending accounted for 16.1, 12.0 and 8.7 in 1988, 2000 and 2015, respectively (SIPRI, 2016b). These latter percentages are higher than China's over the same timeframe but India's much lower GDP during this period (see Chapter 4) accounts for the current difference in their total military spending. Although budgets are increasing, aimed at upgrading India's capabilities, observers argue that 'despite spending huge sums on force modernization and induction of weapons systems, there is limited or marginal accretion to overall capabilities' (Arun Saghal & Vinod Anand quoted in Ladwig, 2015: 7).

These observations are variously attributed to either the extent of modernization required, the slow pace of change in the current programme, the lack of coordination between political and military leaders or an often status- and image-driven dimension to India's acquisition of more advanced weaponry (see the section on nuclear weapons below). Pointing towards the former elements, New Delhi carried out its first comprehensive review of national security in 1999 – efforts that subsequently led to the creation of a Strategic Forces Command to coordinate its three armed forces, as well as the introduction of a Nuclear Command Authority –, whilst India's National Security Council was inaugurated in November 1998. In the early 2000s, a joint command centre for all three armed services (the Far Eastern Naval Command), also known as the Andaman and Nicobar Command) was also created. Additionally, Indian elites have been keen to celebrate their state's past military successes – most notably the fiftieth anniversary of the 1965 war with Pakistan in 2015 through a 'victory carnival'. The event was seemingly designed to stoke nationalist pride as, according to observers like Nitin Gokale, 'the 1965 war has been forgotten by people; . . . this is an effort to revive the memory' (quoted in BBC, 2015a).

Military Forces

Realist-orientated accounts of great power have broadly emphasized the use of military force. Initially, this was in terms of a balance of power: 'a balance of all the capabilities, including physical force, that states choose to use in pursuing their goals' (Waltz, 1959: 205). This understanding was then refined to become one of balance of threat, which additionally included considerations of geographic proximity, aggregate strength (size, population and economic capabilities), offensive capabilities and offensive intentions (Walt, 1990: 22–5). Subsequently, these structural approaches were separated out into offensive and defensive strands concerning how such hard/material power is to be used vis-à-vis other states. These reworkings therefore included an appreciation of the *perception of threat* between states, which provides a clear ideational angle for the analysis of material capabilities that is simultaneously interrelational, interdependent and relative in designation – all of which are critical analytical concerns of this volume and are at the fulcrum of great power. Such an account, however, does not solely relate to states but also concerns how the international system – essentially a collective representation of states – regards military power. Ever evolving, after the end of the Cold War the system 'mov[ed]) away from the emphasis on military force and conquest that marked earlier eras' (Nye, 1990: 170), with a new emphasis on softer diplomacy.

With currently around 1.15 million active troops (Ladwig, 2015: 27), along with an estimated 2.1 million reserve forces, the Indian Army is the world's third largest standing force (behind China and the Democratic People's Republic of Korea [North Korea]). These numbers are further complemented by 1.3 million paramilitaries from the Indian Home Guard and Civil Defence, including the Indian Coastguard, the Assam Rifles and the Special Frontier Force. Apart from having a high level of direct combat experience against both external and internal foes (see above), the Indian Army is also conducting a growing number of exercises with the militaries of other states, increasing their interoperability capabilities. These exercises have been conducted, for instance, with leading powers such as the United States, Russia, China and the United Kingdom. In Asia, there have also been joint exercises with Bangladesh, Indonesia, the Maldives and Singapore – efforts that often rest upon India's vast anti-terrorism experience against opponents in Kashmir and its restive northeastern region. Since 2004, India has signed a series of explicit defence agreements with states across Southeast Asia (including Vietnam, Malaysia, Singapore and Indonesia) and beyond (such as Australia and Brazil), improving its linkages with other militaries.

India is also beginning to train other service personnel, including the Afghan, Bahranian, Qatarian and Singaporean militaries, as well as the Malaysian Air Force, and, at its most expansive, it opened its first overseas military base in Tajikistan in 2007. Beyond carrying out domestic stability operations, the Indian Army is also embracing non-traditional roles – including disaster relief: most notably after the December 2004 tsunami and the September 2011 earthquake in Sikkim, but also following periodic bouts of flooding. Outside India, its armed forces are habitually among the top three contributors to United Nations Peacekeeping Operations (UNPKOs), both historically and at any time, and numbered 7,700 in total or 7.54 per cent of all contributions in June 2016 (UN, 2016b). In addition, as of May 2016, India had lost the greatest number of UN peacekeepers (162) of any state (UN, 2016a).

The Indian Air Force (IAF) has around 170,000 personnel, is a highly regarded entity internationally in terms of experience and skill and holds annual exercises with France and the United States, among others. It is currently undergoing an extensive modernization designed to increase its geographical reach, which has included the planned purchase of 126 Dassault Rafales from France as part of its Medium Multi-Role Combat Aircraft acquisition. Organizationally, the IAF includes the Indian Space Research Organization, which has established an active, visible and successful presence in the last decade. This has included setting up an aerospace command in 2007 and developing the capacity to launch communications and earth observation satellites into geo-synchronous orbit, as well as several lunar probes. Of increasing importance, India has established a reputation as a leading commercial provider and has put satellites into orbit on behalf of (among others) France, Austria, Canada, Denmark and the United Kingdom from its Sriharikota launch centre in Andhra Pradesh. New Delhi plans a manned space mission in the next decade and has sent probes to the moon and Mars – efforts intended not only to bolster its technological capabilities but also to boost domestic nationalist pride.

The Indian Navy has around 55,000 active personnel and in the last ten years has been successfully deployed in most major bodies of water in the world. In particular, ensuring the security of the Indian Ocean Region (IOR) has been a primary goal, so as to secure the transportation of gas and oil from West Asia (the Middle East) and to safeguard sea lines of communication from piracy. This presence includes provision to counter a perceived 'Hormuz Dilemma', whereby the Straits of Hormuz must remain open to ensure India an unabated energy supply. More generally, India's current maritime build-up is targeted at maintaining regional stability, protecting trade and strengthening New Delhi's peacekeeping capacity. In terms of submarines and supporting warships, India is the strongest of the littoral IOR states (Ogden, 2014b: 43). It has also carried out a range of regular large-scale exercises with a host of important global and regional actors, including the United States, France, the United Kingdom, China, Australia, Japan, Nigeria, Mozambique and South Korea, as well as in Southeast Asia with Brunei Darussalam, Indonesia and Singapore, among others. Most critically, in 2015 India had two aircraft carriers in service (the INS *Viraat* and INS *Vikrant*) and it has plans for several others in the next decade – a capability that would place it second only to the United States. Moreover, India has set up naval staging and listening stations on Madagascar, Mauritius and the Seychelles.

Symptomatic of its wider military modernization across all three of its armed services, India is currently ranked as the world's second largest arms importer after Saudi Arabia, and spent $3.78 billion in

2015, accounting for 13.2 per cent of the global total (SIPRI, 2016a). New Delhi was in fact the world's top arms importer overall from 1990 to 2015 (and for each year between 2009 and 2014), with a total of $54.7 billion or 8.5 per cent of all sales (SIPRI, 2016a). In 2015, Russia supplied 63.8 per cent of these weapons, followed by Israel (10.3 per cent), the United States (9.8 per cent), France (4 per cent) and the United Kingdom (4.5 per cent) (SIPRI, 2016a). A series of agreed purchases will ensure that India retains primacy in this domain for many years to come, with current deals totalling $100 billion to buy fighter jets, helicopters, landing ships and submarines. New Delhi's indigenous weapons production remains very low, total-ling only $33 million in 2015, most of which went to Afghanistan and Myanmar (both 45.5 per cent) and the remainder to Suriname (SIPRI, 2016a).

Turning to China, the PLA, with 850,000 soldiers (IOSC, 2013), forms the main part of China's military forces, which, with around 1.48 million personnel in total, can be regarded as the world's largest active armed forces. To these can be added a reserve force of 510,000 and, in the event of invasion, members of the nationwide People's Armed Police (PAP), plus an estimated 8 million militia members (Blasko, 2013: 28–31). Although Beijing has a policy of compulsory military service, this is not enforced owing to sufficient volunteer rates. In 2015, Xi announced that PLA numbers would be cut by 300,000 by 2017 (BBC, 2015d). With very limited combat experience and having fought no major war for over thirty-five years (since that with Vietnam in 1979), paired with its modernization drive, the PLA has actively sought out opportunities for joint military exercises since 2002. Normally very small-scale and focused upon either anti-terrorism, border security or disaster relief, these have occurred most often with Russia and the Central Asian states, as well as with Pakistan, India, Mongolia, Thailand, Singapore, Gabon, Romania, Turkey, Peru, Tanzania, France, Japan and the United States. Joint exercises have also been more frequent, with the PLA (army and marine units) and the PAP carrying out over thirty such operations with different foreign forces from 2011 to 2012 (Blasko, 2012: 207). China is also a regular contributor to UNPKOs, and was the twelfth highest supplier in June 2016 (2,645 personnel or 2.59 per cent), sending more than any of the other UN Permanent Five (P5) members (UN, 2016b).

A desire for continued modernization underscores these activities, centred upon achieving internal control, area denial around China's periphery and limited regional force projection abilities. The PRC is significantly deficient across the gamut of its military capabilities, with observers noting that 'the gap between us and that of advanced countries is at least two to three decades' (Minister of Defence quoted in Blasko, 2013: 35). In 2010, only 'about 26% of [China's] naval surface forces, 25% of air forces and 40% of air defence forces were modern' (US Office of the Secretary of Defense quoted in Blasko, 2013: 35). Pointing to relative stages of development between states beyond the headline military budget figures, such an imbalance also explains Beijing's focus upon attaining asymmetric means to achieve advantage in selected areas rather than across the full spectrum of its military. Thus, there is an emphasis on developing area denial and anti-access strategies around China's periphery, as well as a focus on electronic, hi-tech and space warfare (including a successful anti-satellite test in 2007). On this basis, China is now regarded as having 'the most extensive and most practiced cyber-warfare capabilities in Asia' (Dombrowski & Demchak, 2014: 77). China's space programme aids these efforts, including a first manned space mission in 2003 and satellite broadcasting capabilities, which go 'beyond enhanced power projection, . . . [and] tell the rest of the world that China is on a trajectory for greatness' (Lampton, 2008: 59) and create prestige.

Although the PLA is occasionally involved in managing China's internal security, it is the PAP that is in charge of safeguarding security and maintaining public order. Formed from the PLA in 1982, and numbering 1.5 million from the domestic security forces (via the Ministries of Public and State Security), the PAP is primarily responsible for 'containing and suppressing unrest; disaster relief; border security; counter-narcotics work; guarding critical Party, government, economic and infrastructure facilities; [and providing)]logistical and security support to the PLA during time of conflict' (Tanner, 2013: 91). Significantly, China's internal security budget has exceeded its military budget since 2010 (Blanchard & Ruwitch, 2013), underscoring the regime's domestic instability concerns (see below).

With a focus more representative of the PRC's geopolitical trade interests, including energy security, the People's Liberation Army Navy (PLAN) deals with China's maritime affairs. As such, its remit is not just to protect coastal areas but also to move towards a '"blue-navy" posture and expansion of scope of maritime strategic defence . . . [including] control of China's adjacent waters' (Yuan, 2013: 103). Enveloped within this mission is the mantra of area denial, whereby China's leaders seek to fashion a protective buffer around its continental and maritime periphery, so as to deter military attacks against the mainland, and the focus of which not only relates to its peripheral relations (see Chapter 5) but also reflects the fact that the majority of

China's GDP and population are based in coastal areas. Beijing is also concerned with securing the state's energy security, and in this regard faces both a 'Hormuz Dilemma' and a 'Malacca Dilemma' regarding the supply and transportation of oil and gas from the Middle East. The PLAN carries out anti-piracy, anti-smuggling and search-and-rescue missions, and in 2011 and 2015 evacuated Chinese nationals from Libya and Yemen, respectively.

With 235,000 personnel (IOSC, 2013), the PLAN is undergoing a major modernization focused upon gaining power projection capabilities, including the development of the world's first anti-ship ballistic missile. Within this domain, Beijing 'strongly favoured submarines over aircraft carriers, given the latter's high cost and technological complexity, as well as the political issues that carriers would raise because of the major threat they could pose to regional states' (Yuan, 2013: 103), revealing a perceptual element within a hard power calculus. Regardless, the refitted aircraft carrier *Liaoning* was commissioned in 2012 (although it is yet to enter full service) – itself an embodiment of national prestige. Building up its interoperability capacities, the PLAN has held maritime exercises with states ranging from Pakistan, India, the United Kingdom, the United States, France, Canada, the Philippines and Australia, to Chile, Peru and Brazil. In 2016, China signed an agreement to build a naval supply station in Djibouti, a key geographical chokepoint with regard to its trade security and anti-piracy efforts.

The People's Liberation Army Airforce is the world's third largest such force (after the United States and Russia) and the largest in Asia, with 398,000 personnel (IOSC, 2013), but has very limited combat experience and is far behind Western capabilities. Reflective of security issues relating to its periphery and area denial aims, 'the modernization of China's air force over the past decade has focused on short-range fighters, not long-range bombers' (Fravel, 2008: 135). This has included the development of indigenous planes, including the J20 'stealth' fighter, through China's domestic defence-industrial base, which also manufactures other major weapons systems, including fighter aircraft and nuclear submarines, some of which are under PLA control. Overall from 1990 to 2015, China was the world's second largest arms importer behind India, as noted above ($41.6 billion or 6.4 per cent of the global total – SIPRI, 2016a), and led imports from 1999 to 2006. In 2015, Russia supplied 67.9 per cent of the PRC's arms imports, including submarines, destroyers and missiles, followed by France (14.3 per cent), Ukraine (8.1 per cent) and the United Kingdom (3.3%) (SIPRI, 2016a). Beijing is still under wider international embargoes from the European Union and the United States dating from the 1989 Tiananmen Square incident. The arms traffic with the PRC is not all one-way, however. China is the world's fifth largest arms exporter, accounting for $2 billion or 6.7 per cent of the global total in 2015, mainly supplying Pakistan (28.7 per cent), Bangladesh (24.1 per cent), Myanmar (14.6 per cent), Algeria (12.9 per cent) and Venezuela (7.5 per cent) (SIPRI, 2016a).

Nuclear Capabilities

In addition to being defined in terms of conventional military resources, great power status is often associated with the possession of nuclear weapons, not only as the ultimate destructive offensive means but also as a capability that inherently defends states from threats through deterrence. Moreover, states' nuclear weapons fulfil Morgenthau's 'politics of prestige' by 'maintaining a façade of military might or impressing their peers of their potential (if not actual) strength' (Suzuki, 2008: 48), thus assuming a perceptual and ideational role. China was quick to develop its nuclear weapons capability in the 1950s, which – within Mao's foreign policy outlook of total war – meant that 'the top security priority . . . was surviving a massive and surprise aggression, . . . therefore huge natural and human resources were diverted toward acquiring a second-strike capability' (B. Wu, 2001: 276–7). Such efforts were based upon deterrence and principles of assured retaliation in which a small arsenal could be used to inflict retaliatory damage upon an enemy. This strategy was interrelational and ideational – in the sense of presenting the perceived ability to counter an imagined threat rather than desiring to deal with it materially. As Deng put it, 'we have [nuclear weapons] because they [the US] also have them' (quoted in Fravel & Medeiros, 2010: 65). Fundamentally, such weapons had a symbolic prerogative, resting upon a belief that there was a need for China to appear powerful versus its adversaries in order to deter – rather than initiate – any nuclear attacks, and they were thus Mao's 'paper tigers': an instrumental resource to allow its population not to be intimidated.

China carried out its first nuclear weapons test in October 1964 in Lop Nor and has built 'a small, unsophisticated, and, arguably, highly vulnerable nuclear force' (Fravel & Medeiros 2010: 48), based upon minimum means of reprisal and limited deterrence and a no first use (NFU) policy. Rejecting principles of security maximization, as per the dominant protocols/outlooks of other great powers (most notably the United States and Russia during the Cold War), China's behaviour countered structural realist approaches to international security. In this way, the rationale for its conservative posture is 'both ideational and technical in that nuclear weapons have been viewed largely in the context of rejecting nuclear coercion [rather] than as weapons for use in military combat, and that technology . . . [is central to achieving] nuclear modernization' (Yuan, 2013: 104).

Thus, whilst possessing a nuclear triad (the ability to launch nuclear weapons from land, air and sea), China has a limited (and dispersed) inventory of between 178 and 260 deployed warheads (Kristensen & Norris, 2015a). Its intercontinental ballistic missile capabilities – the DF-41 has a range of between 12,000 and 15,000 kilometres – plus several nuclear submarines and strategic bombers collectively suffice to realize this deterrent. On this basis, signing the Nuclear Non-Proliferation Treaty (NPT) in 1992 and the Comprehensive Test Ban Treaty (CTBT) in 1996, as well as being a 'champion of nuclear disarmament' (Dittmer, 2004: 477), has resulted in China being a 'forgotten nuclear power' (B. Roberts et al., 2000). Reinforcing this position, China did not develop a nuclear doctrine until the 1990s, which would lead to the 'nuclear counterstrike campaign' (*he fanji zhanyi*) of the mid-2000s based upon a 'self-defensive nuclear strategy' (*ziwei fangyu he zhanlue*) – the core principle that had been pursued by all CCP leaders since 1949. Overall, Beijing's nuclear doctrine and force modernization are dictated by three guiding principles: effectiveness (*youxiaoxing*), sufficiency (*zugou*) and counter-deterrence (*fanweishe*) (Pan, 2010).

India's nuclear programme from 1948 also focused upon ensuring greater levels of self-reliance versus external powers, along with concurrent elements of economic advancement, technological achievement and accompanying international prestige. In the earliest years of the Cold War, in line with the strategic outlook of Nehru and Mahatma Gandhi, India was more concerned with peaceful means, and 'focused on technological advancement in terms of nuclear energy [rather] than on developing a nuclear arsenal' (Ogden, 2014b: 47). However, India's scientists realized that even though their initial efforts were to build nuclear energy reactors, developing nuclear technology could be weaponized if necessary. In conjunction with this dual focus, its leaders called for universal nuclear disarmament from the 1950s onwards – an element that would persist even after New Delhi began explicitly to develop nuclear weapons – lending an ambiguous dimension to this issue. Only after the 1962 defeat against China (and Beijing's acquisition of nuclear weapons in 1964) did the need for an explicit 'nuclear option' emerge, so as to ensure India's existential survival as a force equalizer, and to heighten its strategic autonomy by averting the need for nuclear security guarantees from either the United States or the Soviet Union.

In this context, a succession of Indian leaders supported having a nuclear weapons programme yet concurrently supported – but did not sign – the 1967 NPT, as they resented 'being locked into what [they saw] as an inferior status due to the regime's politico-legal stratification' (Walker, 1998: 511) between the 'haves' and 'have-nots'. In turn, the 1965 war with Pakistan, closer China–Pakistan ties, the 1972 US–China rapprochement, plus a perception among elites of India being faced with the negative triple entente of US–China–Pakistan, increased domestic pressure to begin nuclear testing. These events led to the 1974 Peaceful Nuclear Explosion, which – widely seen as a weapons test – resulted in sanctions from the United States and international anti-proliferation efforts (namely the creation of the to-be Nuclear Suppliers Group) that sought to curb India's nuclear programme. By the 1990s, India's nuclear stance thus appeared to be one of 'ambiguous recessed deterrence' (Bajpai, 1998: 184). Facing the indefinite extension of the NPT and the CTBT, along with the loss of the Soviet Union as a strategic partner and Pakistan's own nuclear development, Indian leaders of most hues held the opinion that all great powers have nuclear weapons and, so as to achieve this status, India must also acquire them (W. Anderson, 2001: 772–3).

The ascendency of the Hindu nationalist BJP to power in 1998 broke this deadlock, as it quickly fulfilled a manifesto promise to induct nuclear weapons. Along with validating India's longstanding aspirations to become a great power (including an appreciation that all P5 UN powers also have nuclear capabilities), the May 1998 tests were as much about enhancing self-image as material capabilities. Although initially criticized by several large powers, the tests would eventually earn India 'grudging recognition as a major player in international relations' (Chaulia, 2011b: 26), thus elevating its prestige. In accordance with an approach whereby 'nuclear weapons do deter, and yet are "non-useable"' (Basrur, 2001: 184), India's defensive nuclear posture is based upon 'credible minimum deterrence', a NFU policy and universal nuclear disarmament – elements enshrined in its 2003 nuclear doctrine. Via 'restraint, stability and minimalism' (Basrur, 2001: 181), nuclear weapons have remained as powerful emblems of India's technical proficiency and status, thus retaining a purpose that is more ideational than material. In 2003, India created the above-mentioned Nuclear Command Authority, and with an arsenal of 110 to 120 nuclear warheads (Kristensen & Norris, 2015b), it also possesses a full nuclear triad, with the Agni V having an estimated range of 5,500 to 8,000 kilometres. Whilst still actively pro-nuclear disarmament, New Delhi also remains a non-signatory of both the NPT and the CTBT.

Internal Stability

The ability to ensure internal stability is essential to any state, intimately linking together as it does territorial extent, geography and location, as well as its ethnic, religious and cultural make-up, and for a great power it is a marker of the legitimacy, constancy and competence of its ruling regime. In an era of non-traditional and comprehensive security, which has broadened the number of non-state actors, the rise of threats such as (international) terrorism, insurgency and communal violence all serve to show how the nature of conflict has changed, becoming more intra-state than inter-state. Such a change not only reveals the difficulty of comparing the rise of different great powers in different eras and thus within different international systems, but also potentially undermines 'the capacity of Great Powers to physically defend themselves against armed violence' (Lasmar, 2012: 400. In a globalized age, how states deal with such threats also impacts upon their international image, as the perceived repression of some groupings may negatively affect the validity of any ruling elite, even if their subjugation may be essential for asserting internal control.

Domestic instability has been a longstanding and mounting security concern for New Delhi, and its ruling elites face several sources of separatism, insurgency and terrorism emanating from within and outside India's borders. The ongoing issue of the status of Kashmir vis-à-vis Pakistan has been the most critical (and established) of these problems (see Chapter 5), and in addition there are multiple separatist groupings present across the northeast (especially in the states of Assam, Manipur, Nagaland, Tripura and Mizorum). In mid-2016, the Ministry of Home Affairs listed thirty-nine such banned organizations under the Unlawful Activities (Prevention) Act of 1967 (MoHA, 2016). As of August 2015, thirty-nine different terrorist, insurgent and extremist groups were deemed to be active across India, with 123 others being inactive plus another twenty-four involved in peace talks or ceasefires (SATP, 2016c). Many of these groups receive funding, training, shelter or arms from India's neighbours – in particular

Pakistan, China, Nepal, Bhutan and Bangladesh – or have done so his-tiorically. Currently, the most prominent of these terrorist groups are the indigenous Indian Mujahideen, the Students Islamic Movement of India, Lashkar-e-Toiba (which orchestrated the Pakistan-sponsored November 2008 attacks in Mumbai) and Jaish-e-Mohammed – all of which have conducted bomb attacks across several Indian states in the last decade.

There has also been evidence of Sikh- and Hindu-based terror-ism (especially in the 1980s and 2000s, respectively), which links to communal, ethnic and political violence that often results in rioting, looting, arson and bomb attacks. Such frictions are longstanding, and date from the violence that accompanied India's Partition in 1947 (see Chapter 1). Between 1994 and July 2016, over 65,000 deaths (civilian, security forces and terrorist) were attributed to these sources of violence and instability (SATP, 2016b). This total includes 722 fatalities in 2015 alone, although this is a significant decline from the 5,839 deaths recorded in 2001. Regardless, such numbers are on a scale simply unrivalled by any other (great) power, and significantly occupy India's (under-developed) security forces. Observers were additionally highly critical of New Delhi's under-preparation for and slow response to the 2008 Mumbai attacks despite receiving prior warning, stating that 'India's claim to be a future world power was embarrassingly undermined by the gross inadequacies of its security institutions, on full display during the assault and ensuing siege' (Fair, 2012: 160). In terms of ethnic make-up, the majority of India's popu-lation (80.5 per cent) is Hindu, then Muslim (13.4 per cent), Christian (2.3 per cent) and Sikh (1.9 per cent), followed by a plethora of other religious denominations and groupings (Census of India, 2011). The presence of at least thirty national and regional languages, and more than 2,000 dialects, further highlights the complex heterogeneity of Indian society – a diversity that can serve to raise inter-communal tensions drastically.

The most powerful of the insurgent groupings are the Naxalites, who are active in a third of India's states and to whom 7,125 deaths have been attributed between 2005 and July 2016 (SATP, 2016a). Adopting a Maoist ideology, the Naxalite movement largely repre-sents indigenous tribal communities (Adivasis) and civilians affected by issues relating to land rights, unemployment and the socio-eco-nomic exclusion – all of which are symptoms/consequences of India's recent embrace of liberal capitalism (see Chapter 4). Naxalites have been responsible for widespread attacks against police stations, army camps, state infrastructure, businesses, the bombing of trains, stations and markets, as well as numerous bank robberies and kidnappings. They remain highly active, and in May 2013 assassinated INC officials for the first time. Given all this, Manmohan Singh referred to the Naxalites as 'the single biggest internal security challenge ever faced by our country' (quoted in Thottam, 2010), particularly since they are opposed to India's economic growth and modernization programme, which is so central to fuelling its present rise to great power.

Functioning in a one-party state, the CCP sees the maintenance of internal control as essential to combat any political competitors to its authoritarian legitimacy, and to reduce social unrest and instability that may threaten China's economic development. The monolithic state control of the CCP thus rests upon 'tightly preventing and sternly striking against enemy forces both inside and outside the border' (Bai Jinghu quoted in Tanner, 2013: 94), namely combating the perceived 'three evil forces' (*sangu shili*) of terrorism, ethnic separatism and religious extremism. Responsibility for achieving these ends rests with the PAP, which must 'now attempt to maintain order in the face of a society that is vastly more mobile, organized, informaticized, assertive and violent than just one generation earlier' (Tanner, 2013: 88). In a population beset by the rapid social and economic change of the last thirty-five-plus years (see Chapter 4), rising social inequality, high levels of environmental pollution and the impact of globalization also play into these perspectives. The CCP's own rise to power through revolutionary means, and its own historical calling as the guarantor against any return to past instability (see Chapter 1), further compounds the import of these issues – an observation tellingly symbolized internally by the 1989 Tiananmen Square incident.

The clearest evidence of these pressures comes from the rise of 'mass incidents', defined as large-scale protests or riots that usually concern economic interests, corruption and civil rights rather than political abuses, and which rose from 8,700 in 1993 to 180,000 in 2010 (Tanner, 2013: 88). Although vast in scale, these protests 'tend to constitute action rooted in mobilizing structures that are localized, rather than the result of national, regional or even smaller-scale social movement organizations' (Reny & Hurst, 2013: 211), and thus typically target a business or CCP cadres in a particular area. They do, however, cover a large spectrum of contentions, including political, social, religious, ethnic, rural/urban and dissident activism/intellectuals, and indicate a population that is less intimidated by the rule of the CCP. It is also of note that criminal cases are rising in China: from 600,000 annually in the 1980s to 5.6 million in 2009, whilst from 1997 to 2007 the violation of social order regulations rose from 3.2 to 11.7 million (Tanner, 2013: 88) – a factor that also demands a commensurate state response in terms of policing and justice.

Although China's population is ethnically dominated by a single group – the Han, who make up over 90 per cent of its people – its scale means that another 110 million people are from ethnic minorities. Posing a challenge to the CCP's uniform control and Hu's vision of a 'harmonious society' through their non-homogeneity in terms of religion, culture and language, the Xinjiang Uyghur Autonomous Region and the Tibetan Autonomous Region are China's most challenging and restive areas. Harking back to the imperial period and specific images concerning the extent/nature of China's landmass, the CCP fears separatism (and calls for autonomy) from these regions, which is seen by its leaders as concerning 'China's sovereignty and territorial integrity, . . . [rather than] a religious or ethnic issue' (Hu Jintao quoted in Clarke, 2013: 232). With its separatists increasingly cast as terrorists from the 1990s onwards (a sentiment fully realized after 9/11), but also conjoined with external concerns relating to human rights issues (including the use of the death penalty, torture and re-education camps), Tibet – in particular – has become 'a lightning rod for criticism of Beijing' (Clarke, 2013: 231). In turn, there has been a rapid rise in Uyghur-related terrorist incidents in China in the last decade, involving indiscriminate gun, knife and (suicide) bomb attacks, and which have on occasion descended into mass inter-ethnic violence. For these reasons, observers note that these issues will overshadow CCP policy for the foreseeable future and, most significantly, that Beijing 'is simply too preoccupied with its mounting internal problems to risk external military adventures' (Li, 2013: 399).

Ideational Meets Material

Military power plays an increasingly significant role in the foreign policy outlooks, values and behaviour of our two emergent great powers. Confirming to a degree that given 'the necessity of taking care of one's interests, one may wonder how any state with the economic capability of a great power can refrain from arming itself with the weapons that have served so well as the great deterrent' (Waltz, 2000: 34), both China and India possess large nuclear-equipped military forces that are currently being heavily modernized. Crucially, this process has been in response to myriad other dimensions of their security affairs, ranging from a need to secure energy and trade routes so as to bolster rates of economic growth, to protecting self-conceptions of their territorial integrity, and ensuring political control versus external and internal adversaries. Reinforcing and interconnected, such usages serve to create 'a virtuous cycle in which power projection is a product of the elements of national power and, when employed, contributes itself to the development of greater comprehensive national power' (Kamphausen & Liang, 2007: 136). As such, we can expect the military power capabilities of both states to continue to increase.

Based upon the particular historical experiences, precedents and recollections of elites in both New Delhi and Beijing, this interlinkage also indicates an equilibrium between ideational and material power resources concerning the desired/expected use of military power. Here, we can recall that foreign policy can be regarded, 'at bottom, as the external form of domestic political values and objectives' (Mel Gurtov & Byong-Moo Hwang quoted in Li, 2013: 391). Furthermore, as seen in this chapter, although now displaying some shared commonality, for at least the 1940s and 1950s leaders in India and China regarded military power very differently. These responses were symptomatic of their differing independence struggles but also demonstrate that 'being a "great" power . . . implies certain attitudes and policies, . . . "great" states have both a class identity and an ambition' (S.P. Cohen, 2002: 31). In these ways, the principles elucidated in Chapters 1 and 2 directly impact upon the security predilections of both China and India concerning the use of force, and, through their innate difference, further confirm how foreign policy attributes are state-specific (not generalizable) and are informed by domestic determinants and ideational concerns. Moreover, how these differing state attitudes coalesce to form dominant (but not sacrosanct) system-level attitudes *also* impacts upon state behaviour, thus manifesting the system's co-constitutive nature. On this basis, military (and more generally material) power has a *particular meaning* for states, which can alter dependent upon various – past, present and future – needs, fears and expectations.

Our account emphasizes not only the interconnection between different kinds of power but also their interrelational, relative and evolutionary qualities, as expressed either conceptually (concerning the very definition of great power itself) or empirically (between states or between states and the system). Underpinning these notions is the observation that 'which behaviours are conceivable, that is which norms are accepted, varies over time' (Finnemore & Sikkink, 1998:

896), as shown by military means being used either offensively or defensively for activities such as war and conquest; protecting borders and trade routes; ensuring energy security; achieving technological advances; combating internal founts of instability; or amalgamating national pride and status. Areas of tension in international affiars are highlighted where the symbiosis of perception concerning these uses overlaps and diverges. Hence, fears of China's international rise are 'a matter not of absolute Chinese capabilities but of Chinese capabilities relative to those of others' (Nathan & Ross, 1997: 236), an observation just as applicable to Indian capabilities. Thus a state interacts with others through the lens of how it regards certain kinds of (great) power, and invariably increases or decreases its conception of threat based upon this perceptual calculus.

4

ECONOMIC DRIVERS

Intimately underpinning the acquisition of military capabilities, economic power has long rested at the fulcrum of great power, whereby 'money and material resources are convertible forms of power – they purchase coercive capabilities, confer normative power, are attractive, and provide the means to disseminate ideas' (Lampton, 2008: 78). This attribute not only further confers potential wider elements of authority, interdependence and control within the international system but also gives the most economically powerful states a system-determining centrality. In turn, as a result of any significant changes in the overall hierarchical distribution of material capabilities across states – first evidenced by China's economic rise and now India's similar emergence –, the structure of the international system also evolves in its underlying nature, make-up and polarity in keeping with the relative standing of states vis-à-vis one another. From this largely materialist and objective perspective, economic power provides one of the most direct and consequential measurements of a great power, with resultant political clout displaying a close correlation with economic prowess and its myriad translations.

This interlinkage between relative state-to-state power balances and their ensuing authority within the international system underscores how 'processes of interaction produce and reproduce the social structures – cooperative or conflict[ual] – that shape actors' identities and interests and the significance of their material context' (Wendt, 1995: 81). It is thus the concurrent core values, perceptions and understandings emanating from the more materially preponderant states that then determine the orientation, essence and characteristics of the international system that they co-constitute. Here, this linkage relates to the workings of international trade and global finance, and further segues into the basis of multilateral institutions and regimes (see Chapter 6). In the present era, it is globalization that significantly alters our notion of what makes a great power, as it represents a 're-negotiation of . . . [great power] identities and roles in the post-Cold War world' (Lasmar, 2012: 400). Such geo-economic forces bypass traditional state characteristics, such as physical borders, by making territorial integrity less and less relevant, and serve to 'shift the currency of power, in particular devaluing hard military power' (Hurrell, 2006: 7). Given its essential impact upon the *functioning* of international relations, such structural change redefines the context of great power itself. Globalization further epitomizes how the overarching international system is an evolving entity that develops, morphs and varies across time between different eras. Compared to earlier generations, the world – and hence the great power quotients upon which it functions – is more inherently interconnected.

This shrinkage applies to the increased movements of goods, services, people, ideas, organizations, finance and culture across international borders. Pointing to complex interconnectivity, globalization also highlights new elements of interaction, including action at a distance (from multilateral bodies to corporations, manufacturers and speculators), time-space compression (via twenty-four-hour transport and communication networks, the internet and multimedia) and accelerated interdependence (as institutions and technologies are integrated, adopted and relied upon) (see Held & McGrew, 2003: 3). Critically, in developing/transitioning states in particular, it produces disjuncture, disunity and developmental tensions – elements experienced by both India and China (as shown below). Globalization also intrinsically provides the shared international environment within which both states are rising to prominence, and includes non-traditional elements (and non-state actors) that have typified the broadening of security to become more comprehensive in scope. In these ways, the contemporary context in which our two emergent great powers are rising is fundamentally different from that of other great power ascents in terms of its highly interconnected and relational dynamics.

This intersecting also underpins notions of recognition, whereby a rising great power may act like a 'self-conscious outsider or social upstart' and seek 'to conform as closely as ever possible to the rules which govern life in a certain social setting . . . by conforming to the rules he makes it possible for others to recognize him as the kind of person to whom these rules apply' (Erik Ringmar quoted in Suzuki, 2008: 50) – an assertion evident for China and India through their acquiescence to global liberal trade from the 1980s and 1990s, respectively. For India and China, economic power furthermore harks back to their past great power status: in 1750 they respectively accounted for 24.5 and 32.8 per cent of world manufacturing output, levels that fell to 1.7 and 6.2 per cent by 1890 (Madisson, 2003: 261). In 1985, both states accounted for 3.3 per cent of world GDP, whilst in 2000 and 2010 these levels correspondingly rose to 7.4 and 13.7 per cent for China, and to 4.3 and 6.1 per cent for India (IMF, 2015).

Economic strength inter-associates with other factors, most notably the size of a state's population. Having large working populations, as well as large landmasses (and commensurate resources), under-pins, sustains and facilitates the ability to acquire economic power. Currently, 'China (1.4 billion) and India (1.3 billion) remain the two largest countries of the world . . . representing 19 and 18 per cent of the world's population, respectively' (UN, 2015: 1). In turn, India's population is expected to overtake China's by 2022 and will be younger in structure, hence enabling a larger potential workforce (UN, 2015: 4). Whilst giving our emergent great powers a numerical advantage versus less populous states, such huge populations can act as a major disadvantage concerning the financing of internal infra-structure, education, health and social services provisions – a factor especially relevant to states that are seeking to modernize domesti-cally. This issue can constrain a state's foreign policy behaviour, scope and ambitions, as rulers seek to placate domestic constituencies. Drawing attention to relative stages of development, some observers have also questioned whether a state can be a great power without, say, adequate public health facilities (Huang, 2011) – an assertion that currently applies to both China and India.

Encapsulating these themes, and the central leitmotif of China and India's expanding global interaction and significance, here we concentrate upon how their attitudes and reasoning towards eco-nomic power have evolved over the last sixty to seventy years. From an initial basis focused upon self-reliance (in India) and isolationism (in China), as well as respective socialist five-year plans and autarky, both states' economies have gradually embraced more liberalist principles. Such an adaptation has become critical to their common contemporary rise, has formed the basis of many of their expanding relations over the last decades, and underscores how economics is the key driver in fulfilling their great power goals. These perspectives further inform other matters of growing significance in both India's and China's external relations, especially with regard to ensuring energy and trade security needs in order to maintain sustained high rates of growth. We also highlight a number of issues affecting both states that may impact on their long-term trajectories.

The Pre-Reform Period

Reflecting the guiding argument of this volume that states can be seen to 'interpret historical experience through the lens of their own analytical assumptions and worldviews' (Levy, 1994: 283), the attitude of Indian and Chinese elites towards economic power was influenced by their early involvement and interaction with the international system, especially in the immediate period after both gained independence in the 1940s. The *modus operandi* of these states, as an engrained process, highlights – as per earlier chapters – 'a particular set of interests and preferences' (Hopf, 1998: 175) structuring specific policy responses and behaviours that are particular to China and India, and which variously converge and diverge in designation. As with military power, we must also note that different states, and – collectively – different consensuses/institutions, will have different meanings associated with economic prowess. GDP can thus be seen as being a social fact 'produced by virtue of all the relevant actors agreeing that . . . [it] exists' (Ruggie, 1998: 867), whose construction of material reality is dependent upon interpretation.

After decades of colonial rule, which had siphoned off much of India's national wealth, in 1947 the INC 'inherited an economy that was one of the poorest in the world per capita, totally stagnant, with industrial development stalled and agricultural production unable to feed a rapidly growing population' (Malone, 2012: 76). Vulnerable, weak and under-developed, India adopted prudent *swadeshi* (economic self-reliance) as the mainstay of its economic approach, with Nehru noting that basing 'our national economy on export markets might lead to conflict with other nations and to sudden upsets when those markets were closed to us' (1946: 403). In turn, the INC's efforts to alleviate domestic poverty led to an internal, protective focus away from the bipolar machinations of the Cold War. These beliefs emphasized principles of socialist self-sufficiency, complete autonomy and development via domestic production and state-led industrialization, so as to enhance India's steel, chemical and power industries. With liberalization regarded with suspicion in light of its negative colonial experience, India had very low levels of engagement with international capitalist forces, it limited foreign direct investment (FDI) and it eschewed any major spending on its military capabilities (until after 1962).

On this basis, New Delhi adopted a range of state-controlled and inward-orientated strategies based upon a synergy of autocracy and socialism. With the state acting as the key determinant of economic policy, the public ownership of the means of production via state-owned enterprises (SOEs) was expanded in order to control private-sector activities in support of the government's developmental aims. The first five-year plan of July 1951 pooled together all available national resources, with all major industries having been nationalized via the Industrial Policy Resolution of 1948. An import-substitution system was central to this economic approach via extensive regulations, high import tariffs and a non-convertible rupee that protected India from external speculation. This system 'reduced competitiveness and innovation, [and] led to low productivity and efficiency through an over-dependence upon the state' (Ogden, 2014b: 55). State protectionism and the highly complex 'licence-permit Raj' (the process required to set up a private business), moreover, led to widespread corruption as political connections were often abused for material advantage. Regardless, Nehru's actions saw India's economy grow 'three times as fast during the 1950s and 1960s as during British rule' (Thakur, 1997: 15).

Under Indira Gandhi, India continued to strive for self-sufficiency – in particular to avoid any dependence upon external aid, which in 1966 Washington had linked to the devaluation of the Indian rupee. As part of this agenda, Gandhi launched the Green Revolution in 1966, which would transform India into one of the world's foremost agricultural producers. Instabilities remained, however, within New Delhi's economic approach, especially its high trade deficits, the impact of the 1973 OPEC oil crisis and the cost of the 1962 war with China and the 1965 and 1971 conflicts with Pakistan. Whilst, from 1950 to 1980, average annual Indian economic growth was 3.7 per cent (Srinivasan & Tendulkar, 2003: 8), Indian exports – which had constituted 2.2 per cent of world exports in 1948 – declined to only 0.5 per cent by 1983 (WTO, 2003). In turn, the 1980s saw some slow and intermittent reforms, with the rupee being pegged to the US dollar and some controls removed concerning the setting up of private businesses, as well as the lowering of taxes and the removal of state subsidies. During this period, Rajiv Gandhi sought to reinterpret self-reliance to mean 'the development of a strong, independent national economy dealing extensively with the world, but dealing with it on equal terms' (1985: 87).

While future Prime Minister Manmohan Singh would later state that 'there can be no doubt that protection was essential in the initial phase of our industrial development, so that we could go through the learning period without disruption' (1991: 4), the structural weaknesses underpinning India's economy became conspicuous. Also stemming from a conflagration of wider issues – namely the end of the Cold War and the collapse of the Soviet Union (one of India's major trading partners) in the late 1980s, the 1990 Gulf War (which increased oil prices and cut off foreign currency remittances from Indian workers in the region) and a historically inadequate tax base (which did not match government expenditure) –, in June 1991, India had a balance of payments crisis. With government debt rising from 35 per cent of GDP in 1980 to 53 per cent in 1990 (Malone, 2012: 81) and only enough foreign exchange reserves to pay for three more weeks of imports, New Delhi was forced to secure a $2.2 billion loan from the International Monetary Fund (IMF). Dependent upon a promise to reduce state control significantly, New Delhi was forced by the crisis to liberalize its economy and to submit to dominant global capitalist forces – itself a notable indication of the system-determining influence of the key great power (the United States) at that time.

In many ways mirroring India's experience, at least in the earliest years of its modern incarnation, China also emerged as an impoverished state in 1949. Decimated by the interference of outside powers from the mid-1850s, and shattered by decades of instability, civil war, external invasion and the Second World War, China's economy was stagnant and under-developed. This was clearly evident in the policy perspectives of the earliest generations of CCP leaders: Mao thus remarked that China 'has always been a great, courageous and industrious nation; it is only in modern times that [we] have fallen behind ... and that was due entirely to oppression and exploitation by foreign imperialism and domestic reactionary governments' (quoted in Kirby, 1998: 13). Apart from underscoring a desire to reassert China's perceived rightful status, such a belief also inculcated elements of suspicion and wariness towards international finance and trade. However, the benefits of external trade were not lost on its leaders, and since that time 'the driving force behind all of China's foreign economic relations – to make China stronger, more modern and more self-reliant – has not wavered' (Ross, 1998: 437).

Emblematic of its political ideology, the CCP adopted a command economy model based upon China's membership of the global socialist bloc, through which ideological indoctrination surmounted material incentives. Aligned with and (via loans and technical assistance) dependent upon the Soviet Union, in its earliest years this model rested upon state ownership, urban heavy industry and collectivized agriculture, in order to maximize state interests and control via a totalitarian outlook. These facets resulted in an isolated command economy with direct state control over all industries, production processes, wages and prices, which stressed self-reliance and restricted ties to the world economy. Centred upon periodic five-year plans (the first of which was in 1953), such 'tight state control over imports and exports and a limited number of state trading corporations meshed well with China's traditional desire to keep foreign commerce at a minimal level and to limit contacts with foreigners' (Ross, 1998: 439). Within China there were no private markets and there was no private industry, whilst the national currency was non-convertible and the system remained opposed to foreign investment on anti-imperialist and anti-colonial grounds.

Following an ideological schism with the Soviet Union in response to Moscow's perceived over-proximity to dominant Western economic practices, 'from 1958, we [China] decided to make self-reliance (*zili gengsheng*) our major policy' (Mao quoted in Ross, 1998: 440). Regarding aid as a source of foreign exploitation, the CCP re-focused inwards onto the Chinese masses as the means to achieve modernization. In this scenario, 'revolutionary enthusiasm was supposed to compensate for the absence of foreign technology and capital' (Roy, 1998: 82). Such a highly autarkic stance isolated Beijing from the dominant global world order, and led to policy undertakings such as the Great Leap Forward from 1958 to 1961. Intended to transform the Chinese economy through the rapid development of its agrarian and industrial capabilities, so as to leap across the capitalist stage of development and achieve a socialist society (as per Marxist thought), the policy resulted in failure. Beset by bad weather, poor communication and misplaced ideological fervour, it 'plunged millions into poverty, accelerated widespread famine [killing 20–45 million people] and very nearly destroyed the Chinese economy' (Lanteigne, 2013: 5), further resulting in shortages of food, goods and products.

In response to such an ineffective system, the early 1960s saw some slow liberalization efforts, included the introduction of private plots and sideline production. Although highly isolated from other great powers (such as the United States, which had a trade embargo against China from 1950 to 1971), Beijing also developed some low-level partners in the latter 1960s and 1970s 'as trade and aid became tools China actively used to win friends and counter Soviet influence in the Third World' (Ross, 1998: 435–6). Internally, however, further ideological experiments – primarily the 1966–9 Cultural Revolution, followed by the radical politics of the Gang of Four from 1969 to 1976 – resulted in production declining and the economy stagnating. In the latter phase, China's leaders believed that 'foreign economic influence would destroy the socialist revolutionary spirit and leave China vulnerable to foreign manipulation' (Roy, 1998: 85). However, by 1978, the Maoist economic model had essentially impeded China's economic development. Although annual growth rates from 1953 and 1978 were between 6.7 per cent – according to Chinese officials – and 4.4 per cent – according to outside analysts (W.M. Morrison, 2015: 2–3) –, how China could achieve such rates in a consistent and stable manner was less evident. Additionally, and of special note, China had no international debt.

Economic Transformations

By the late 1970s, the CCP's second generation of leaders recognized that the unsettled – and often dire – economic situation of the Mao era, in conjunction with the near civil war conditions engendered by the ideological excesses of Cultural Revolution, had left the Party with a 'political legitimacy crisis' (Shirk, 1993: 23). Seeing what he regarded as an over-concentration of power combined with an inefficient bureaucracy and political strictures that hindered fiscal growth, Deng intended to rejuvenate the economy across the fields of agriculture, industry, national defence and science and technology through his 'Four Modernizations' policy. In turn, CCP elites agreed that more explicit foreign economic relations were a necessary step in realizing their developmental aims for modernizing China. Key to this consensus was the need for modern technology and international cooperation, which Deng aimed to accomplish via an 'open door' policy so as to access foreign trade, expertise and investment. Based upon a new cost–benefit calculation, this policy enabled China to become a resurgent great power via (controlled) international engagement rather than through its continued economic isolation and estrangement.

Through the introduction of pricing, fiscal and financial reforms, the CCP began to focus the state's efforts towards increasing material standards rather than Maoist class struggle, as Deng completely changed party lines to focus upon the mantra of 'to get rich is glorious'. Decentralizing much (but not all) of the state's control of the economy, Beijing encouraged the use of private plots to lead to more private/sideline production (as it had tried in the early 1960s), with any surpluses being permitted to be sold on private markets. Such efforts served effectively to marketize the Chinese economy as a whole, leading to newfound founts of consumerism/materialism in the population. Special Economic Zones were opened up to stimulate industrial production and foreign trade, whilst SOEs were reformed, signalling the end of the state's 'iron rice bowl', which had guaranteed work, housing and other benefits to its workers, but now left them open to market forces.

Besides domestic reform, the CCP's economic liberalization policy rested upon further elements of both *qingjinlai* ('inviting in') and *zouchuqu* ('walking out') (Lanteigne, 2007: 163). This led to intensive efforts to bring in technology along with FDI, which rose from $2 billion in 1985 to $38 billion in 1995 and up to $72 billion by 2005 (W.M. Morrison, 2015: 15). Externally, China joined the World Bank in April 1980, and at the same time reasserted its ties with the IMF (of which, pre-PRC, it had been an original member in December 1945). Via an official policy of striving for opening up, peaceful cooperation, harmony and 'win-win' economic ties, thus fitting with liberalist rather than realist self-interest perspectives, China began to have a growing influence in the international economy. Moreover, as it became economically interlinked with other states and institutions, China grew more cooperative than confrontational in its foreign policy. In turn, as market reforms were boosted, and as supply and demand dynamics increased, the party's (micro) control of the economy relaxed, as private business was encouraged in all domains, including commerce, real estate and tourism. Via a further re-crafting of CCP ideology under Jiang to become a 'socialist market economy', China's GDP (in current US dollars) rose faster than any other rising power in history: from $189 billion in 1980, to $359 billion in 1990, to $1,205 billion in 2000 and to $6,040 billion in 2010 (World Bank, 2016b). In GDP per capita terms this equated to $193.30 (1980), $316.20 (1990), $954.60 (2000) and $4,515.90 (2010). By 2015, with a growth rate of 6.9 per cent (World Bank, 2016c), China's overall GDP stood at $10,866 billion (World Bank, 2016b), or $7,924.70 GDP per capita (World Bank, 2016d). This in turn followed annual growth rates averaging 9.8, 10.0 and 10.3 per cent in the 1980s, 1990s and 2000s, respectively.

As the result of such dramatic change, economic prosperity has become absolutely central to the continued political rule of the CCP. By conjoining with enhancing development *en route* to restoring China's great power status, economics 'underpin[s] [its] perceptions of [its] place in the world' (D. Scott, 2008: 15). The CCP has also intertwined political legitimacy with economic prosperity, making it an existential issue for the party that has blurred the line between domestic and foreign policy in China. Moving from 'a brutal communist/socialist past to an intense capitalist/commercialist/consumerist present' (Horner, 2009: 148) has in turn revolutionized Chinese society, and has gone some way to achieving domestic modernization and alleviating poverty. It has also represented a dramatic perceptual change in terms of Beijing's (self-)image, rapidly switching from one of poverty and isolation to one of wealth and integration with the international economic system.

Underpinning this explosive transformation, Beijing's 2008 'National Defense White Paper' stated that 'China cannot develop in isolation from the rest of the world, nor can the world enjoy prosperity and stability without China' (IOSC, 2009). Implying an explicit level of synergy, its economic success is due, in part, to foreign markets (primarily the United States, Japan and Europe) desiring China to become the 'factory of the world' and hence a key part of the global system. By 2015, this had resulted in China becoming the world's largest exporter and third largest importer (CIA, 2015a). Apart from raising questions as to who exactly benefits from Chinese growth (in 2007 only four of China's twenty-five top exporters were owned by Chinese companies – Meredith, 2007: 68), such role-giving indicates a level of recognition by other states towards Beijing. The level of interdependence is also revealed by increasing amounts of FDI, with net inward flows into mainland China totalling $14.76 billion in the 1980s, rising to $283.08 billion in the 1990s, then to $1,011.25 billion in the 2000s, and amounting to $249.86 billion in 2015 alone – making it the world's second largest recipient after the United States ($409.87 billion in 2015) (World Bank, 2016a). Observers thus note how 'any major economic failures in the PRC will quickly become world problems' (Lampton, 2008: 114), as exemplified by large global stock market falls in the autumn of 2015 on news of falling Chinese demand for commodities. Some analysts also maintain that in order to ensure internal stability, China's GDP growth must not be allowed to dip under 7.0 per cent (Kang, 2007: 3). From 2016, China's yuan gained reserve status at the IMF, alongside the dollar, euro and yen, giving it an enhanced role as a core global currency.

Although beginning a decade or so later than Beijing, and in response to an economic rather than political crisis, from the early 1990s New Delhi also sought to transform India's economy. Based upon a transition 'from the primacy of politics and geo-strategic

87

considerations to a new emphasis on economic ties and interests' (Malone, 2012: 76), India gradually liberalized its economy. Such an undertaking represented a conclusive ideological change after decades of inward self-reliant socialism that had left it isolated from mainstream economic dynamics. Underscored by the collapse of the Soviet Union (whose economic model New Delhi has heavily mirrored) and China's economic success, the 1991 balance of payments crisis demanded a fundamental overhaul of India's approach to foreign and domestic security. In turn, its leaders desired to make India 'free from poverty . . . [by] becoming a major global power in the world economy' (Manmohan Singh quoted in Ciorciari, 2011: 67). These stimuli were further complemented by some foreign powers' growing perception of India as a potential 'swing state' through its possession of a large and growing economy, its geo-strategic position and its domestic democratic credentials. Other states thus supported its liberalization process, sought out its markets and gave New Delhi recognition.

For these myriad reasons, India's elites came to recognize the status and leadership benefits to be derived from enhancing their state's international economic relations, as well as the essential convertibility of such power. Via the 'Statement of Industrial Policy' of July 1991, they slowly dismantled the controls typifying the pre-reform era, as well as reducing taxes and tariffs. This 'alleviation of the investment and trade policy . . . encouraged foreign investors to India, [whilst] the devaluation of the rupee . . . ma[de] exports more competitive' (Panagariya, 2004: 34). Banking, insurance and telecommunication were also freed from state control, and the rupee was made fully convertible in March 1992 as New Delhi accepted the founding agreements of the World Trade Organization (WTO) to increase imports into India. With agreement across all political parties (except communist entities), the agency of India's elites was critical, as 'the seriousness and the sweep of the reforms . . . demonstrated that the driving force behind the reforms was equally . . . our own conviction that we had lost precious time' (T.N. Srinivasan & Jagdish Bhagwati quoted in Johri & Miller, 2002: 87). Via incremental reform, average annual GDP growth rose from 5.7 per cent in the 1980s to 5.8 per cent in the 1990s and 6.9 per cent in the 2000s, reaching 7.6 per cent by 2015 (World Bank, 2016c).

For these reasons, the economic reforms in 1991 can be seen as a pivotal turning point in India's proactive acquisition of great power capabilities. By opening up to the international system, Manmohan Singh 'framed India's great power ambitions in strictly economic terms, excluding any aspirations of being an exemplary civilization or paragon of international virtue' (Malone, 2012: 148) via an approach (the Manmohan Doctrine) of mounting international interaction centred upon economic growth and consumption, not borrowing. Global engagement thus became necessary to India's foreign policy, so as to achieve greater levels of autonomy in all spheres and as the collective means to becoming a great power. In addition, growth was critical for domestic development, whereby economic regeneration and revitalization also fed into the worldview of India's elites. With a large potential (middle-class) market and needing ever-increasing amounts of energy, trade, commodities and investment, New Delhi also found itself ideally positioned to appeal to other states, signalling enhanced levels of global interdependency, recognition and status. Thus India's current economic emergence is its 'main claim for entry into the hallowed portals of influential states, and this attribute is likely to keep impressing itself on the rest of the world with an even bigger voice in the decades to come' (Chaulia, 2011b: 32).

Such efforts have, however, been beset by an 'image of politics as usual' (Jenkins, 2000: 6), with, for instance, many companies still remaining under state control. This observation underlines the difficulties of carrying out rapid reform in a democratic setting, within which those domestic interests and constituencies adversely affected by (economic) change are able periodically to remove political elites from office, if they so wish. That said, as India's economy has continued to grow, so has the wider acceptance of the virtues of global capitalism, which drives forward the liberalization process in the belief that it will increase investment, production technology and access to world markets. In this former vein, India has been a rapidly rising recipient of FDI, which rose across the 1980s, 1990s and 2000s, with net inflows (in current US dollars) totalling $1.05 billion, $15.06 billion and $156.29 billion in each decade, respectively, and amounting to $44.21 billion in 2015 alone (World Bank, 2016a).

Whilst still ranking some way behind China, albeit with a less lengthy (indeed potentially fifteen to twenty years shorter) period of liberalization, in conjunction with a more accountable political system, India can still be regarded as an emerging economic behemoth. Thus, its GDP (in current US dollars) rose rapidly from $190 billion in 1980 to $327 billion in 1990, to $477 billion in 2000 and $1,708 billion in 2010, totalling $2,073 billion in 2015 (World Bank, 2016b). Of note is the fact that India's GDP in 1980 was actually higher than China's at the same juncture. In turn, from 1980 to 2010, GDP per capita in India (in current US dollars) also rose significantly, from \$271.90 in 1980, to \$375.20 in 1990, to \$452.40 in 2000 and \$1,387.90 in 2010, standing at \$1,581.6 in 2015 (World Bank, 2016d) – an achievement that has taken at least 200 million people out of poverty. While these figures are positive, however, in 2015 India was only the world's seventeenth largest exporter and eleventh largest importer (CIA, 2015b), thus not sharing the same global economic centrality currently enjoyed by China. Over time, though, its expanding economic base will allow New Delhi to pursue an independent and self-reliant foreign policy aimed at giving India 'equal status to world powers such as the US, Russia and China' (Adeney & Wyatt, 2010: 216). The need to gain economic growth therefore remains paramount in the self-perception of Indian policy-makers, as 'India is not respected because it has acquired the capacity to launch rockets or satellites, or because of the size of its population, . . . the world respects India because of its capacity to emerge as an economic powerhouse' (Chidambaram, 2007: 3).

Implications of Economic Power

Gaining economic power has a range of implications beyond a state simply gaining greater levels of national wealth, development and prosperity. From the perspective of great power accounts, primary amongst these impacts are elements of interdependence and cooperation, whereby 'the proof of power lies in the ability to change the behaviour of states' (Nye, 2004: 69). This impact can be either largely positive (attractive) or largely negative (coercive), and is intrinsically persuasive and instrumental. Furthermore, owing to its intimately hierarchical essence, in that states have more or less than others, amassing economic power implies some degree of heightened standing within the present economics-driven international system. Critically underpinning this perspective, however, is the assertion that great power status is measured not solely by material capacity but also through recognition by others. As we have already seen above, China and India are gradually receiving this wider recognition, most notably the former, such that other states are able to profit with them via increased levels of economic interaction.

Most immediately, economic power bolsters relationships with other states, and creates synergies and interdependencies between various state, multilateral and corporate entities. In these ways, a state's trading power – or 'commercial diplomacy' – translates into political power that can result in gaining potential leverage and influence over others. Critically, such power can overshadow other quotients, with Perkovich noting, for example, how the possession of nuclear weapons 'cannot grow an economy, gain international market share, or win political support for a nation's demands to shape the political-economic order' (2004: 138). Given these attributes, economic strength underpins the rise of great powers but is also a highly convertible resource. At its most essential translation, both China and India have amassed large foreign exchange and gold reserves with which to protect their economies from speculation, as well as to absorb any external shocks affecting their export markets, and these allow them to settle any payment obligations. By the end of 2015, these reserves stood at $3.22 trillion for China – the world's largest (and 150 per cent above second-ranked Japan) – and at $0.37 trillion for India (CIA, 2016f). Both states are also increasing their outward FDI flows: India's rose from $4 million in 1980, to $6 million in 1990, to $0.51 billion in 2000, to $15.93 billion in 2010, and to $9.85 billion in 2014 (0.62 per cent of the overall global total); China's figures for the same years were were $0.00, $0.83 billion, $0.92 billion, $68.81 billion, and $116.00 billion (7.31 per cent of the global total) (UNCTAD, 2016).

The conversion of residual economic power to overt great power influence also occurs via its (potential) conversion to other types of power, most notably military – as shown in Chapter 3 by India and China's mounting expenditure and material acquisition in this area. This transfiguration points to a degree of interconnected power enhancement across different yet intimately tied quotients, whereby, say, economic power is strengthened through the enhanced ability of a state to use military force to protect trade, commodity and energy security navigational routes. Moreover, it has a co-constitutive property, such that the resultant power attainment can be used to reinforce further this (military) or another source of power. In these ways, power has a self-replicating but also exponential element to it as it begins to blossom in scale.

Additionally, a state can derive structural power from economic power if it has a key role in global trade. In this way, such is the current central attractiveness of China in the international system that in 2014 it imported 57.7 per cent of the world's iron ore, 31.0 per cent of its copper ore, 57.7 per cent of its soya beans, 31.8 per cent of its integrated circuits and 14.4 per cent of its oil, creating major trade dependencies with (among others) Chile and Peru, Australia and Brazil, the United States and Brazil, Taiwan and Hong Kong, and Saudi Arabia and Russia, respectively (BBC, 2015c). This role has led some analysts to speculate about a 'Beijing Consensus', although this has been criticized as being 'a misguided and inaccurate summary of China's actual reform experience' (S. Kennedy, 2010: 461). Regardless, the undeniable success of the CCP's authoritarian capitalism over the last thirty years appears to threaten Western liberal democratic models ideationally, and hence, to some degree, the values currently underscoring the workings of global finance. Such ideational competition points to Beijing's structural power and its (potential) ability to re-orientate the basis upon which the international system operates – itself a veritable sign of great power influence. Further ideational tensions with dominant (Western) trade norms also relate to widespread child labour in India (which is regulated but not banned), as well as well-established allegations against China relating to industrial and cyber-espionage, reverse engineering and large-scale hacking.

Hard economic abilities can also be translated into soft power: the 'ability to get desired outcomes because others want what you want' (Keohane & Nye, 2008: 85). Innately non-coercive, aspirational and co-optive, economic sources of power can thus be a source of attractive normative power. Much of India's soft power relates to its core political values of non-violence, democracy and peaceful mediation, which are 'broadly compatible with those of the West' (Nayar & Paul, 2003: 271). The importance of ideas is of contemporary significance, and is perhaps a more critical element for great powers to consider than in previous eras, since 'we live in an information world and information depends on its credibility . . . countries that are more credible are more likely to be believed and more followed' (Joseph S. Nye quoted in Pocha, 2003: 8). This being the case, international relations act as a form of 'international public relations' (L'Etang, 2009). Culturally, India's Bollywood film industry is now being exported across the world, whilst its authors have a key international presence. By 2015, there were also thirty-five cultural centres set up by the Indian Council for Cultural Relations 'to foster and strengthen cultural relations and mutual understanding between India and other countries' (ICCR, 2015). China has also set up equivalent Confucius Institutes, which will number 1,000 by 2020 (Volodzko, 2015), to propagate Chinese language and culture. In terms of projecting a desired vision of their state globally, Beijing's biggest act of public diplomacy was hosting the 2008 Olympics, whilst for New Delhi it was the 2010 Commonwealth Games, although the latter was beset by a host of logistical difficulties. Beijing will host the 2022 Winter Olympics, and India will certainly bid for Olympics in the future.

Tensions and Issues

As China and India undergo expectant economic transitions from being large developing states to modernized developed entities, the pace of their reform periods has led to a series of tensions. Many of these relate to the necessity of continued fiscal growth, which brings with it deepening issues that straddle the domestic and external domains of their foreign policy behaviour and interaction. In turn, these problems highlight how the trajectories of both states are not necessarily guaranteed, and are indeed exacerbated by economic power being the most convertible power source for a would-be great power to have, which makes them somewhat dependent upon the current financial system.

The clearest example is the attitude of Beijing and New Delhi towards globalization, which is regarded by both as a necessary balance between global immersion (and the accompanying trade, FDI, technology and market benefits which it brings) and state protection (against multinationals that attack local business, and alien ideas that threaten to dilute indigenous culture). This tension highlights competing identities between Asia's emergent great powers and an international system still regarded with caution and suspicion courtesy of their negative colonial experiences – underscoring the continued role of history, memory and experience in their global interactions. The 1997 Asian Financial Crisis compounded such perspectives, when (Western) external investment was withdrawn from states across Southeast Asia that had rapidly liberalized their economies, resulting in the decimation of their financial systems. Hence a globalized economic order is seen to potentially threaten Indian and Chinese independence, self-sufficiency and autonomy. This sentiment is implicit in their gradual economic liberalizations, with both states fearing any reduction in their sovereignty and thus preferring preferential and free trade over global agreements. International law, 'Western' ideas and external stock market and commodity speculation are all seen as unwanted and potentially destabilizing extra-national pressures.

Reflective of this conundrum is the continued search for, need for and exploitation of energy resources. For both China and India, a steady and uninterrupted supply of energy (principally oil and natural gas) is key to their continued economic growth and increasing (great) national power. This explains why both states are frequently willing to deal with entities regarded as international pariahs (such as Iran, Sudan, Myanmar and some Central Asian states), for rising needs outweigh any international criticism. In this context, energy security is defined by the UN as 'the continuous availability of energy in various forms and in sufficient quantities at reasonable prices' (quoted in Noronha & Sudarshan, 2011: 5). Critically, all sectors of an economy – including agriculture, industry, services and households – depend upon energy, and without it their economic growth will rapidly decrease. Thus, it is commonplace for any great power to protect its energy security routes.

As New Delhi experiences continued economic growth, its search for energy has increased, with analysts estimating in 2007 that India's energy dependence will 'grow five-fold over the next 25 years' (Sahni, 2007: 24–5), making it the world's third largest oil importer. In this regard, Jaswant Singh states that 'energy is security . . . any deficiency in energy will compromise the nation's security' (quoted in D. Scott, 2008: 17), whilst Manmohan Singh adds that 'the quest for energy security is second only . . . to food security' (quoted in H. Zhao, 2012: 60). By 2020, it is estimated that 90 per cent of India's energy needs will be met from external sources (Pham, 2007: 344). For these reasons, India does not discriminate in its international dealings with states accused of having questionable government or poor human rights records. New Delhi's non-ideological and unconditional approach to purchasing energy resources thus aids its efforts in this regard, and in 2013 60 per cent of India's crude oil imports came from West Asia (including 20 per cent from Saudi Arabia and 14 per cent from Iraq), 16 per cent from Africa (half of which came from Nigeria) and 12 per cent from Venezuela (MarEx, 2014). In 2015, New Delhi was importing over 4.1 million barrels of oil per day, making it the world's fourth highest consumer, while domestically it produced nearly 1 million barrels per day (USEIA, 2016b). In 2005, New Delhi set up a Strategic Petroleum Reserve. It also has coal supplies for 200 years, but as these are highly polluting, it is diversifying towards nuclear power, which will provide up to 50 per cent of its energy production needs by 2045 (Wyatt, 2005: 172).

Beijing faces similar energy security needs, and is also not averse to dealing with energy-rich – if despotic – states, as shown by its apolitical international investment behaviour. Economic interdependence in terms of supply and demand is central to its energy security dynamics, and as noted by Hu Jintao: 'oil is the crux in the rivalry between various forces in the world . . . [and] China must guard against attempts by other powers to strangle Chinese oil supply routes' (quoted in Lanteigne, 2008: 149). From 1985 to 2013, China's oil demand quintupled (USEIA, 2013), in 2015 it overtook the United States to become the world's largest oil importer with 7.4 million barrels per day (McSpadden, 2015), and it is estimated that it will be importing 80% of its oil by 2020. Such changes have led to Beijing broadening the scope of its oil imports, including via transnational pipelines, having a Strategic Petroleum Reserve from 2001 and promoting domestic production and energy efficiency. In 2014, 52 per cent of China's oil imports came from West Asia (including 16 per cent from Saudi Arabia and 9 per cent from both Iran and Iraq), 22 per cent from Africa (including 13 per cent from Angola), 13 per cent from Russia and Central Asia and 11 per cent from the Americas, while domestically it produced 4.6 million barrels a day (USEIA, 2016a).

A direct consequence of such rising levels of energy consumption has been mounting environmental degradation and pollution in both states, often as a result of unchecked economic growth in largely unregulated (or at least legally unenforced) circumstances. In 2011, China and India were ranked as the largest and fourth largest carbon emitters in the world, with emissions of 2,460 million and 566 million metric tons respectively (CDIAC, 2015). Such emissions are resulting in low air, land, water and health quality in both states, and although the overall situation is currently worse in China, in recent years charts citing the world's most polluted cities are now resoundingly dominated by India. These high rates of domestic environmental destruction are also a shared focal point for intensifying protest, unrest and instability, and have the potential to delegitimize the role of leaders in both New Delhi and Beijing. They are also resulting in public health crises, especially concerning respiratory illnesses and childhood diseases, and the damaging of indigenous natural resources – factors that represent a significant present and future cost that will retard the speed of modernization in both states. The material gains of high economic growth have thus resulted in often destructive and very longstanding societal consequences.

The economic transformations of the two states have also seen life expectancy at birth increase between 1980 and 2014 – from 66.5 to 75.8 years in China, and from 53.9 to 68.0 in India (World Bank, 2016f) – and have pulled many millions out of poverty. That said, in 2010 and 2011, respectively, 11.2 per cent of China's population and 21.3 per cent of India's lived on less than $1.90 a day in 2011 PPP (price purchasing parity) terms (World Bank, 2016g). Although these are significant reductions from 1987 levels (when the figures for China stood at 60.8 per cent and India at 50.3 per cent – World Bank, 2016g), for New Delhi, current levels point to a 'glaring and unsustainable discrepancy between India's apparent influence abroad and the poverty of its domestic politics' (Narlikar, 2007: 994), and have the potential to undermine global perceptions of it as a great power. Such a credibility gap is worsened by low healthcare, housing, pensions and education provision, and represents a significant internal challenge for its ruling elites. It further 'raises obvious doubts about the wisdom of characterizing India as a global economic power' (Panagariya, 2008: 207). Although Beijing's problems in this regard are smaller in scale, Xi Jinping (2012) has noted that 'China is still a developing country facing a series of grim challenges', echoing sentiments from Hu Jintao that 'improved social order [is] essential for ... continuing economic growth' (Tanner, 2013: 89). Vast social inequalities compound these perspectives, with the richest 1 per cent in China and India owning 70 per cent and 49 per cent of national wealth, respectively, in 2012 and 2014 (Garofalo, 2012; *The Hindu*, 2014) – differences exacerbated when urban areas are compared with poorer rural ones.

Coalescing with these inequalities, both states are experiencing prevalent corruption, which 'feeds the sense of inequity, inequality, and procedural injustice that fuels rage' (Lampton, 2008: 238). Symptomatic of a transitioning economy, some officials in both India and China have sought personal gain from their states' newfound wealth – actions that frequently delegitimize the status of their political leaders. The leaders of China, as rulers over a one-party state, often view the seriousness of these issues in very existential terms; outgoing President Hu stated in November 2012 that 'if we fail to handle this issue well, it could ... cause the collapse of the party and the fall of the state' (quoted in BBC, 2012b). In its turn, India in recent years has become swamped by a sequence of high-profile corruption cases, including large telecommunication and mining scandals when national assets were sold for fractions of their real value, as well as during parliamentary votes and arms purchases. Such incidences have threatened India's political leaders by undermining its democratic standing, as well as reducing multinational investment confidence. India's economic liberalization process has thus not been accompanied by an 'evolution of its structures and institutional competence' (Krishnappa & George, 2012: 1), which has produced a political deficit. Overall, India and China respectively ranked 85 and 100 on Transparency International's 2014 Corruption Perceptions Index (TI, 2014). Still, given the sheer size of their internal markets, such corruption may not significantly dissuade external investment, with continued growth effectively trumping any domestic legitimacy issues.

Interdependence, Interpretation and Recognition

Economic prowess represents perhaps the purest material power source linked to the attainment of great power status. Enabling the acquisition of other kinds of power, it is highly fungible, flexible and co-constitutive. In turn, other states are drawn towards those amassing significant amounts of economic power – especially large states with large populations like China and India –, which signals further elements of liberal interdependence through exports and imports, inward and outward FDI and foreign aid. States that can provide a great power with the material means to facilitate its continued growth, such as raw materials, commodities and energy resources, are also pulled in by these attractive centripetal forces. Great powers stand to gain the most from these recognition-based interplays, and thus economic strength presages international behaviours based upon often mutually beneficial and transactional interactions. This interlinkage is simultaneously fiscal and ideational in nature, as international trade reflects the dominant consensuses and values – created via historical state-to-state interaction and experience – regarding how such great powers function, and these are presently based upon globalized, liberal, free-market economics.

Moreover, economic power is interconnected with other (great) power sources. As shown by China and India, attitudes towards a source of great power can change over time. For example, when both Beijing and New Delhi chose to embrace liberal economic principles, transcending their earlier autarkic proclivities, this evolution 'deemphasized the ideology of both states, rejecting in large part the image of American economic-imperial ambitions while incorporating insights regarding the use of America's economic . . . strength to achieve its goals' (Braumoeller, 2012: 78). Their embrace of liberal capitalism also reflected new global realities that shifted from a political-military to a political-economic footing in the 1980s/1990s – a reality itself predicated upon the internal principles and outlooks of existing great powers, in the guise of the United States but also Western states in Europe. That the economic dominance of these states allowed them to determine the underlying nature of global finance indicates that (economic) systemic principles in the future could also innately reflect those states who will have global (material) preponderance. Hence, there is much validity in assertions that 'countries like China [and] India . . . are acquiring enough power to change the face of global politics and economics' (Mark Garten quoted in Hurrell, 2006: 2), and this underscores the need to understand the domestic values/identities of great powers.

On some measures, China already achieved this material preponderance by 2014, when its GDP in PPP terms outstripped those of the United States and the European Union to become the world's highest (CIA, 2015a). Some observers argue that China's economic power will lead to its hegemony (Jacques, 2009), although its long-standing belief in multipolarity may undercut such an outcome (see Chapter 6). There is also evidence of Chinese self-awareness, as exemplified by the 2006 China Central Television series entitled *The Rise of the Great Powers* (*Daguo Jueqi*), within which 'the US and Britain . . . are upheld as typical examples of great powers that rose to eminence *without* relying on force, and therefore are objects of emulation' (Suzuki, 2014: 643) – a viewpoint that seemingly marries with many of China's values as explicated in Chapters 1, 2 and 3. Nevertheless, there are many externally derived negative perceptions towards China's rapid rise concerning its various growing trade surpluses (unbalancing economic interdependencies), anxieties over its monopolistic behaviour (regarding textiles, steel and 'rare-earth' materials – 97 per cent of which are in the PRC –, among others), and speculation as to the true value of its currency (externally as the renminbi [RMB] and the yuan domestically), which is not yet fully convertible – all of which give China unfair trade advantages.

Of note here is that the RMB is being slowly internationalized – facilitated by clearing hubs opening across the world, the signing of multiple RMB Bilateral Swap Agreements and the introduction of the RMB Qualified Foreign Institutional Investor scheme in 2014. Having a fully convertible RMB as a global currency, and the interdependencies that it may bring, will give China a systemic centrality/recognition that is a critical requirement of any true great power. In the coming years, the PRC's leaders will also have to confront whether or not their state is still developing – something that will change its institutional relations, responsibilities and status (see Chapter 6). Apart from the many internal challenges faced by Beijing, be they related to the environment, corruption or inequality, when GDP is seen in per capita terms, China is far behind most Western states. This viewpoint reminds us of the relative nature of great power status, especially when comparing emergent Asian entities with their already developed/modernized (Western) peers. In turn, it further indicates that much of China's (economic) power will need to be directed inwards for some time to come, so as to achieve its longstanding development and modernization goals.

Whilst not fully comparable to China in terms of scope, scale and centrality, India is also liberalizing its economy, by means of which it is becoming more interwoven within the fabric of international capital. And, through some increasingly interdependent dynamics, New Delhi is developing into an essential international actor via a mixture of market, trading and resource linkages. US officials thus note that 'as the economic power, cultural reach, and political influence of India increase, it is assuming a more influential role in global affairs' (Department of Defense, 2010: 60) – further illustrating the interplay between economics and other factors. Given India's soon to be world-leading largest population, other analysts predict that it will have the world's largest GDP by 2050 (Hawksworth & Cookson, 2008), which will significantly reinforce its modernization/development goals, as well as bolster its great power status across all power dimensions. As with China, India also faces some monumental shortcomings in terms of its internal infrastructure, along with challenges concerning poverty, the environment, corruption and inequality, which will require significant material resources – as well as considerable political will – to ameliorate successfully. In this regard, large demographics are either a material windfall or an Achilles' heel, and may signal a different kind of great power that needs to be less globally focused/active in intent. Indian values relating to equality, development and democracy (see Chapters 1, 2 and 3) will affect this behaviour, such that the domestic realm seeps into the global. This reflection may be more valid for post-colonial states, such as India and China, who intuitively regard international affairs with suspicion.

5

PERIPHERAL RELATIONS

Encapsulating elements of relative positioning, physicality, latent influence and status, from a geopolitical perspective, the 'advantages and vulnerabilities that territorial and maritime space may bring to foreign affairs and national security' (Phil Kelly quoted in D. Scott, 2008: 3) inform great power debates. A state's geographical extent, nature and location are all of significance concerning its international relations. By moving beyond notions of mere territorial scale (and viable expansionism) – and when conjoined with notions of regional status, pre-eminence and hegemony –, a state's physical positioning further highlights the role of perceptions. As these have evolved through past and present state-to-state/state-to-region interactions, historical memory and relative/desired power hierarchies, a state's peripheral relations therefore critically encompass elements of experience and self-image, as well as role-giving and role-taking. Given that a state's neighbours are basically immovable, these elements gain ever-greater credence.

Regional standing represents a combination of diplomatic, military and trade dominance, along with a degree of proximate ordering and management. Inherently hierarchical, these notions echo realist outlooks on power as 'the ability of one state to exert influence or control over the actions of other states' (Carey, 2008: 61), which represents an innately relative and interactional exchange. Moreover, as Prys notes (2008: 8), by enveloping material *and* perceptual qualities – including intent, desire, ambition, fear and threat, often buoyed through positive/negative interactions, experience and history –, 'perceptions', 'projection' and 'provision' are key to regional ordering. Proactive ambition plays into these understandings, whereby the willingness of states to pursue (regional) hegemony is seen as a requisite in international affairs (Keohane & Nye, 1977). Notably, such dominance need not be coercive, with smaller states often able to benefit from a hegemon even when the distribution of goods is skewed in the latter's favour – an observation particularly valid in terms of trade ties, markets and capital. In these ways, 'the manipulation of material incentives . . . is the dominant form through which hegemonic power is exercised' (Ikenberry & Kupchan 1990: 283), and which complements the rising economic authority of both China and India, who now possess the largest economies in East Asia and South Asia, respectively.

Furthermore, constructivist accounts note that the effects of power are also 'a function of culturally constituted ideas' (Wendt, 1999: 41) that impact upon quantifiable power quotients. Thus, following on from previous chapters, identities and the 'historical, cultural . . . and social context' (Hopf, 1998: 176) under which they are conceived significantly influence inter-state relations, and can be almost as indelible as geography (consider India vis-à-vis Pakistan and China vis-à-vis Japan as two examples of regional contestation – see below). When great power identity is regarded as 'a reciprocal construction composed of the interplay between a state's view of itself and the view of it held by other members of international society' (Buzan, 2004: 61), these factors gain even greater salience. Here, recognition by others can help establish an identity, potentially limit any proclivity for violence and indicate a form of (regional/global) legitimacy. However, when recognition is not forthcoming, it can lead to competition and tension, and these oppositional dynamics can be especially problematical – particularly if they relate to ordering, pre-eminence and ranking. With roles being formed through interaction and socialization, they are also influenced by precedent, experience and perception, and can potentially produce a negative projection of the past into the future. Perceptions of material power (as per chapters 3 and 4) play into such equations, as do the beliefs and agency of political elites and nationalism (as delineated in Chapters 1 and 2). For both China and India, all of these interconnected factors are present regionally, in particular the weight of history and prior interactions.

This chapter investigates the development of Asia's largest entities' peripheral relations, which stem from a shared physical dominance regarding their respective neighbourhoods (China in East Asia, and India in South Asia). The main focus of examination rests upon how India and China's elites conceptualize of their states regionally, and whether or not they can be regarded as their region's (accepted) hegemon. The chapter draws upon case studies that reflect ongoing recognition, status and territorial disputes within both Chinese and Indian foreign policy, most pertinently for the latter concerning unsettled relations with Pakistan, and for the former concerning ongoing historically driven tensions with Japan. It further focuses upon the strategic priorities of both states' elites concerning their wider peripheral relations, as well as their attitudes concerning primacy towards the IOR (for India) and the South China Sea (for China), which are regarded as 'natural' extensions of their territorial influence/sovereignty.

Strategic Priorities

Constituting in excess of 75 per cent of the region's overall population, territory and GDP, as well as comprehensively outstripping its neighbours in terms of military spending, India has an 'asymmetry in South Asia [that] is obvious and overwhelming' (Wagner, 2005: 1). For these reasons, it is a benign regional hegemon, whose capabilities allow it to dwarf all of its bordering states through a combination of hard and soft bilateral strategies. Such understandings are replicated in the outlook of its leaders, who have 'inherited the Raj tradition . . . [of] an influential, if not dominant, role over the wide arc from Aden to Singapore' (Pramoda Panda quoted in Ogden, 2014b: 75). As part of this hegemonic discourse, India's perceived sphere of influence widens to include Iran, Afghanistan, Thailand and Tibet, and the IOR. Furthermore, New Delhi appears as an isolated democratic beacon within a highly volatile region, with all but one of its neighbours featuring in the top forty of the 2015 *Foreign Policy Fragile States Index* – Pakistan, Myanmar, Nepal, Bangladesh and Sri Lanka ranking fourteenth, twenty-sixth, thirty-third, thirty-sixth and forty-third, respectively, whilst India ranked seventieth (FP, 2016). For these reasons, the major strategic priority of India's elites is to manage their immediate strategic neighbourhood, so as to ensure heightened stability and control.

Overall, India has land borders with six other states (five before 1971), amounting to over 13,888 kilometres, and is the only state to border all of the states of South Asia, thus acting as its natural fulcrum. Two of its neighbours – Bhutan and Nepal – are landlocked and rely on India for sea access, whilst the Indian coastline is over 7,000 kilometres in length and has proximity to two other states (Sri Lanka and the Maldives). Cognizant of the primacy of core principles relating to unity, coherence, 'national identity and survival'

(Chaturvedi, 2000: 214), India's elected leaders have carried out a process of ongoing – and often forceful – territorial consolidation. Resting upon a clear conception of its physical extent, this process has included the military annexation of Hyderabad and Junagadh in 1947; the regaining of Goa in 1961 (from Portugal and also via military force); the eventual return of Pondicherry from France in 1963; and the absorption of Sikkim in 1975. Against this, however, it should be noted that India returned one of the Coco Islands to Myanmar in 1951, revealing that its leaders have a clear conception of the extent of its borders, rather than harbouring unfettered expansionist desires. India's major 'cartographic anxiety' (Krishna, 1994) now rests upon unresolved land disputes with Pakistan (over Kashmir) and China (over Arunachal Pradesh, Aksai Chin and a portion of Kashmir). Unclear border demarcations dating from the colonial era are at the root of many of these issues, with the Curzon and McMahon lines variously seen as responsible for contested borders with China but also with Nepal, Bhutan and Bangladesh, while the Mountbatten Plan is seen as responsible for territorial disputes relating to Pakistan (Kashmir and pre-1971 East Pakistan).

Related not only to ensuring New Delhi's regional pre-eminence, along with protecting India against security threats linked to terrorism, migration and smuggling, preserving autonomy in its foreign policy-making and behaviour has also been an overriding concern. Indian foreign policy has thus involved the frequent projection of military force into bordering states during the Cold War (primarily via the Indira Doctrine, as elucidated below), and a general bilateral rather than multilateral slant to its regional diplomacy. Although 'India has sought primacy and a veto over actions of outside powers' (Mohan, 2006: 17) so as to reduce external interference, New Delhi has struggled to maintain its sphere of influence, in particular vis-à-vis the United States and China in Pakistan. Furthermore, the presence of a host of unstable neighbours, buoyed by some often toxic and schismatic historical relations, has led many observers to contend that such volatility may hinder India's (short-term) economic growth (Dash, 2001: 210). In sum, others assert that 'becoming one of the principal powers of Asia will depend entirely on India's ability to manage its own immediate neighbourhood' (Muni & Mohan, 2004: 318) – itself a key sign of being a great power.

China's physical size and economic/military capabilities have long been seen to allow it to assume a leading role in Asia. As with its Middle Kingdom status and the hegemonic pre-eminence of its imperial period, China appears set to re-become Asia's hegemon. Chinese

exceptionalism, premised upon the superiority of the Chinese civilization over the region for many centuries, also contemporarily colours
the thinking of domestic leaders and audiences. Hence, the desire for
'international status' (*guoji diwei*) – so as to achieve power, security
and respect – has dominated Chinese foreign policy discourses since
the 1990s. These elements inform both Chinese foreign policy and the
perceptions of many of its neighbours (fourteen by land, seven by sea)
along its 22,447 kilometre-long border. In addition to its 14,500 kilometre-long coastline, China has the world's longest land borders and
the joint highest number of neighbouring land states. Beijing also has
a clear conception of the physical extent of the PRC, as exemplified
by territorial disputes over Taiwan, Arunachal Pradesh (with India,
and referred to as Southern Tibet) and several small islands (with
Japan and several Southeast Asian states – see below). These disputes
are often seen as 'sacred commitments' aimed at restoring the honour
of great national unity (*da yi tong*) and reversing past humiliations.
With this aim, in October 1950 the PRC invaded and annexed Tibet
as part of the territorial assertions of its leaders.

Reflective of the ideological fervour of the Maoist era, China's
elites sought to export the communist revolution across Southeast
Asia, whilst being immediately distanced from Japan (courtesy of
Tokyo's pre-Second World War occupation) and eventually distant
from the Soviet Union (after their 1960s political split). In line with
the Dengist transformation of Chinese foreign policy in the 1970s,
the CCP then sought 'to abandon ideology as the policy guide and
to develop friendly relations with neighboring countries regardless
of their ideological tendencies and political systems' (S. Zhao, 2004:
214). After the events in Tiananmen Square in 1989, Beijing was also
keen to repair regional relations, and to present China as a politi-
cally benign and non-hegemonically inclined state that could foster a
secure neighbourhood that would also aid Beijing's internal modernization programme. As Chinese Premier Wen Jiabao remarked, this
'periphery policy' (*zhoubian zhengce*) aimed to present China as 'a
good neighbour and a good partner, to strengthen good neighbourly
ties, to intensify regional cooperation, and to push China's exchanges
and cooperation with its neighbours to a new high' (Wen Jiabao
quoted in Beeson & Li, 2012: 37).

Becoming progressively more proactive and self-confident, China's
peripheral diplomacy thus aims to present Beijing as 'an indispensable partner and potential alternative to American-led Western
Power' (Lanteigne, 2013: 109). Through mutual 'peaceful development' (*heping fazhan*) based upon a stable regional environment

104

with foundations of equality, trust and win-win cooperation, in 1992 China normalized many key relations (with South Korea, Russia and the new Central Asian states) and significantly deepened regional relations via enhanced trade cooperation. As a result, by the early 2010s, 'China [wa]s one of the top five export destinations and top three import sources ... [for] all its neighbouring states (except Afghanistan)' (Womack, 2013: 918), indicating a high level of liberal hegemonic interdependence between Beijing and its periphery. China also resolved many of its border disputes: for instance, signing agreements with Laos, Bhutan and Mongolia in the 1990s; with Russia in 1991, 1994 and 2004; with Vietnam in 1999; and with the Central Asian states. These deals often came about through clear sovereign compromises by Beijing: settling for 20 per cent of disputed land with Kazakhstan, 30 per cent with Kyrgyzstan and conceding the majority of its claim to Tajikistan's Pamir Mountains (Lampton, 2008: 48). Observers claim such behaviour stems from imperial China's cultural, rather than physical, hegemony over its periphery (Kang, 2007).

Of particular significance, however, are the wider security dynamics of the East Asia region, which currently encompasses many of the world's largest economies, largest militaries and a host of nuclear (and nascent nuclear) states. Specifically, this conflux points to two contender (or actual) great powers in the guise of Japan and Russia, plus the significant external presence of the United States, which results in China having 'an offshore power dominant in its own home region' (Twomey, 2008: 405). It is also a region where a violent and traumatic past continues to cast a long shadow, fostering historical animosities/volatilities and restricting multilateralism. As such, the US-centred hub-and-spoke system remains critically essential to regional stability, and is unlikely to give way in the short term to a different kind of regional order, such as one centred upon a China-dominated hierarchical Asian arrangement. For these reasons, the current situation is one that defies realist axioms that the 'strong do what they have the power to do and the weak accept what they have to accept' (Thucydides quoted in Kim & Lee, 2002: 131), and instead centres on structuralist/liberalist economics, and is informed by constructivist identity accounts.

Principal Contestations

Within their regional relations, both India and China are faced with a principal contestation with another state – Pakistan and Japan, respectively – which is premised upon a combination of status, territorial and ideational parameters. Highlighting an interplay and interconnection between different material factors (primarily military and economic) and perceptual elements (such as prestige, trauma and humiliation), these rivalries underscore the role of identity and (self-) image in the delineation of great power. History is critical in this regard as it acts as a chronological tool (and temporal manager) that traces a state's interactions, and provides a depository of experience and precedents about policy-making and behaviour. Time therefore acts as a necessary variable, serving to confirm that a state's security is not an ageless essence but is instead historically contingent and contested. It also indicates the historical specificity of any great power emergence.

The roots of Beijing's regional rivalry with Tokyo lie in the Sino-Japanese war of 1894–5, which resulted in China's defeat and its ceding of regional centrality (and supremacy) to Japan. China's lack of complete territorial integrity continued during the same period, as exemplified by Japan's occupation of parts of the north via the Manchukuo puppet state in the 1930s. The occupation also precipitated the loss of Taiwan (then called Formosa) to Japan, as well as the control and eventual splitting of the Korean peninsula. Tokyo's physical presence would only end with the conclusion of the Second World War in 1945. These damaging events collectively formed a major emotional mainstay in China's perceived Century of Humiliation, which shattered notions of its longstanding Middle Kingdom dominance. Casting a shadow over Sino-Japanese relations, they indicated how 'historical traumas can heavily influence future perceptions' (Jervis, 1969: 470). After the establishment of the PRC, such negative tensions were subsumed by Japan's focus on modernization aided by the United States' occupation and then protection, as per the 1960 'US–Japan Mutual Security Treaty'. Although Japan's Yoshida Doctrine had clear anti-communist elements, Beijing favoured Japan–US security ties over any re-militarization by Tokyo, and thus further benefited from the highly pacifist Article IX of Japan's Constitution that 'forever renounce[d] war as a sovereign right of a nation' (quoted in Lanteigne, 2013: 125).

Via increasing economic linkages in the 1960s, relations between China and Japan were normalized in 1972, along with some accommodation of historical issues. Article 2 of their 1972 'Treaty of Peace and Friendship' further stated that 'neither party will seek hegemony within the Asian and Pacific region or in any other region, and that both shall oppose any attempt by any country or group of countries to establish such hegemony' (TPF, 1978). Fomenting largely good economic and diplomatic ties, relations broadly improved as the century progressed. Japan did initially perceive the 1989 events in Tiananmen Square in a negative light (on account of its US ties and democratic basis) but then went on to help pull China back into the international mainstream. Although the economic benefits between the two states are clear, however, questions concerning regional superiority remain, underscoring their pressurized interplay of (economic) interdependence and status issues.

Heading the list of major tensions are those relating to China's national memory of Japan's pre-PRC imperial occupation. Notwithstanding that their 1972 Joint Communiqué stated that 'the Japanese side is keenly conscious of the responsibility for the serious damage that Japan caused in the past to the Chinese people through war, and deeply reproaches itself' (quoted in Hoshiyama, 2008: 100), there is a well-established sentiment of a 'perceived . . . whitewashing [of] Japanese World War II atrocities in China' (S. Zhao, 2004: 223). With tensions periodically triggered by disputes over the accuracy of Japanese history textbooks (including denials concerning the 1937–8 Rape of Nanjing), visits by Japanese Prime Ministers to the Yakasuni Shrine in Tokyo (which interred several war criminals in 1978) and never-ending accusations of Japan's failure to confess fully to its wartime atrocities, history remains an emotive touchstone between the two sides. Such tensions are heightened by the historical view in Japan 'that the Pacific War was not a war of aggression but was a war of self-defense' (Mochizuki, 2007: 758), itself highlighting an ongoing battle of perceptions, history and memory. Overall, this issue has had a blossoming impact upon China's foreign policy (see Chapter 1), informing not only Sino-Japanese relations but also its great power aspirations/reassertion; search for respect, recognition and prestige; and regional standing. Scholars further link this negative interface to the CCP's ruling legitimacy, seeing it as the most effective 'history card' that its leaders can play when facing internal nationalist criticism.

Further characterizing Sino-Japanese rivalry are several acute territorial issues, which serve to add a physical dimension to their ideational enmity. Principally, these relate to the Diaoyatai (for China)/Senkaku (for Japan) Islands, which Beijing claims as part of Taiwan and which Tokyo considers to be part of Okinawa. In 1992, China passed a territorial seas law to assert its claim, and regards the islands as falling within its exclusive economic zone (EEZ) according to the UN's Convention on the Law of the Sea, allowing it to explore potential oil and natural gas deposits. This EEZ overlaps with Japan's own EEZ, which conversely forms the basis of Tokyo's own claims. Acting as a trigger for periodic mutual nationalist outbursts, individuals from both states have landed on the islands, there have been face-offs between civil and naval craft from both sides, and in November 2013 Beijing declared an Air Defence Identification Zone over the islands, which was ignored by Japan, the United States and South Korea, all of whom promptly flew aircraft through it. A further flashpoint centres on the maritime boundaries of the East China Sea, in particular the offshore Chunxiao gas field, in which China began drilling from 2003. Also involving mutual shows of military force, 'Japan ... asserts the view that the intermediate line is the line of demarcation, and China ... argues the theory of the natural extension of the continental shelf' (Hoshiyama, 2008: 87). Given that anti-Japanese protests and riots occur as a result of these tensions, balancing between 'rising nationalism and popular indignation against Japan, while ... pursuing a pragmatic policy ... are huge challenges for the Chinese leadership' (Panda, 2012: 136).

As two of the world's largest economies – ranked second and third in 2014 according to the World Bank –, China and Japan have experienced bouts of financial competition and now increasing interdependence. Resulting in what some observers see as 'cold politics, hot economics' (*zhengleng jingre*), both sides have periodically deployed a mercantile realist emphasis on financial and technological growth so as to provide state security. Thus, despite growing levels of inter-state trade, including 'currency swap mechanisms, regional bond markets, and central bank coordination initiatives' (Beeson & Li, 2012: 48), as well as mounting mutual FDI, the necessity of economic growth has often resulted in rivalry. Hence, for instance, China's state-centred approach towards energy security (see Chapter 4) has led to greater efforts to control its gas and oil supply routes, actions that then feed into its territorial claims and expanding naval capabilities (see Chapter 3), and thus potentially further exacerbate nationalist tensions with Japan. The economic dimension also pertains to matters of status, prestige and agency. Economic leadership in the region appears to have passed to China through key events such as Beijing's non-depreciation of the yuan during the 1997 Asian Financial Crisis and its fiscal stimulus after the 2008 global credit crunch, both of which protected the region, plus its escalating outward FDI.

Wider contentions remain as to which power (if either) will claim regional hegemony in East Asia courtesy of their historical experience and prior status. Such a process is both relative and interactional, with analysts asking 'whether or not China recognizes Japan as a regional political great power, not solely as an economic great power' (Hoshiyama, 2008: 74), whilst Beijing fears a resurgence of Japanese nationalism and a potential re-run of the Century of Humiliation. Hence, China does not support Japanese efforts to become a permanent member of the UN Security Council, and is wary of any reinterpretation of Article IX that may lead to a re-militarized Japan. On the latter point in particular, perceptions are shown to be very much co-constitutive, oppositional and reinforcing. In 2014, Japanese Prime Minister Shinzo Abe lifted the fifty-year ban on the export of military weapons – an action that appeared to confirm Beijing's fears, especially given evaluations that Japan's air and naval capabilities remain far superior to China's (Swaine, 2005: 274). The role of the United States underscores these tensions, since 'as long as Japan refuses to possess nuclear weapons of its own, it will have to rely on America's extended nuclear deterrence' (Mochizuki, 2007: 742), but any withdrawal by Washington may lead to a resuscitation of frictions, and Tokyo's possible military nuclearization. East Asia therefore evidences signs of a fluid great power concert with multiple entities vying for prominence.

In South Asia, India's principal contestation is with Pakistan, which is 'the only South Asian state that has tried to resist Indian predominance through military and ideological means' (S.P. Cohen, 2002: 229), and their longstanding rivalry rests upon a mélange of territorial, systemic, nuclear and perceptual dimensions. Both formed from the Partition of British India in 1947, modern India and modern Pakistan have founding principles that are dichotomous and schismatic. At its heart, India remains committed to religious plurality and coexistence, which contrasts with Pakistan's devotion to the single religion of Islam as the guiding basis for its national and territorial identity. Such differences result in the two sides' guiding principles and national identities being intrinsically incompatible. Upon Partition, the ensuing territorial dispute over Kashmir personified this ideational split, resulting in a war in 1947–8. In a dispute that has been variously sustained ever since, the status of Kashmir was at the root of further fighting in 1965 and 1999, featured in the East Pakistan conflict of 1971 and would underlie the frequent occurrence of insurgency and terrorism in the region from the late 1980s onwards.

Despite New Delhi's pre-eminence in all of the direct conflicts between the two states, Pakistani claims concerning Kashmir, by challenging India's secular credentials, represent a significant ongoing challenge to the former's physical, political and ideological identity. As noted by Nehru in the 1950s, this is an unresolved issue undermining India's territorial integrity: 'what was broken ... was something very vital, and that was the body of India, ... [which] produced tremendous consequences ... in the minds and souls of millions of human beings' (quoted in Krishna, 1994: 509). Conversely, for Pakistan, the loss of its eastern wing courtesy of the 1971 liberation of East Pakistan, as facilitated by India's involvement – purportedly on humanitarian grounds – resulted in a second Partition that reinforced the need to protect Kashmir at all costs. The 1971 conflict also 'transformed South Asian geo-politics and left India more than ever in a position of hard power military supremacy over its rival Pakistan, and in South Asia generally' (D. Scott, 2011: 120). Notably, although the Line of Control (LoC) as delineated by the 1972 Simla Agreement would act as a *de facto* border through the Kashmir region from then onwards (splitting the disputed area 60 per cent to India, 30 per cent to Pakistan and 10 per cent to China), the ideational proclivities of India's elites (see Chapter 1) restrained them from taking further land. Thus, after the 1971 war, India 'relinquished substantial territorial gains that it had made ... and returned 94,000 prisoners of war' (Ogden, 2014b: 78), seemingly preferring to gain international status via responsible – rather than coercive – conduct.

For these reasons, and as sustained and engrained by their repeated direct (and indirect) conflict concerning Kashmir, this issue remains unresolved and acts as the undoubted ideational flashpoint issue between the two sides. This situation persists despite multiple efforts to try to resolve the conflict, including the holding of peace summits and talks, and periodic ceasefires declared across the LoC. Relatively regular cross-border incursions (by troops and militants) and a still hazy border demarcation also continue to exacerbate this issue between the two states. Thus, by producing a state of psychological demonization between New Delhi and Islamabad that has been entrenched over the last seventy years, and by being a continual and shared issue of mutual national legitimacy, Kashmir has become essentially zero-sum – whereby completely losing the territory would equal an emasculating and devalidating experience for either side. Beyond these intertwined territorial and ideational dynamics, if India were to lose Kashmir entirely, New Delhi elites fear a wider negative demonstration effect concerning its overall territorial integrity, which may legitimize separatist movements – especially in the restive provinces of its remote northeast. In particular, India's ethnically and culturally complex heterogeneity has the potential to play into such contentions, whereas – until now – New Delhi has largely been able to subsume myriad sub-national identities within the wider paradigm of a cohesive 'idea of India' (Khilnani, 1997).

This territorial and ideational schism has been replicated in India and Pakistan's divergent interaction within the wider international system. India helped found the multilateral NAM – designed to counter the bipolar Cold War world so as to create Third World solidarity by avoiding military alliances, and based upon anti-colonial and anti-imperialist sentiments (see Chapter 6). In contrast, Pakistan joined the US-backed Southeast Asian Treaty Organization and the Central Treaty Organization, focused upon mutual cooperation, protection and collective defence. From the mid-1950s onwards, Pakistan gained substantial US aid and military training, with Washington variously keen to set up listening stations close to Soviet territory, then to counteract Soviet military action in Afghanistan in the 1980s, and latterly to aid its post-9/11 'war on terror' in the same state. Recently, Washington has become more inclined to support India regionally, to some extent debasing its relationship with Islamabad (see Chapter 7). Further exemplifying this split, India tilted towards the Soviet Union during the Cold War via its socialist political basis, received industrial and military aid and built a solid strategic partnership based upon military, economic and diplomatic ties. These links were substantiated by the 1971 'Peace, Friendship and Cooperation Treaty' signed prior to the East Pakistan war that protected India vis-à-vis Pakistan's links to the United States and China (see below). In turn, New Delhi has been regularly shielded from external criticism/involvement concerning Kashmir thanks to Moscow's UN Security Council permanent veto power – a benefit that persists until the present day.

Pakistan has also enjoyed close ties with China, resulting in an 'all-weather relationship' boosted over time by episodic inflows of military aid, technological cooperation and strategic land swaps in Kashmir (of which Beijing, as noted, now has 10 per cent). For China, such efforts are aimed at maintaining 'India's preoccupation with Pakistan[, which] reduces India to the level of a regional power, while China can claim the status of an Asian and world power' (Pant, 2011a: 237). These linkages have been maintained through the multiple conflicts over Kashmir, although they have not resulted in China's explicit military support (via troops) in regard to the Pakistani cause. Beijing also benefits from having deep-water ports in Pakistan that afford it a vital trade route for its energy supplies from the Middle East. It is worth noting that in recent years, enhanced India–China relations have led to Beijing's neutrality on the Kashmir issue along with greater anxiety concerning Pakistan's links to terrorism, which have the potential to create wider regional instability. Overall, by essentially appropriating power from extra-regional states, such efforts have helped Islamabad to modernize its military forces and aided its continued regional competition with India. Pakistan's sustained – if fluctuating – ties with the United States and China further intensify the perception among Indian elites of their state being encircled and contained within South Asia – perspectives that may serve to counteract and thus potentially restrict its great power ambitions.

Significantly underlying this combination of ideational, territorial and regional rivalry is that both India and Pakistan are armed with nuclear weapons. Although there are uncertainties as to the extent of Islamabad's capabilities following its 1998 tests in retaliation to India's of the same year, the sheer physical proximity of the two states exacerbates existing tensions. Regionally, Pakistan's acquisition of nuclear power also 'somewhat nullified India's advantages, ... [serving] as a "great equalizer" for the weaker party between two otherwise unequal powers' (Nayar & Paul, 2003: 51–2), and conversely increased the possibility of low-intensity conflicts (as in Kargil in 1999), as well as supporting Islamabad's pursuit of terrorism against New Delhi (see Chapter 3). Uncertainties concerning Pakistan's internal balance of power (between the government, the military and the security services), as well as inherent social instabilities and fears of a system collapse, increase these concerns – especially when seen through a historical/ideational lens. Thus, although India–Pakistan relations appear by some measures to be normalizing – including rising trade levels and the supply of energy –, competing identities, self-images and status concerns continue to dominate. These elements have also made South Asia a necessary touchstone for other (great power) states (such as the United States, China and Russia), and India a necessary part of their foreign policy calculations.

Wider Regional Relations

Aside from Pakistan, India's wider peripheral relations concern a host of smaller powers in South Asia (Bangladesh, Bhutan, the Maldives, Nepal and Sri Lanka), one state on the fringes of Southeast Asia (Myanmar) and a large coastline projecting downwards into the IOR. Through its physical and material dominance, India has historically initiated a succession of unequal treaty-based security arrangements across the region – for instance, with Nepal (1950), Bhutan (1949),

Bangladesh (1972) and Sri Lanka (1987) – which have given it a decisive and controlling influence concerning its internal (particularly military) affairs. Such treaties represent a continuation of regional preponderance from the British colonial era and are 'a diplomatic hard power strategy' (Wagner, 2005: 9) designed to enhance India's peripheral stability through coercive political means.

Such interactions also reveal the worldview of Indian elites, with Nehru's leading diplomat Krishna Menon stating, 'why should we get involved with these third-rate powers? . . . Our interests lie with the great powers' (quoted in Varkey, 2002: 161). Building upon its imbalanced security treaties and reflecting the more pragmatic sentiments that entered India's foreign policy lexicon in the mid-1960s, principles of domination and tacit hegemony paired with the brandishing and deployment of military power as the means to safeguard New Delhi's regional pre-eminence. This attitude manifested itself in the Indira Doctrine, named after Nehru's daughter, through which India would not tolerate 'intervention by an outside power; if external assistance is needed to meet an internal crisis, states should look within the region for help' (Ayoob, 1999: 256). In conjunction with this stance, India used its military forces as a deterrent and as an interventionist force for regional stability against Nepal, Sri Lanka, the Maldives (see below) and Pakistan. For some, this strategy was specifically intended 'to create a regional order in which the ranks of South Asian nations are determined by the nature of their relations with India' (A.K. Gupta, 2008: 62).

For critics however, the 'concept of exclusion of the non-regional powers from the region . . . [was] a thin disguise of the hegemonistic status and a claim to establish one's own sphere of influence' (former Pakistani Foreign Minister quoted in Devotta, 2003: 368). Others have argued that such a policy was 'motivated by a fear, bordering on paranoia, of outside intervention in Indian affairs' (Gilboy & Heginbotham, 2012: 57). Fundamentally, it indicated that a state's foreign policy precepts can often be conditional, situation-specific and circumstance-specific (for instance, Indian elites profess non-intervention as a guiding principle [see Chapter 1], but they do not adhere to it in their own region). Moreover, the policy demonstrated that New Delhi's policy-makers proactively sought autonomy and prestige via India's periphery as a crucial step *en route* to becoming a great power. Displaying self-sufficiency plays into this self-image, whereby, for example, India's 1988 Maldives intervention concerning a failed coup d'état was motivated by reports that the Maldivian Foreign Minister had asked the United States and the United

Kingdom for help (Hagerty, 1991: 359). Crucially, whilst certainly projecting material power (in the form of military troops) and ideational influence (via the idea that it was the region's natural protector and guarantor), not all of India's interventions were positive – such as that in Sri Lanka from 1987 to 1990, which was a fiasco resulting in many Indian deaths.

With the end of the Cold War and India's nascent economic liberalization (see Chapter 4), along with a more benign global strategic environment, its policy of intervention, deterrence and mutuality as the means to retain regional hegemony evolved into the Gujral Doctrine. Based upon good will and benevolence, whereby 'India does not ask for reciprocity but gives all it can in good faith and trust' (D. Scott, 2011: 121), the Gujral Doctrine specifically aimed to build more cooperative ties across the region. While dissuading the influence of Pakistan, China and the United States, the policy sought to reassert core values of equality, peaceful means and respect for territorial integrity, and to establish a positive stability for the region while enhancing New Delhi's regional standing and legitimacy. It further recognized how a more concessionary stance (though excluding Pakistan) could enhance India's trade, energy and power relations across South Asia. Consequently, 'the strategy of blockading and rejecting external actors [was] replaced by a strategy of cooperation' (Prys, 2013: 289), and an effort to heighten India's soft power via an emphasis upon development and comprehensive security rather than assertive military power. Such positive asymmetry was also regarded as enabling India's eventual 'strategic release' from South Asia.

Reflecting an ability to adapt India's foreign policy behaviour and to be flexible in the face of new geostrategic realities, New Delhi has therefore displayed consistent attributes of great power management with the lesser South Asian states. Whilst demonstrating the attempt to actively craft its regional security environment, it continued its emphasis upon consolidation, mutuality and reciprocity (and hence away from brute military force) into the 2000s. This involved fresh forms of cooperation, including deterring its neighbours from harbouring and supporting separatists, insurgents and terrorists within their borders, as well as reducing cross-border smuggling and infiltration (of all kinds). However, many of India's borders still remain unclear and badly demarcated (although in 2015 New Delhi and Dhaka signed a land-swapping agreement in this regard). Myriad cross-border identities exacerbate this problem and encourage regional sub-nationalisms to emerge, which demand New Delhi's ongoing control and supervision.

PERIPHERAL RELATIONS

Additionally, India has been creating energy and trade dependencies (such as hydroelectric projects with Bhutan and Nepal, and gas supplies from Bangladesh), as well as permitting zero-duty access to the Indian market (for Bangladesh, Bhutan, Nepal and Sri Lanka). In this regard, India actively promotes economic growth and development (see Chapter 4) as a win-win situation for its neighbours by convincing its periphery 'that far from being besieged by India, they have a vast, productive hinterland that would give their economies far greater opportunities for growth than if they were to rely on their domestic markets alone' (Shyam Saran quoted in Kugiel, 2012: 364). Juxtaposed with this assertion, however, are observations that South Asia is characterized by 'enmeshed dissonance' (Gordon, 2014: 43), whereby sometimes New Delhi effectively imposes its position on its weaker neighbours without their full consent or agreement. This proto-hegemonic position was typified during India's 1989–90 trade dispute with Nepal (in response to the latter's closer ties with China) and its prevention of Bangladesh from signing a force-stationing agreement with the United States in the 2000s. Such domineering behaviour can be seen to be operating within a 'brahmanic framework' (A. Gupta, 1990: 712), with India asserting its caste primacy over all others. Such a self-conception is exemplified by then NSA M.K. Narayanan's assertion in 2007 (in relation to Sri Lanka) that 'we are the big power in this region. Let us make it very clear . . . they should come to us. And we will give them what we think is necessary. We do not favour their going to China or Pakistan or any other country' (quoted in Destradi, 2012: 79). This underlying dictatorial stance explains the lack of a substantial regional regime (see Chapter 6).

Further commensurate with the more conspicuous elements of pragmatism evident within their strategic thinking from the 1990s (see Chapter 1), Indian elites also endeavoured to re-frame relations with Myanmar along pragmatic – as opposed to idealistic – Nehruvian lines (Ogden, 2014b: 89–91). As a result, relations have come to rest upon resolving mutual security issues such as gaining energy resources, preventing cross-border incursions by terrorist groups/smugglers and increasing connectivity through the funding of infrastructure projects that link India to the wider Southeast Asian region via Myanmar's landmass. Economic aid and arms sales have further bolstered these linkages, and in 2007 New Delhi ignored Myanmar's crackdown on pro-democracy supporters in a blatant display of political realism. A (re-)focus upon shared cultural, social, religious and historical heritages has also fruitfully informed such links, and serves as another example of New Delhi successfully projecting its security concerns

115

outwards across its borders. Confirming this extrapolative stance, in June 2015 India was permitted to send troops into Myanmar's territory to attack rebel camps in an effort to reassert its regional control.

Apart from a belief in dominating the South Asia landmass, New Delhi's elites also consider that their sphere of influence extends to the wider IOR. This conviction dates from negative historical experiences (invasion from the sea by colonial aggressors) to consistent efforts to deter any external great power involvement in the wider region (initially via assertions in the 1960s and 1970s to declare the IOR to be a 'Zone of Peace'). With the IOR now forming part of India's 'extended strategic neighbourhood', its significance in terms of ensuring trade and energy security has become ever more apparent: indeed, 90 per cent of all India's trade by volume and virtually all of its oil needs are dependent upon sea access (Ogden, 2014b: 92). Conjoining key great power elements, India's self-conception in South Asia impacts upon its development, modernization and status goals, and further intertwines with its gradual acquisition of a blue-water navy and establishment of naval command centres in the IOR (see Chapter 3). By having the IOR's most advanced navy, setting up institutional bodies (such as the Indian Ocean Naval Symposium), making efforts to proactively manage the region via anti-piracy and disaster relief operations and declaring its 'strategic footprint as a "super regional power"' (Manmohan Singh quoted in H. Zhao, 2007: 138), New Delhi claims regional hegemony in this regard, asserting itself as a self-confident and regionally central great power.

Similarly interweaving innately superior material qualities (geographical extent, economic clout and rising military capabilities) with more ideational elements (past, and potentially current and future, great power status), China also appears to dominate many of its smaller neighbours within East Asia. These include the lesser states populating Southeast Asia (Laos, Myanmar and Vietnam by land, and the Philippines by sea), as well as North Korea. Such an assertive positioning remains juxtaposed – as it analogously does for India with Pakistan – with the presence of Japan (as above) and the United States (see Chapter 7) – two entities largely unwilling to accept Beijing's supremacy (materially or perceptually) within the gamut of great power competition. During the imperial era, and reflective of its Middle Kingdom complex, China held suzerainty power over its smaller neighbours in the form of subservient tributary relations. With the emergence of the PRC, and within the Cold War context, Beijing continued a policy of forceful domination, including the support of regional communist movements and regimes (variously in Cambodia, Indonesia and Vietnam). The Association of Southeast Asian Nations (ASEAN) was partially set up in 1967 in response to China's aggressive ideological exportation, whilst Beijing (abortively) invaded Vietnam in 1979 and would have many border clashes with Hanoi until 1990.

In line with Deng's ideological softening and the CCP's embrace of economic growth (see Chapters 1 and 4), China's regional approach became more benign. In particular, after the events of Tiananmen Square in 1989, in concert with the downfall of the Soviet Union, Beijing sought better regional relations through its *zhoubian* (peripheral) diplomacy. Recognizing that the Asia-Pacific region is 'fundamental to China's core economic interests, which include sustaining dense trade, investment, and social flows' (Calder & Ye, 2010: 164), this approach was largely based upon reciprocal trade relations, combined with the PRC being a proactive and non-obstructionist regional actor. China's actions during the 1997 Asian Financial Crisis typified this stance, with Beijing aiding Southeast Asia's eventual recovery through the provision of loans and its non-devaluation of the yuan. In addition to providing regional leadership (and a foil to Western liberalism), as the 2000s progressed, China became 'so economically important to the region that other states ha[d] no choice other than to cultivate good relations' (Beeson & Li, 2012: 46). This attractive influence thus drew other states within Beijing's orbit in a manner that recognized its mounting regional centrality, prominence and status. The predominantly neo-liberal 'win-win' basis of these interactions, along with amplified institutional linkages (such as with ASEAN – see Chapter 6), also defied realist predictions that China would have 'a more assertive foreign policy' (Roy, 1996: 759).

On this basis, China quickly became the pivotal influence concerning the region's political, economic and diplomatic affairs. As reflected in its 'new security concept' (as detailed in Chapter 2), China's approach eschews the use of military force and instead emphasizes soft power and public diplomacy, in conjunction with maintaining the bedrock of economic ties. Highly self-aware and role-projecting, Beijing presents itself as a 'benevolent great power' via its rhetoric of a 'peaceful rise', and assertions that it 'neither interferes in other countries' internal affairs nor imposes its will on others, . . . it will never seek hegemony no matter how strong it may become' (Xi, 2014b). This approach is historically aware, in that, 'unlike Japan's abortive attempt at regional hegemony, . . . China is using diplomacy and a sophisticated "charm offensive" to win over neighbours' (Beeson & Li, 2012: 35). Reflecting regional voices that would wish China to behave as a trustworthy great power, Beijing states that it will not compete for hegemony or particular spheres of influence, with the purposeful reassurance that East Asia's largest power 'constitutes no threat to other countries' (Wen Jiabao quoted in Lampton, 2008: 61).

Consequently, regional states 'view China as more benign than malign' (Shambaugh, 2004: 67) and are accommodating themselves to Beijing's 'amicable, tranquil, prosperous' (*mulin, anlin, fulin*) neighbourhood strategy. Acting as its economic lynchpin is the China–ASEAN Free Trade Agreement (CAFTA), which came into force on 1 January 2010 and created the world's largest free trade area, incorporating around 2 billion potential consumers. Of particular note is the fact that 'Chinese policymakers were prepared to accept relatively disadvantageous terms' (Beeson & Li, 2012: 44) in order to facilitate the CAFTA, indicating an altruistic rather than coercive approach. Conjoined with its great power aspirations, China is also further nurturing its image as a responsible power that is productively involved in tackling and resolving various regional security issues. Centred upon collaborative security and multilateralism, primarily via the 2003 'Treaty of Amity and Cooperation' with ASEAN, these efforts encompass combating shared non-traditional security concerns, such as terrorism, insurgency and smuggling and improving border security. Notably, Beijing may be less ready to assert its (implicit material) superiority owing to the presence in the region of other actual or potential great powers (such as the United States and Japan), whilst also understanding that status is further based upon recognition, perception and leadership, gained from being a non-threatening 'constructive partner [and] careful listener' (Shambaugh, 2004: 64).

Other dimensions of China's self-perception – primarily territorial – do, however, pose significant obstacles to regional stability. When combined with domestic nationalist pressures, in conjunction with any given leader's need for legitimacy within and without the CCP (see Chapter 1) and the global system's scrutiny of Beijing's contemporary rise, such issues undercut positive factors. Specifically, both China and Vietnam claim the entire area of the South China Sea and its assorted islands, while Brunei, Indonesia, Malaysia and the Philippines all have claims to its adjoining areas. Providing myriad flashpoints for potential conflict, the area has witnessed rival military exercises, blockades, disputes over fishing and ocean (including oil) resources and attempts to physically 'claim' the islands by small groups of nationalists. From the mid-2010s, Beijing has pursued an assertive policy of land reclamation, including constructing an airstrip on the Fiery Cross Reef, which exacerbated sovereignty disputes.

As more than half of global shipping tonnage traverses the South China Sea, which is also vital for over 80 per cent of oil imports to Japan and South Korea, the great power that controls this region 'will dominate . . . Southeast Asia and play a decisive role in the future of the western Pacific and the Indian Ocean' (Jose Almonte quoted in H. Zhao, 2012: 220). It is further estimated that at least $5.3 trillion in annual trade crosses the South China Sea (Glaser, 2012). When combined with the modernization and expansion of China's naval capabilities (see Chapter 3), many of its neighbours now see it as an ever 'hungry tiger . . . [rather than as a] peaceful elephant' (Lansdown & Wu, 2008: 222).

China's relations with the Democratic People's Republic of Korea (DPRK – North Korea) are further symptomatic of Beijing's desire for regional stability, the prevention of external influence and efforts at great power management. Based upon their Marxist-Leninist 'lips and teeth' unity during the Cold War (including China's role in the 1950–3 Korean War), their alliance was codified in 1961. Although now ideologically split – given China's economic liberalization – Beijing remains one of the DPRK's few allies and has the capability to shape the peninsula's long-term future. Desiring a buffer state, and wishing to avoid the DPRK's political and economic collapse, which would threaten regional stability (and economic development), from 2003 Beijing took a lead role in the Six-Party Talks (along with Japan, Russia, South Korea and the United States) to resolve tensions. This role became more difficult after Pyongyang tested a nuclear device in 2006 (and again in 2009, 2013 and 2016), leading Beijing to support international sanctions and UN Security Council Resolutions against it. Pyongyang's nuclearization also highlights China's *huolian* (fire-chain) fear, whereby Japan and South Korea gain nuclear capabilities to balance against the DPRK. Revealing the limits of its efforts (or indeed those of any state) to be a responsible/managerial great power, China now openly criticizes the DPRK, with President Xi stating that 'no one should be allowed to throw a region and even the whole world into chaos for selfish gains' (quoted in Gao, 2013).

Proximity, Attraction and Transcendence

Whether based upon their physical authority, economic clout, military capabilities or diplomatic prowess, there is a consistent assertion that great powers are the key actors 'whose involvement in the affairs of . . . [a] continent is a necessary factor in the calculations of

119

others' (Braumoeller, 2012: 68). Again underscoring the interconnection of several factors, both material and ideational, being a region's *essential state* is central to the calculation of great power status. Such 'influence is often the result of economic flexibility or technological innovation' (Genest, 2004: 126), as well as providing leadership to others so as to fulfil their needs and prospects. Both Beijing and New Delhi are increasingly proactive in these regards, as is evident from their evolving efforts to provide direction, aspiration and elements of ordering/management to their relative peripheries. The role of perception also persists as a critical factor, with both powers facing enduring regional challengers (Japan and Pakistan, respectively), who dispute and contest their (actual and desired) status – roles exacerbated by their immovable proximity. Thus, every great power must deal with specific regional dynamics that are not the same for others.

China has emerged as an indispensable actor in East Asia. It is economically (and hence diplomatically) interwoven with virtually all of its neighbours, forming dynamics that are central to Beijing's great power rise. Such a centrality suggests a return to China's prior Middle Kingdom status, whereby contemporary security practices of symbiosis and superiority serve to convey the same cultural meaning. As economic growth remains vital to China's domestic and international aims, so does maintaining a stable periphery through liberalist-inclined interdependence rather than realist-minded outright domination. Constructivist-based perceptions serve effectively to trump any such dynamics, particularly if Beijing's economic fortunes decline and nationalist forces gain ascendancy, especially concerning a Japan that does not recognize China's emergent status. Such subtleties reveal the limits of great power role-taking, -giving *and* -making, whilst underscoring how Beijing seeks to 'increase China's soft power, [and to] give a good Chinese narrative' (Xi, 2014a), so as to reduce such fraught status anxieties and prevent historically driven interactions from critically boiling over.

Although New Delhi is also using public diplomacy and soft power 'to advocat[e] and explain the Indian "brand"' (Rao, 2010), South Asia remains 'one of the least integrated and most unstable regions in the world' (Kugiel, 2012: 351). Undoubtedly dominant in material terms, and tacitly perceptually accepted by most of its neighbours (with the exception of Pakistan), New Delhi has peripheral relations that are largely stable and based upon ever-increasing diplomatic and economic ties, with shared trade and energy security concerns gaining ascendancy. However, although India is essential to the strategic calculations of its surrounding states, its wider asymmetry places it in a somewhat circular quandary, whereby 'unless its region becomes more cooperative (and prosperous), India is unlikely to develop into more than a regional power, but it is as well true that it cannot be a global power unless it reaches beyond its neighbourhood' (Malone, 2012: 128). Through its preference for largely unconnected bilateral relations, rather than developing wider management strategies to deal with overarching security concerns, India is also currently unable to exercise effective regional leadership. Consequently, New Delhi fulfils the great power criteria of regional dominance and strategic centrality but without the embedded core of managerial aspects enjoyed by Beijing, which for the latter transcend to a global – rather than solely local – level.

6

MULTILATERAL INTERACTION

Often premised upon a combination of common interests and mutual threats, multilateralism is a 'particularly demanding form of international cooperation [which] requires a strong sense of collective identity in addition to shared values' (Hemmer & Katzenstein, 2002: 575–6). Representative of historically entrenched interaction and communal perspectives, on a global or a regional level, such regimes give 'expression to international society over historical time and geographical space' (Martin Wight quoted in Bull, 1977: 17). Sustained by rules and practices embodied from the shared values of their participant states, multilateral bodies, moreover, aid the creation, maintenance and sustenance of international order, which binds members together and reduces negative misperceptions. Courtesy of their global scope, interests and impact (largely cultural, military and economic – see Chapters 1, 2, 3 and 4), great powers regularly dominate such regimes, translating into a wider sense of global responsibility. Such a notion dates from the 1815 Congress of Vienna – the first great power institution – and currently encompasses the full gamut of non-traditional security concerns (see Introduction).

Within the multilateral context, great powers display a dynamic combination of quantifiable power with more idealistic components – interweaving their material capabilities with a social role. In these ways, being a great power demands holding top ranking across all of 'the primary global structures – economic, military, knowledge and normative' (Samuel Kim quoted in Nayar & Paul, 2003: 31). These latter elements underscore this volume's core emphasis that states and great powers comprise and construct each other via the interplay of their values, perceptions, experience and political culture. Multilateral institutions hence act as 'normative and cognitive maps for interpretation and action' (Ikenberry, 2000: 15), and are social groupings that reflect the identities of their major constituent states. As such, international relations can be regarded as 'inter-cultural relations' (Iriye, 1979). Notions of soft power (see Chapter 4) again inform these contentions, whereby attraction outplays compulsion. For some, however, 'soft power is merely the velvet glove concealing an iron hand' (Colin Gray quoted in Ferguson, 2004: 24), pointing to an interplay with other power sources.

Through their often superior positioning within multilateral regimes, great powers also traditionally desire a managerial role. As such, the rules and practices underpinning regimes serve to prescribe and proscribe acceptable and unacceptable behaviour. Because these rules are often set by the great powers as a consequence of their relative (material and ideational) power preponderance, 'leading states have sought to shape ... their international environment ... [to] further enhance their wealth, power and status' (Goldstein, 2005: 17). For power-maximizing realists, multilateral institutions are therefore 'merely arenas for acting out power relationships' (Tony Evans & Peter Wilson quoted in Lanteigne 2005: 15), rather than promoting any pure realization of collective purpose. Given this positioning, great powers effectively act as gatekeepers who are able to preserve their conception of world order, and enforce what they regard as 'legitimate' in international society. Entry into major global groupings thus indicates a form of wider social recognition and validity by confirming rights, privileges and peer-derived status, which is also role-giving – especially concerning being seen as a 'responsible' power.

In these ways, the various multilateral institutions created by Washington after the Second World War have served to create the present US-led world order. Critically, however, these groupings only represent *current* power balances within the *current* international system, meaning that, in the same way as they replaced the world order of the late nineteenth century, they can also be supplanted. Rising multilateralism after the end of the Cold War is symptomatic of such developments, as is the emergence of China and India and an 'Asian Century'. In this regard, it is worth noting that 'challenges to the legitimacy of international order ... [come] from those states ... with the capacity and political organization to demand a revision of the established order and of its dominant norms in ways that reflect their own interests, concerns and values' (Hurrell, 2006: 2). Contemporary globalization, which transfers power and authority from states to global institutions (see Chapter 4), as well as non-traditional threats that defy state borders (such as the 2008 credit crunch, international terrorism, disease, smuggling and environmental degradation), bolsters the relevance of multilateralism but also heightens the visibility and influence of India and China, as they become solidly embedded in and essential to global regimes.

Building upon these elements, this chapter analyses how India and China engage with the wider international system through the conduit of multilateral institutions. It begins by considering the core attitudes of both states towards such groupings, and traces their development over time to determine how policy-makers/elites in Beijing and New Delhi desire to project certain core foreign/domestic policy values outwards into the international system. This analysis includes an appreciation of how China and India are increasingly attempting to spread their soft power influence globally through a higher degree of pragmatism and *realpolitik*, as well as shared positions on a multipolar world order, equality, peaceful development and non-intervention. The chapter then studies select examples of how both states – historically and contemporarily – carry out their multilateral engagement both globally and regionally, and looks at their potential to be effective vehicles for fashioning new forms of great power multilateralism.

Attitudinal Development

The core political and cultural values, norms and beliefs structuring foreign policy-making in India and China are crucial for understanding their interaction with multilateral bodies. Continuing on from previous chapters, domestic determinants and inter-perceptions – as derived from historical experience, national identities, security cultures and the agency of leaders/elites – are the means 'through which processes of structural change are articulated and projected on the one hand, and potentially channeled and institutionalized on the other' (Gill, 1997: 7).

China's multilateral attitude is 'strongly conditioned by its historic relationship to the outside world' (W. Shen, 2008: 201). Dating from the 1842 'Treaty of Nanjing', which marked the start of the Century of Humiliation, China's sovereignty was consistently weakened by external powers. Via a series of unequal treaties that included the loss of ports, trading rights and territory, and continued through the imperial period prior to the CCP's ascendancy in the 1940s, the perception of China as a victim of imperialism became engrained in elite thinking. As a result, the multilateralism of international law was seen as an unfair legal cover to 'establish sovereignty of the strong over the weak' (Lanteigne, 2013: 58). China's negative treatment prevented the PRC from entering the international system as a unified state, and it was also shut out of the Western-fashioned UN, the General Agreement on Tariffs and Trade (GATT) and the IMF – all of which significantly reduced Beijing's reconstruction efforts after the Second World War had ended. Consequently, Mao regarded such organizations as anti-socialist 'instruments of Western imperialism and hegemonism' (Johnston, 2008: 34) that threatened China's sovereignty and autonomy, and contributed to the focus upon isolationism and self-reliance under his rule. When Chinese troops fought US-led UN troops during the 1950–3 Korean War, the veracity of this attitude was essentially compounded for Beijing.

The approach of 'opposing imperialism, revisionism and reactionaries' (*fandui di xiu fan*) (H. Wang, 2000: 478) continued throughout the 1950s, and was intensified by China's ideological split with the Soviet Union in the 1960s. Only in the late 1960s did Mao's worldview start to shift, primarily through the development of his 'Three Worlds Theory' (*sange shijie*), consisting of capitalist, socialist and post-colonial spheres, and his efforts to portray China as a large developing state. Beijing also continued to limit its multilateral engagement and declined membership of the NAM and the G77. Such attitudes were transformed under Mao's successor, Deng, who changed China's cost–benefit equation towards global institutions. Seeking capital, investment and information regarding the norms and practices central to international trade and economics (see Chapter 4), the PRC now saw contact and engagement with external regimes as both necessary and beneficial. Although initially very weak in terms of diplomatic capabilities and institutional knowledge, Deng's 'Open Door Policy' rapidly shifted attitudes towards a pragmatic stance, and was the precursor to China's membership of intergovernmental groupings, which rose from one in 1971 to thirty-seven by 1989 (Hempson-Jones, 2005: 707), eventually reaching 266 by 2004 (Qin, 2007: 333).

Heightened interaction was also compelled by a desire to 'dispel mistrust' (Johnston & Ross, 2006: 201), and to enhance Beijing's international image by no longer presenting China as a revisionist and obstructionist power. These efforts aimed to combat negative perceptions that China's rise represented a threat and to present it as a responsible global actor. High degrees of self-awareness among CCP elites continued to guide these efforts, particularly given China's rapid military and economic rise (see Chapters 3 and 4), which led some observers to see it as the 'hegemon on the horizon' (Deng & Wang, 1999: 3). With the shift from a zero-sum to a positive-sum perspective (under Mao and under Deng and all of his successors, respectively), the management of external perceptions also helped Beijing's ongoing quest for great power status – the realization of which especially involves peer recognition, acceptance and enshrinement. Multilateral regimes were thus platforms for positively promoting China on the world stage via a mutual two-way process based upon reciprocity, cooperation and common learning. Given the CCP's heavy emphasis on economic growth and regional stability (see Chapter 5), its understanding that ultimately 'both China's welfare and its security depend heavily on its interaction with the outside world' (Yunling & Shiping, 2005: 49) additionally underpinned its embrace of multilateral engagement.

China's increasingly advantageous economic positioning, especially the size of its markets, also encouraged other states to cooperate with it, giving Beijing enhanced leverage. While it was still typically gradual and cautious in its approach, China's eventual joining of the WTO in 2001 (see below) involved adapting to existing international rules, with the CCP, for example, having to revise over 2,300 national laws to meet the organization's demands (J. Scott & Wilkinson, 2011: 11). Similarly with the IMF, China rapidly assimilated itself to the prevailing requirements of the global market economy, which subsequently aided its advantageous integration into the current global fiscal system. Such acquiescence underscored the necessary interdependence of such membership but also Beijing's greater willingness to socialize and morph to meet international rules and norms, especially if the financial pay-offs (for example, greater FDI and market access) were clear. As Christensen observes, China also joins many regimes 'to avoid losing face and influence but . . . [still] pursu[es] its own economic and security interests' (1996: 38). Beijing thus remains wary of entering multilateral international security regimes, where the gains are less clear and the longer-term risks and costs are potentially much higher, and still prefers to engage in select bilateral security partnerships.

Therefore, Beijing's elites began to accede to and follow the Western-led international order rather than seek to revise it, as their attitude towards multilateralism 'evolved from suspicion, to uncertainty, to supportiveness' (Shambaugh, 2004: 69). However, as China became more embedded in the interactive and social practices constituting any regime, its leaders also saw how it could begin to frame their international rules via its heightened engagement – acknowledging how these groupings have historically reflected the prevailing power balances within, and the character of, the international system. Regime membership, principally in groupings which Beijing had not initially helped form – and hence not based upon its core norms, understandings and values (especially in terms of development, equality and non-intervention – see Chapter 1) –, can thus be especially constraining. For this reason, by the 2000s, China began to form its own institutions in its own image, in keeping with its national interests and specific strategic culture (see Chapters 1 and 2). This proactive innovation included the Shanghai Cooperation Organization (SCO) and the Brazil–Russia–India–China–South Africa (BRICS) grouping (see below), with Beijing mimicking a 'trick used by the US to realize its own strategic designs' (H. Wang, 2000: 482).

Chinese elites have a preference for multipolarity (*duojiha*), whereby there would be multiple great powers vying for influence through a 'democractization of international relations' (Sohn, 2012: 81) that would balance out any hegemonic power, and allow emerging great powers greater international influence. Central to China's self-image and status is the belief expressed by Deng that 'in the so-called multipolar world, China too will be a pole . . . we should not belittle our own importance; one way or another, China will be counted as a pole' (quoted in He, 2009: 125). Longstanding as a core strategic understanding, this notion has consistently been used by Beijing to variously criticize Cold War bipolarity and post-Cold War US unipolarity, and to bolster its own anti-hegemonic pretensions (see Chapter 2). This aspiration has, however, been adapted, and by the mid-1990s CCP elites noted that although multipolarity is an expected 'long-term trend, . . . the international system would be characterized by one superpower and many major powers for a comparatively long time' (He, 2009: 129). Within the context of this chapter, Beijing sees that 'multilateralism is instrumental to the formation of multipolarization' (Jianwei Wang, 2005: 163), and as the fundamental means to make its own vision of the global order more salient and realizable.

Deployment of a specific *Chinese* soft power has complemented the promotion of China's values into the international system, which are central to building openness and commonality within multilateral settings. Now that China's 'national cultural soft power' (*guojia wenhua ruan shili*) is a core dimension of its foreign policy, it has become a central concern. As a Foreign Minister has asserted, by 'cultivating and enhancing China's soft power, we will . . . try to make China's voice heard' (Y. Wang, 2013). A Minister of Culture further noted how such power, as carried out through public and cultural diplomacy, 'create[s] a good atmosphere for Chinese overall diplomacy, . . . it promotes trustiness and alleviates doubts when developing relations with neighboring countries, . . . it serves to win people's hearts' (Sun, 2004). In turn, the mandate of the China Public Diplomacy Association, set up in 2012, is to 'enhance mutual understanding and friendship between China and the rest of the world, project to the world a positive image of China, . . . and create an international environment conducive to China' (CPDA, 2015). The 2008 Beijing Olympics typified such efforts to project China's image as a regional and global leader.

For India, the core values intrinsic to its national identity and strategic culture (see Chapters 1 and 2) have also acted as major guiding influences upon its attitude towards multilateralism. Built upon foundations emphasizing the primacy of its national interests, for generations of New Delhi elites there has been a belief in absolute sovereignty, as exemplified by independence, non-interference and non-alignment in global politics. In particular, principles of non-intervention stemming from India's colonial experiences bolstered anti-imperial attitudes and proactive efforts to avoid any constraining external influences upon its foreign policy autonomy. The pursuit of non-alignment sought to maintain this sufficiency, and was 'perfectly realist, but also idealist' (Bajpai, 1998: 162) in its strategic aims. Critically, Indian elites distinguished this approach from simple neutralism and saw it as an activist position that would enable the promotion of India's interests, values and overall worldview within the international system. In turn, Mahatma Gandhi's notion of *swaraj* (self-rule) sought to promote a common vision of self-determining states that were not oppressed by any form of domination or hegemony by others.

During the earliest decades of the Cold War, such a realization contrasted with Beijing's isolationist approach, as New Delhi helped to establish and lead the pro-developing world and anti-imperialist NAM (see below). Key to this vision were further understandings relating to the promotion of international peace and security, tolerance, equality and progress – all of which were core domestic values but which had a wider resonance that resulted in India becoming the era's central 'harbinger of [the] Third World's political, economic and moral aspirations' (Jain, 2009: 20). Although some scholars argue that non-alignment was ineffective in that it 'did not lead to a careful assessment of the dynamic international security situation and exploration of options for India (Pant, 2011b: 16), it did present a clear set of values that were easily comprehensible, and thus shared, by a plethora of similarly placed states. Such factors gave these principles (and by extension India) a greater degree of legitimacy within the international system, which other developing and post-colonial states conferred on New Delhi. These core norms further related to notions of recognition and status – attributes sought by India to the present day.

Commensurate with these attitudes and their purported target audience, along with a consistently articulated great power aspiration buoyed by the personality of Nehru, New Delhi maintained a global over a regional focus within its approach to multilateralism. Reflective of the continued impact of negative historical legacies, there was also an opposition to solely collective security regimes and a preference for more economic groupings – where potential gains were far clearer. Underpinning such inclinations was a persistent aim to promote 'a "cooperative multipolar order"' (Atal Behari Vajpayee quoted in Ciorciari, 2011: 64), within which New Delhi was one of the several most powerful entities in the international system. Additionally inclusive and inherently anti-hegemonic, this vision was supported by the concept of *vasudhaiva kutumbakam*, whereby the world is one family, which also became a recurrent reference point for all generations of Indian leaders. Contemporarily, multipolarity has merged with non-alignment to create 'multi-alignment' (Tharoor, 2012) as the most effective means to deal with the non-traditional and comprehensive security threats of the twenty-first century, where neither total autonomy nor outright alliance is fully applicable.

In the post-1947 context, active engagement with (some) multilateral bodies was seen by New Delhi's elites as a means of power equalization to overcome its economic and military deficiencies, as well as to promote Indian norms and advance its global standing. Further strengthened by the self-confidence and visibility of its leaders, India projected a global vision of solidarity for itself and others, with Nehru stating that 'where there is continued domination, whether it is in Asia and Africa, there will be no peace either there or in the people's minds elsewhere, there will be ... a continuous suspicion of Europe in the minds of Asia' (quoted in Pillai & Premashekhara, 2010: 6). This approach further complemented the core assumption that India's self-image was that of a global power. In turn, critical also was the agency and self-perception of Nehru, who took a leadership role in international organizations because he 'was convinced that India had a catalytic role to play in establishing a moral and just world order' (Dixit, 2004: 84). These factors helped establish India as a leading voice for the Third World and marshalled it as a vocal lobbying influence, which proved to be highly effective in the 1950s and 1960s. New Delhi would, however, still suspect the motivations of some bodies – such as the UN (see below) – and display an overall bilateral over multilateral penchant in its diplomatic dealings.

India's multilateral influence waned in the 1960s as more elements of *realpolitik* entered its foreign policy calculus (see Chapter 2) and cast a shadow over the veracity of the core norms perpetuated under Nehru. Key events, such as the 1971 invasion of East Pakistan, ever-closer ties with the Soviet Union and the 1974 nuclear tests, all undercut the promise of values relating to peace, non-intervention and self-reliance. As a result, and despite efforts to establish bodies to represent the Third World (such as the New International Economic Order, NIEO), India's voice in multilateral regimes was side-lined from the 1970s. Only with the ending of the Cold War did the international atmosphere become more conducive to New Delhi, and neatly matched its increasing pragmatism and rising economic needs (especially gaining access to FDI, technology and new markets – see Chapter 4). Highlighting elements of adaption and evolution, as shown within constructivist and strategic culture accounts, national elites displayed the skill of *yugadharma* ('changing with the times').

As the UN Security Council became more active in ordering international affairs in the 1990s, UNPKOs also increased, as did Indian contributions to them (as detailed below). In addition, the amplification of 'global' discussions relating to trade, non-proliferation and the environment led to India's more active, outspoken and often leading (developing) involvement. This context fused with greater domestic political will and clearer economic and development goals concerning great power status – an ambition made realizable via the gaining of international recognition, legitimacy and respect in institutional settings. As a result, India's foreign policy in the multilateral context grew more complex, as the scope and scale of its international interaction increased in line with the trend relayed across all aspects of its international affairs (and as detailed in all the previous chapters in this volume).

Despite these developments, Indian elites remain suspicious of the intentions of other powers in international institutions, which are still perceived as forums within which New Delhi can be criticized. As such, the historical baggage of prior interaction, such as the favouring of Pakistan when the Kashmir issue was brought to the UN in 1948, continues to cloud the thinking of Indian leaders, who are distrustful of over-involvement and entrapment. This wariness has often manifested itself in a defensive, hardline and nay-saying posture (Narkilar, 2006). A lingering disconnect between India's still-increasing material capabilities and its intrinsic belief in being a great power further compounds this issue. As a result, New Delhi continues a preference for a top-down embrace of multilateral regimes, especially if they are created in its own vision and are based upon its particular norms and values – an observation that applies to the NAM and the NIEO but also the G77 (as grouping together developing states in the global South), the G4 (as a means to reform the UN Security Council) and the BRICS grouping (as representing the global interests of emergent great powers). India's multilateral policy thus displays a preference for its own norms, not those of others. Bilateral relations continue to outrank wider regionalism or multilateralism, as marked by the myriad strategic partnerships between New Delhi and all major international powers, which numbered in the thirties by 2016.

Promoting a particular *Indian* soft power has also been a key foreign policy tool for New Delhi over the last decade. Both the Public Diplomacy Division within the MEA and the Indian Council for Cultural Relations were established for this purpose, with a former President of the latter stating that the idea of soft power 'is to project India as a plural multicultural society and to achieve the goals of political diplomacy' (Karan Singh quoted in Shukla, 2006: 24). Such power is premised upon perceptions of Indian culture and religion, and a Ministry of External Affairs official has remarked how 'religious practices were utilized, often for political ends. . . . [As] these constructs spread . . . [they] were an indicator of the "soft power" that India enjoyed in its extended neighbourhood' (Wadha, 2015: 235). On 21 June 2015, after lobbying the UN, Narendra Modi led the first International Yoga Day as part of a 'Brand India' campaign to enhance India's global standing *en route* to becoming a 'soft power superpower' (Mukherjee, 2007). There also remains an ongoing co-constitutive interplay of soft power with other sources, since it frequently requires hard power foundations to become credible, which has been true for India across the last sixty years or so of its interaction with multilateral regimes.

Global Engagement

In the promotion of their core values and norms, as expounded above, both India and China have endeavoured to carry out this projection beyond South Asia and East Asia, respectively. Both states also subscribe to the assertion that 'the special position which has been granted to great powers . . . [is their] main responsibility for the maintenance of international peace and security' (British Government commentary on the Charter of the UN, quoted in Modelski, 1974: 154), but in ways that have eschewed military means, including making alliances. Instead, it is enhanced interaction, rather than forceful managerialism, that has marked their engagement so far. Liberal interdependence itself builds upon the (growing) economic centrality of these states (see Chapter 4) but also their inclusion in major multilateral frameworks gives them the ability to mutually influence and formulate decisions relating to key political and diplomatic exigencies of the day. In these ways, both Beijing and New Delhi seek to advance their global stature through multilateralism, to gradually reshape any regime's orientation and to magnify their overall global influence 'beyond the zenith of their power' (Ikenberry, 2000: 53).

India's engagement with multilateral institutions in the post-1947 period has primarily been with three major groupings, and has often varied in line with its residual power sources at any given time. Hence, in the Cold War, and whilst only genuinely possessing soft power as its anti-colonial and anti-imperialist past and democratic credentials, New Delhi focused upon the NAM. In turn, India's UN ties have fluctuated between supporting its ideational underpinnings in the 1940s to consistent participation in UNPKOs, and a present-day interest in having a permanent veto seat on the Security Council, with the latter element representing a key criterion for New Delhi's wider recognition, legitimacy and status demands. Then in the post-Cold War period, and reflective of an increased appetite to engage with global liberal economics, linkages with the WTO have been amplified and gradually enlarged alongside India's growing economic clout. 'India thus used – and has continued to use – liberal institutional venues, norms, and rhetoric in the service of a foreign policy rooted largely in national interests' (Ciorciari, 2011: 70).

In a dual effort to craft global influence within the confines of Cold War bipolarity, in conjunction with resisting the involvement of the Western powers in South Asia, India co-founded the NAM, which was initiated via the 1955 Bandung Conference. Using its status as one of the first post-Second World War states to gain emancipation from colonial rule, India was 'a self-confident actor' (Khilnani, 1997: 176), with leaders unabashed at projecting their global vision onto the world stage. Via a belief that moral idealism – rather than military, economic or territorial might – was the route to becoming a great power, New Delhi helped propagate the movement's 'Five Principles of Peaceful Co-existence' (also known as Panchsheel): namely respect for territorial integrity and sovereignty; non-aggression; non-interference; equality and mutual benefit; and peaceful co-existence. In a programme that was openly critical of Western aggression in Korea, Congo, Suez and Vietnam, the values promoted by India had a clear resonance with other (developing) states, drawing them towards New Delhi. Such was the attraction of these principles that the NAM would gain 120 members (with twenty observers), making it the second largest international organization at the time, and elements of recognition, innovation, interdependence and (shared) leadership were confirmed as central to great power multilateral engagement. After the Cold War ended, however, the NAM found itself increasingly irrelevant and its efficacy as a platform for India subsequently diminished.

Another stage upon which New Delhi has both sought, and continues to seek, global influence has been the UN. As a founding member, India shared an adherence to the body's key principles relating to cooperation and development, peace and security, and international law and arbitration as means to solve disputes. In these ways, the UN allowed India to enhance its soft power repository, and to promote its international standing by both finding commonality with other members and heavily participating in UNPKOs – to which it would become a leading contributor (UN, 2016b). Such involvement increases its international credibility as a responsible power, with its solidarist principles being superseded by a need for recognition, influence and status. These positive aspects have intermingled with an underlying suspicion of the UN as a seat of impartial great power politics – most clearly shown by the concerted 'nuclear apartheid' against India's nuclear weapons programme (see Chapter 3), and the ongoing presence of UN peacekeepers in Kashmir since the 1947 war with Pakistan. Symptomatic of this distrust, during the 1999 Kargil conflict, Indian Prime Minister Atal Bihari Vajpayee 'summarily rejected' (Chaulia, 2011a: 280) attempts by the UN General Secretary to send an envoy to mediate between the two sides.

Within the spectrum of great power attainment, gaining a permanent veto seat on the UN Security Council remains India's major unachieved goal, as per the understanding that the regime's 'actual power is occupied by the five permanent but unelected members of the UNSC' (Jabeen, 2010: 242). New Delhi's elites have contended that a seat is 'India's rightful due' owing to its economic capacity, civilizational history, democratic basis, large UNPKO contributions and general adherence to core UN principles (J. Singh, 2000). More recently, Prime Minister Narendra Modi stated that 'gone are the days when India had to beg, now we command our rights' (quoted in *Times of India*, 2015) concerning gaining such a seat. Critically here, a state becomes a great power via the status accorded to it by others through formal recognition and by being given membership in key international decision-making organizations, whereby such accordance is both time- and context-specific. Significantly, in the 1950s, Nehru twice turned down the opportunity to have a permanent seat (Chaulia, 2011a: 279), seemingly reflecting the beliefs of India's leaders that it would inevitably gain one in the future. Although New Delhi can be regarded as a (pseudo) veto player insofar as it has extensive hard power credentials, which have a system centrality, only a permanent UN Security Council veto seat would give India enduring agenda- and norm-setting powers. Such a status would thus expressively *guarantee* its already important voice vis-à-vis any key international issue, and also allow it to have a key social role as a responsible contributor in international society.

India was also a co-founder of the GATT, the precursor to the WTO that emerged in 1995. In the Cold War period, non-alignment and representing the Third World dominated New Delhi's attitude to this organization, with Indian diplomats being concerned with solidarity, development, parity and countering external economic dominance. Typifying this position, an Indian delegate stated that 'equality of treatment is equitable only among equals . . . a weakling cannot carry the burden of a giant' (quoted in Narlikar, 2006: 63). However, the fall of the Soviet Union and the 1991 balance of payments crisis forced India's increased involvement in the grouping. Whilst New Delhi recognized how engagement could enhance its economic growth so as to achieve its developmental *and* status goals, the WTO was also still perceived as a base for representing the global South. (Largely) maintaining its maximalist negotiating style, this approach has slowly reaped New Delhi support, influence, leadership credentials and recognition. India also, however, has become a fervent supporter of some forms of economic liberalization, reflecting its growing need for greater investment and market access to continue its own economic success. As such, its multilateral approaches have evolved and adapted, changing from those of 'a poor developing nation relying on strength of numbers to those of an emerging power with the ability to hold its own against the major players in the WTO' (Malone, 2012: 261).

China's multilateral engagement is also balanced between promoting and adhering to the core values that structure its national identity but also increasingly gaining advantages from its enhanced involvement in established international structures. Hence, Beijing's interaction similarly displays elements of learning, adaptation and socialization conjoined with a specific and historically informed approach that reflects its national identity and constitutive norms, as well as the aim of ameliorating its great power status. These ideational and material elements are exemplified by Beijing's dealings with the WTO, membership of which was initially shunned under Mao but then became a necessary ingredient to help fuel China's international (economic) rise from Deng onwards. Similarly vis-à-vis the UN, Beijing's attitude and approach – although constrained by a host of negative perceptions – have also evolved, and other states have validated its international status.

With economic regimes regarded as being more transparent than security groupings, Beijing tried to join the GATT from 1986 but faced concerted opposition from wary (Western) states. This difficult passage was not aided by the negative events in Tiananmen Square in 1989, the break-up of the Soviet Union (which de-prioritized China's entry), worries over the PRC's economic maturity as a developing state and opposition from key international actors – primarily the United States – who saw it as an economic threat. In these ways, recognition by others was essential for Beijing in December 2001 finally to enter the ranks of the GATT's successor organization, the WTO, which noted that 'with China's membership, the WTO will take a major step towards becoming a truly world organization . . . [and] will serve a pivotal role in underpinning global economic cooperation' (WTO, 2001). Although there were fears that Beijing could be selective in its engagement (as noted below) and possibly redefine the WTO's values and roles, in reality, and given the concerted fiscal advantages that the regime brings, it has (largely) accepted the established, and widely shared, norms structuring the organization's institutional practices.

In turn, China's 'longstanding opposition to any normative attack on sovereignty, and consequent suspicion for coercive or mandatory international operations' (Contessi, 2010: 331), made Beijing sceptical of becoming involved in any security regimes. Hence, the UN in particular was regarded as a form of US imperialism and neo-colonialism. However, after being shut out of the organization since 1945, in October 1971 the PRC replaced Taiwan as the only lawful representative of China. Not only now socially recognized by other (great) powers, namely the United States, who had facilitated this switch, Beijing also gained the critical influence of having a permanent veto seat on the UN Security Council, giving it a sanction over the organization's affairs. Henceforth, and from this central structural standing, by the 1990s China strongly supported the UN's 'system-maintaining' nature, praised its security-building and disarmament endeavours and participated in the grouping in a 'selective and symbolic' (Kim, 1999: 45) manner. Beijing has rarely used its permanent veto, doing so only nine times from 1971 to early 2015 (compared with seventy-two times by the United States, twenty-three by the United Kingdom, twenty-two by the Soviet Union/Russia and thirteen times by France) though with six of these occasions occurring since 2000 (versus eleven by Russia and the United States) (UN, 2016c).

Within other UN domains, China has been slowly taking on more responsibility, most prominently in UNPKOs, to which it contributes more personnel than does any other veto-holding power (see UN, 2016a). First taking part in 1981, Beijing has used its involvement to inject its norms of national sovereignty and non-intervention into international politics, portray itself as a responsible great power and build ties with the developing world. In these ways, China is seeking 'to defend a pluralist world order based on cultural and political diversity while the West works hard to make a solidarist world order built on liberal democratic values' (P.K. Lee et al., 2010: 21). Thus, Beijing concurrently fulfils the behavioural expectations of other actors (and as such is recognized by them) whilst projecting is own vision outwards, leading to their mutual socialization. China's participation hence highlights how 'rather than seeing the fulfillment of roles and responsibilities of great powers as a "check-box" to be ticked in the identification of status, the ability to contribute to the definition of those roles and responsibilities should be the determinant of status' (C. Jones, 2014: 598), in a process that is role-giving, -taking and -making.

Regional Arrangements

Multilateral regimes also play a role in regional ordering, feeding into the analysis of Chapter 5 concerning China and India's peripheral relations. Frequently more focused, localized and specific in their emphasis, regional security communities involve 'sharing certain values and identities, . . . [having] sustained interactions . . . [and displaying] strategic altruism' (Adler & Barnett, 1998: 31). Seen to be essential to heightening stability and preventing conflict, they also act as invaluable platforms for states to project, explain and promote their worldviews and values to others. Given their relative geographical positioning, India and China are involved with ASEAN, whilst both states have shown a degree of innovation (with varying degrees of success) in their own regions – most notably the SCO for China and the South Asian Association for Regional Cooperation (SAARC) for India. Of further note, and as based upon their shared status and common interests as emergent great powers, Beijing and New Delhi have also collaborated to create some new and nascent intra-regional groupings: mainly the BRICS grouping and the Asian Infrastructure Investment Bank (AIIB).

China's relationship with ASEAN showcases Beijing's switch from belligerent isolation to proactive pragmatism. As iterated in Chapter 5, when ASEAN was founded in 1967, ideological differences prevented closer ties between the two entities. Since the end of the Cold War, however, and courtesy of China's self-awareness that its rapid rise and dominant imperial past contributed to regional security anxieties, Beijing actively sought to alleviate the Association's fears. In an effort to erase 'a history built on widespread suspicion, painful memories, and lingering tensions' (Shambaugh, 2004: 76), regular meetings after the 1997 Asian Financial Crisis increased ties between the two sides. These led to ASEAN+3 meetings (the ten ASEAN states with China, Japan and South Korea), and then ASEAN+1 meetings (solely with Beijing), while a focus upon win-win economic linkages via the CAFTA built trust and interdependence between the two sides. China also accepted the institution's values and norms – primarily transparency, sovereignty, non-interference and peaceful resolution – as both sides were able to see commonality and mutual gain in each other's guiding ideational principles. Such mutualities are complemented by the 'ASEAN Way': an 'informal, wide consultative, consensus and incremental approach ... [which] enable[s] China to participate in a comfortable manner' (Kuik, 2005: 107–8). Notwithstanding some territorial disputes (see Chapter 5), by managing its self-image, recognizing the fears of others and promoting common norms, Beijing has created a durable relationship with ASEAN.

For New Delhi, its dealings with ASEAN have also been premised upon expanding its regional influence, trade reach and status, based upon the identification of shared principles and values. Although India had initially refused membership in 1967 – seeing the grouping as a proxy Western security regime –, by the early 1990s an emphasis on common religious, artistic, linguistic and political heritages, as well as development linkages, led to prospering ties. Central to these ideational bonds was a shared adherence to the 'Five Principles of Peaceful Co-existence', as well as ASEAN's attractive non-political and non-binding basis. More broadly, the 'maintenance of an equitable strategic balance' (Mohan, 2013: 140) was also deemed essential for New Delhi (vis-à-vis both China and the United States) so as to confirm its dominance of the IOR (see Chapter 5) and to open up influence into the Pacific. Positively managing India's image as it has risen to international prominence also played into these dynamics in order to present South Asia's largest state as a peaceful actor. In December 2002, an annual ASEAN+1 summit was launched, in 2003 India signed the Treaty of Amity and Cooperation with ASEAN and from 1 January 2010 the ASEAN–India Free Trade Agreement was instituted. Through their shared normative basis, along with common economic goals, 'full-fledged cooperation' (Sinha, 2003) has continued to flourish to include naval exercises, counter-terrorism agreements and disaster management, as well as agreements on environmental, food and human security. Confirming these strengths, in 2014 the relationship was elevated to that of strategic partnership.

Apart from possessing the ability to actively manage relationships through an awareness of one's own self-image, identity and interests, and understanding how this interplays with the fears and desires of others, *creating* regional and global groupings may also be a hallmark of a great power. Such constructions display elements of attraction, recognition and commonality, as well as political will and coherence to project particular values, norms and principles outwards. In South Asia, India's vast economic and political asymmetries with its neighbours, along with its various military interventions against them, have nourished the region's collective wariness of New Delhi, meaning that establishing a regional regime has been fraught with difficulties. In addition, 'the legacy of British imperialism and its impact on state formation in South Asia . . . produced an almost permanent set of relations that pre-empt regional economic cooperation' (Reed, 1997: 235) (see Chapter 5). These factors are compounded by India's self-image as the region's hegemon, a global over regional focus and a heavy preference for bilateral engagement.

Nevertheless, since 1947, New Delhi has tried to create a number of regional bodies, based either on economic and cultural cooperation or on perceived collective security concerns (primarily vis-à-vis China). These efforts finally reached fruition with the foundation of SAARC in 1985. Supposedly based upon economic ties (including the signing of the South Asian Free Trade Area agreement in 2004), the grouping was rendered largely ineffective as a result of embedded 'mistrust, rivalry and fear' (Baral, 2006: 267), along with enduring state-specific interests, such that there was an insufficient shared basis among its members to make it a success. Of note are realist accounts which state that India has so little to gain from its far weaker neighbours that engagement is simply not worth it, whilst the very nature of South Asia – unsettled and with so few commonalities – may make it intrinsically impossible for *any* power to build a regime there. Only with the intra-regional IBSA (India–Brazil–South Africa) Dialogue Forum based upon common multiracial, multicultural and democratic characteristics has New Delhi come close to initiating and building an effective multilateral institution. Formed in 2003, and aimed at enhancing South–South cooperation, reforming global governance structures and collaborating in the agriculture, trade, culture, and defence fields, IBSA has been overshadowed by the wider BRICS grouping, as detailed below.

Conversely, Beijing has been much more successful in creating a regional organization: the SCO. Originally founded in 1996 as the Shanghai Five, the grouping brings together China, Russia and the Central Asian states (Kazakhstan, Kyrgyzstan, Tajikistan and Uzbekistan) under the norms of the 'Shanghai Spirit': confidence, communication, cooperation, common interest and peaceful co-existence. Hence, reflecting the CCP's own vision of international relations, the SCO promotes China's specific brand of regional diplomacy, is an organization built upon its particular values (and consequently projects them into its neighbourhood and internationally) and counters Western (US) influence in the area. As 'a norm- and rule-based security order in the region' (Yu, 1999: 183) working on consensus rather than alliance, the SCO initially focused upon countering three shared regional threats: terrorism, secessionism and extremism. Underpinning these foci is an ethos that 'advocates mutual trust, mutual benefit, equality, and consultation, respects cultural diversity, and seeks common development' (Yuan, 2010: 862) – key elements that are symptomatic of Beijing's overall multilateralist attitude, as delineated above.

Through the acceptance of these guiding principles by others, China gains recognition, respect and acceptance, whilst displaying an ability to actively manage regional affairs and craft them in its image. In particular, it is by being able to socialize other states into its worldview, integrate them into an institution of its own creation and then enhance positive interdependence between them that Beijing has had success with the SCO. These can also all be seen as key great power attributes vis-à-vis multilateralism. On this basis, the grouping has been portrayed as 'an alternative framework for Asian-exclusive regional politics and security' (Chin, 2010: 84), which has also enhanced China's reputation for confidence-building and effective collaboration, whilst giving it a leadership and managerial role in the area. From its initial basis, the SCO's remit has further gradually expanded to encompass Asian peace-building efforts, including the coordination of joint military operations. Beyond these factors, China currently seeks to use the regime 'to facilitate greater regional economic integration, gain and maintain access to energy supplies, and advocate a new security concept based on dialogue and consultation, mutual benefits and respects, and equality and peaceful resolution of disputes' (Yuan, 2010: 856). The SCO has a number of observer and dialogue states from across Asia, and both India and Pakistan are set to accede as full members by 2020, expanding its remit and appeal beyond Central Asia.

Collaboration based upon shared interests, outlooks and threats also typifies the joint formation of intra-regional regimes by India and China, and indicates their mutual partnership. The foundations for such cooperation can already be seen in global negotiations on trade (such as the WTO's ongoing Doha Round) and the environment, with (on the latter) the 2015 Copenhagen talks seeing 'virtually no difference in Indian and Chinese negotiation positions' (Qiao, 2014: 326). In this vein, in December 2005, both states supported the establishment of the East Asia Summit, which originated as an extension of ASEAN+3 to also include India, Australia and New Zealand. In 2011, the body expanded to incorporate the United States and Russia and can be regarded as a useful primer for building a wide-ranging regional community. These mutual efforts (and others, as noted below) highlight India and China's active willingness to promote alternative regimes to challenge existing Western-originated and Western-dominated international organizations that over-represent the United States and particular European states, as well as to intensify, explore and institutionalize their own foreign policy and multilateral cooperation.

More pointedly, the post-2009 BRICS grouping best exemplifies the clumping together of a set of developing and rising states keen to be great powers. With shared norms relating to non-interference, anti-hegemony, pro-multipolarity, development and equality, the regime is bound by a shared vision of a preferred world order. Jointly representing these interests internationally serves to bolster the achievement of these goals through strength in numbers, whilst their growing shared economic and demographic clout underlines their structural significance. In these ways, the BRICS grouping's 2012 'Delhi Declaration' stated that 'we envision a future marked by global peace, economic and social progress . . . [and] strengthened representation of emerging and developing countries in the institutions of global governance' (MEA, 2012). In July 2014, the regime launched the New Development Bank (NDB) to fund sustainable development and infrastructure projects in developing states, with an initial capital stock of $100 billion – approximately half that of the World Bank. Whilst still transitional and emergent, the NDB explicitly seeks to rival such Western-based institutions, along with the IMF, and has the shared aim among BRICS members to progressively reform the architecture of global finance.

Complementing these efforts but on a global scale, has been the AIIB. First proposed by Beijing but then established in concert with New Delhi in October 2014, the AIIB convened its inaugural meeting in January 2016. Drawing together fifty-seven Asian and Western states (including France, Germany, Italy and the United Kingdom) by early 2016, it excluded the United States and Japan, who declined to join the regime (amid concerns over labour and human rights). With a preliminary capital stock of $100 billion, the AIIB is an even greater rival than the NDB to the World Bank and the IMF, and some observers have regarded its foundation as 'the moment the United States lost its role as the underwriter of the global economic system' (Larry Summers quoted in H. Wang, 2015: 1). Whilst not having overturned the status quo concerning the basis of international economics, the AIIB does provide an alternative arrangement, as well as a vehicle for both New Delhi and Beijing to promote their particular worldviews to others within the context of a major power shift as part of an 'Asian Century'. Enhanced representativeness also plays into these dynamics, with China and India having the largest voting shares in the AIIB (26.06 and 7.51 per cent, respectively), which are considerably higher than in either the IMF (at 6.00 and 2.60 per cent) or the World Bank (at 5.10 and 3.21 per cent) (AIIB, 2016; IMF, 2016; World Bank, 2016e).

Acceptance, Influence and Ordering

Being a great power demands that a state has 'an extensive foreign policy agenda, a wide range of international interests, the ability to project power globally, and to be recognized for it' (Levy, 1983: 17).

141

In these ways, multilateral regimes – with an associated commonality premised upon shared values, principles and interests – are key arenas for the realization, possession and enactment of great power. Such groupings are also innately cross-pollinating and interdependent in that 'international structures exist only through the reciprocal interaction of actors employing constitutive rules and social practices' (Chen, 2003: 168). As such, great powers must be recognized, accepted, validated and effectively enshrined by others. Notwithstanding the role of soft power, also having hard power capabilities (primarily in the form of economic prowess) provides a certain inevitability to this attraction. Elements of ordering and managing – either explicitly or tacitly, and through a combination of diplomacy based on hard and soft power – have also been central to Western-derived notions relating to the running of international society. As social groupings, however, and formed upon norms, identities and perceptions, multilateral regimes change their basis over time. Thus – through processes of evolution and alteration – international society will 'have different specific expressions' (Ruggie, 1993: 12) commensurate with the wider distribution of material, ideational and social capabilities among its great powers.

As displayed in this chapter, the core values structuring India and China's dealings with multilateral institutions are often quite divergent from the central understandings of many Western-created regimes. Notions of multipolarity, peaceful equality and non-intervention are testaments to some of these more fundamental differences. Concerning the latter, observers note that both Beijing and New Delhi reject 'the origins of great power managerialism and the long shadow that European imperialism [has] cast in the[ir]) countries' (Bisley, 2012: 163). Whilst both states evidently wish to inform the basis of (new) institutions via their own specific values and worldviews – most clearly with the SCO and IBSA, and the BRICS grouping and the AIIB –, this is conveyed within an atmosphere of consensus not coercion. Consequently, for leaders in both states, 'the idea of an elite group of states managing relations is not seen as acceptable in an egalitarian world order' (Bisley, 2012: 182), and they thus appear not to aspire directly to the classical model of how a great power ought to behave within an institutional setting. Additionally regarding sovereignty, what distinguishes China and India from Western perspectives is that they 'apply this principle not only to themselves but also to other[s]' (Vezirgiannidou, 2013: 650), which may suggest a more equitable, more benevolent and less oppressive vision of the world.

As India and China continue to rise, such essential differences will impact upon the prevailing world order. With both states now being able to lure others to institutions of their own making – albeit with Beijing (presently) being more successful than New Delhi –, this divergence will only widen, and potentially form the foundations of an alternative world order. Intrinsic here is the desire – or not – of India and China to grasp such an opportunity, such that when they are able to possess the 'ability to shape the world, they shape it according to the imperatives of power' (Khilnani et al., 2012: 69).

7

ENGAGING WITH US HEGEMONY

As the previous chapters have shown, whilst the power capabilities of China and India have doubtlessly increased in scale, scope and significance over the last thirty years, and will continue to do so, neither is the most important actor in the contemporary international system. Rather it is the United States which can be regarded as representing the quintessence of great power. To return to this volume's Introduction, the United States excels in all of Nayar and Paul's 'Ten Virtues' and is often preponderant in them. In hard power terms, it ranked highest in terms of military spending in 2015 (SIPRI, 2016b); had the third largest GDP in PPP terms in the same year – behind China and the EU (CIA, 2016d); attracted the most FDI in 2013 (UNCTAD, 2016); had the fourth largest population (following China, India and the EU) in 2015 (CIA, 2016e); the third largest landmass (CIA, 2016a); and a world-leading level of technological advancement. On softer quotients, US norms have also critically informed the making, institution and leadership of the world's most significant contemporary multilateral regimes (the UN, the World Bank and the IMF, among others). In turn, US popular culture is the world's most attractive/pervasive; the state possesses the largest diplomatic capabilities (Markey, 2009: 83–4); and it displays strong national leadership, which – via a clear strategic culture (Walton, 2012) – has the agency and desire to dominate the global system.

For these reasons, and notwithstanding the relative decline of some of these capabilities over the last decade, the United States is – in many senses – the only complete international power, which is why it is perceived as the system's superpower and (at times) enjoys a unipolar status. For our study, the United States therefore acts as a source of aspiration for India and China, in terms of measuring their progress so far, their relative strength and positioning versus other great powers in the (current, if malleable) international system, and their prospective trajectories as they rise. Through its global central- ity, the US further conditions important understandings concerning the structure of the system but from which Beijing and New Delhi appear to deviate palpably. The most noteworthy divergence concerns hegemony, where the goal is to be 'a state that is so powerful that it dominates all the other states in the system' (Mearsheimer, 2001: 40). Central to realist thought, it is coercive hegemonic stability that allows for the creation and existence of international order within an anar- chic system. Liberalism, meanwhile, asserts that hegemony is required to 'maintain the essential rules governing interstate relations" (Robert O. Keohane quoted in Clark, 2011: 18), including the functioning of the world political economy and multilateral institutions.

Further allowing it to control the prevailing hierarchy underpin- ning the system, and to an extent other great powers, the hegemon determines 'whether, how much, and how fast the existing interna- tional distribution of benefits is adjusted to reflect the changing power balance' (Chan, 2004: 112). Thus, and reflecting its Greek etymology, which means dominance *and* leadership, the hegemon is the system's ultimate gatekeeper and manager. In these ways, the United States can extend legitimacy to states (including their re-entry to the politi- cal mainstream, as occurred with China after 1972 and India after 1998 – see below), and by proxy can anoint any new great powers. Acceptance of the hegemon by others plays into these dynamics, as based upon 'the combination of force and consent, which balance each other reciprocally, without force predominating excessively over consent' (Gramsci, 1971: 215). The acceptance of this domi- nance by others simultaneously legitimizes a hegemon's leadership, which points to constructivist accounts relating to the intersubjective recognition/tolerance of shared values, common norms and mutual interests. From this perspective, hegemons 'rule through the realm of culture and ideas' (Steans & Pettiford, 2001: 114). Here soft power supplements hard power quotients, whereby a hegemon must provide not only leadership but also the means for other consenting states to fulfil their own needs, capabilities and prospects, primarily in the form of territorial, financial and existential security.

Apart from hegemonic assertion and hegemonic consent, we finally note that the definition of hegemony is dependent upon who is making it, and (for constructivists) it is thus reflective of a state's particular values, norms and principles – as derived from its specific historical experience, behaviour and interaction. Central to the contemporary meaning of Western-derived hegemony is a belief that the hegemon (and indeed other great powers) ought to be responsible. To this end, it pays 'a large share of system-maintenance costs', but in return it can take 'a disproportionate share of the benefits' (Beckley, 2011: 48). As such, the bearers of this responsibility are given (and indeed take) exceptional rights, and 'are not beholden to the sorts of moral, legal and political constraints experienced by normal members of international society' (Bisley, 2012: 9). However, as we have seen throughout this volume, and as will be reiterated below, it is far from guaranteed that the core norms structuring Chinese or Indian foreign policy are congruent with such an ordering and vision of the world. As the international system reflects historically gestated, material and ideational power balances between its major constituent actors, this basis will therefore continue to evolve as they continue to rise.

Building upon these tenets, and moving beyond the region- and issue-specific foci of the preceding chapters, here we analyse India and China's foreign policy dealings with the system's current hegemon – the United States. To this end, the chapter shows how their interaction has comparatively developed in political, economic and military terms across the Cold War and post-Cold War periods. Historical and contemporary relations are both examined, including a particular emphasis on how shared interests, values and strategic aims have variously coalesced and diverged over the last seventy years. Apart from indicating how Beijing and New Delhi interact with the current dominant norms and practices typifying hegemony, great power status and wider system dynamics – as premised upon Washington's present-day supremacy –, the chapter also stresses their potential divergent pathways away from Western security trajectories. It further investigates Indian and Chinese attitudes towards the international system as a whole – in particular a mutually shared desire for their autonomy, equality and self-reliance in a multipolar, rather than hegemonic, world.

Cold War

Although supportive of the anti-colonial basis of its independence movement, Washington largely sidelined New Delhi within its post-1945 strategic worldview owing to India's material poverty and a dearth of any obvious cultural, economic or social linkages. Key Indian principles of non-alignment bolstered these differences and clashed with the US bipolar worldview that 'those who are not with us are against us' (John Foster Dulles quoted in Malone, 2012: 154). State visits to Moscow and Beijing in the 1950s by Indian leaders confirmed these differences, as did New Delhi's criticism of Washington via the NAM, along with the socialist political proclivities of the INC. The entrenched desire amongst Indian elites for self-reliance and self-sufficiency deepened this ideational schism, with Nehru stating that 'for far too long have we of Asia been petitioners in western courts and chancelleries. That story must now belong to the past. We propose to stand on our own legs. . . . [T]he countries of Asia . . . [will] no longer be used as pawns by others' (quoted in R. Srivastava, 1995: 3). More pointedly, New Delhi viewed US foreign policy as aimed at world domination and capitalist imperialism. Henceforth, Indo-US interaction was defined by suspicion and resentment.

Apart from their direct ideological divide, further divergence occurred as the Cold War progressed. Despite New Delhi's periodic receipt of technology, agricultural, military and food aid as part of US efforts to counteract the Soviet Union's presence in South Asia, such aid was often conditional upon India limiting its military expansion (including towards Pakistan), embracing economic development and restricting relations with Beijing and Moscow. It was also inconsistent: for example, military aid was given in 1962 (at the time of the war with China) but withheld in 1961 (when India reclaimed Goa), and food aid was provided from 1954 but stopped in 1965 during a famine (in part due to the 1965 war with Pakistan). In the midst of these erratic interactions, mounting US ties with Pakistan – India's South Asian nemesis and competitor (see Chapter 5) – 'not only brought the Cold War to India's doorstep . . . but [also showed that the United States was] striving to negate India's natural pre-eminence in the sub-continent' (Pant, 2013: 2). As ties between Islamabad and Washington deepened, India became increasingly aligned with the Soviet Union – especially around the 1971 East Pakistan war. With relations ruled by mutual distrust, and New Delhi seeing itself as being treated as a minor international actor (in stark contrast to its self-conception as a would-be great power), the dichotomy of the Cold War marked a period of ideological dislocation between the two sides' worldviews. The depth of these schismatic sentiments in Indo-US relations was summed up by Indira Gandhi, who asserted that 'it is better that we die than give in to constant pressure from the US' (quoted in Jayakar, 1992: 185).

On this basis, and through the Cold War prism, Washington was 'unable to find for India a position in its global strategy which would satisfy India's national self-esteem and ambitions' (Shah, 1983: 175). As the period progressed, further examples of differing/competing conceptions of the world punctuated Indo-US relations, most notably New Delhi's 1974 Peaceful Nuclear Explosion, which seemingly countered the US-led NPT of 1967 (which India had sponsored but refused eventually to sign) and led to US sanctions (see Chapter 3). Renewed US interest in links with, and military aid towards, Pakistan after the 1979 invasion of Afghanistan by the Soviet Union further disassociated Washington and New Delhi, leaving their relations typified by alienation, hostility and disillusionment. Only through the visits of a host of Indian leaders to the United States (primarily Indira Gandhi and Rajiv Gandhi) and a 1978 visit to New Delhi by President Jimmy Carter did relations slowly improve, based upon increased trade levels, the limited transfer of defence-related technology and an increase in US work visas for Indian citizens. However, Indio-US relations remained vitally defined by the structural constraints of the Cold War. Also critically indicating the perceptual gulf between them in terms of core values, practices and worldviews, Pentagon officials stated that 'while India is playing chess, the United States is playing checkers – we are not even on the same board' (quoted in Ogden, 2014b: 142–3).

For China, official relations with the United States stretched back before the emergence of the PRC in 1949. First contact made in the late 1700s, and throughout the nineteenth century Washington was seen as a pragmatic partner who did not exploit China. These sentiments were enshrined in the 1844 'Treaty of Wanghiya', which was far less unequal than other treaties foisted on China at this time. Reflecting Chinese admiration for 'America's wealth, its powerful military and its technological prowess' (Moore, 2010: 129), the Mandarin name for the United States was *Meiguo* ('beautiful country'). After the 1911 Revolution and during/after Japan's imperial occupation, the United States treated China as an ally, including for the duration of the Second World War. However, Washington would eventually support the nationalist Kuomintang party, who lost the ensuing civil war with the CCP. Continued US support for the Kuomintang after they fled to Taiwan, along with direct conflict between US and Chinese troops during the 1950–3 Korean War, shattered their once-positive bilateral relations. Then, within the bipolar Cold War context, which pitted differing political conceptions against each other – of both themselves and the prevailing world order –, the roots of the US–China mutual opposition would include their divergent sociocultural arrangements.

148

Henceforth, and reflective of the core values permeating its political elite (see Chapter 1), Beijing regarded Washington's diplomacy as being both anti-CCP and anti-PRC (neither of which the United States recognized), as well as fraudulent and divisive. On the international stage, the United States' mounting dominance was imperialist, with Mao describing it as based upon a coercive 'politics of aggression . . . [for which they] will be hanged' (quoted in Piao, 2005: 79). Such a basis helped to spur on Beijing's 'leaning to one side' policy of closer ties with the Soviet Union, and the first Taiwan Straits crisis of the 1950s led to an era of near-severed diplomacy. This was not to last, however. With Stalin's death in 1953 precipitating an ideological split with Mao, and China looking increasingly isolated within the international community, a new opportunity to thaw relations emerged. In the late 1960s, Richard Nixon proposed a reopening of relations based upon *realpolitik* not ideology, so as to prevent Chinese revisionism, protect against nuclear proliferation, balance against Moscow and protect the United States from criticism concerning its (emergent) military efforts in Vietnam. Closer ties would thus aim 'to pull China back into the family of nations' (Nixon, 1967: 122). Facilitated by the secret visit of Henry Kissinger in July 1971 (as it was initially difficult to convince domestic audiences of the necessity of having enhanced ties with a communist state), Nixon travelled to Beijing in February the following year. This visit saw the signing of the 'Shanghai Communiqué', which publicly opposed great power competition and included a US declaration that Taiwan was part of China. The return of China into the global mainstream (along with its gaining of a UN permanent veto seat), which it viewed as commensurate with its status, highlighted how 'membership of the club of great powers is a social category that depends on recognition by others: by your peers in the club' (Hurrell, 2006: 4).

Chinese elites now acknowledged the need for improved relations, with Deng stating that 'Sino-American relations must be made good' (quoted in S. Zhao, 2004: 248). This coincided with a re-imagining of Chinese foreign policy that embraced economic and multilateral cooperation (see Chapters 4 and 6), and a rising coalescence concerning the dominant material and ideational basis of the international system. Central to this new perspective was the resolution of a 'contradiction between "conformity as subordination" and "rise to equality" . . . [whereby] China . . . gains the respect and trust of the world through conformity' (Shih, 2005: 756). On this basis, China and the United States became useful allies, with the former, for instance, helping Washington's efforts in Afghanistan in the 1980s. Diplomatic ties were damaged, though, by the 1989 Tiananmen Square incident, and although economic relations were quickly resumed, sanctions banning weapons sales were placed on Beijing, whilst incompatible differences over human rights also re-emerged.

Post-Cold War

With the fall of the Soviet Union, China became the primary communist state in the international system, which was founded on a mix of mutual pragmatism and underlying suspicion (and nascent great power competition). Beijing's worldview also clashed with the United States' triumphant unipolar moment as Washington embraced the role of global hegemon. The US's declaration of a 'new world order' after the 1991 Gulf War was opposed by a China which perceived not only a 'new international order' (*guoji xin zhixu*) but also a system encompassing 'one superpower, many great powers' (*yichao duoqiang*). Within this context, and despite mutual calls by leaders of both states to 'build towards a constructive, strategic partnership' (Jiang Zemin & Bill Clinton quoted in Shambaugh, 2002: 98), political differences relating to democracy, the status of Taiwan and the South China Sea disputes were revived.

Buoyed by these dynamics, combined with China's own rapid economic growth and increasing military spending, a 'China threat' school of thought emerged, citing the high probability of a Sino-US conflict. Premised upon realist accounts that 'China is a rising power and that, as such, it is unlikely to behave differently than others of its type throughout history' (Friedburg, 2005: 20), this approach designated Beijing as a strategic competitor and potential threat to US hegemony. Core ideational differences relating to politics, individuality, nationalism and global economics also re-emerged. Distrust permeated such arguments, as typified by accounts stating that whilst Chinese foreign policy does not provide 'clear evidence of an active effort by the PRC to fundamentally alter the distribution of power regionally or globally, [this] does not mean that such a desire does not exist' (Johnston, 2008: 209). Such perceptual claims rose to prominence despite the emphasis in China's cultural identity on the pacific nature of Confucianism and self-restraint, among other norms (see Chapter 2). Instead, the PRC was regarded as identical to previous great powers, whose rise would lead to imbalances in the system resulting in conflict, and who would attempt to change the system for its own ends. At heart, this outlook echoed the self-perception and self-image held by

US elites that when a rising great power meets another great power concerned with maintaining its position, the two states will inevitably progress towards conflict.

Underpinning these accounts is the understanding that power is relative, so that if that of one state increases (here China) it will lead to the decline of another (here the United States). Such fears arise from a combination of ideational and material perspectives highlighting intangible uncertainties concerning how Beijing's apparently tangible capacities will be utilized, thus culminating in a potent inter-relational and inter-perceptual exchange between the two states. In response, US policy appeared to fluctuate between two positions (see Kirshner, 2010: 53). The first, realist containment, sets out to limit China's power acquisition by deterring its regional or international expansion in any form, as maximized by the expansion of formal US-led alliances (with Japan, South Korea and Australia, and across Southeast Asia). The second, liberalist engagement, aims to co-opt and socialize Beijing into the current system's dominant Western-led norms, whereby its 'immersion in a variety of international institutions will discourage nationalist policies and reward global citizenship' (Hook & Pu, 2006: 168). Contemporarily, and as demonstrated by the raw attraction of China's economy and the PRC's membership in various fiscal regimes (see Chapters 4 and 6), US policy vacillates between these two policies, leading to 'congagement'.

From the Chinese perspective, this duality is recognized as a pragmatic reaction, although it does heighten Beijing's fears of encirclement and limit its influence in East Asia. In response, China's policy – in line with Beijing's heavy self-awareness of being a rapidly rising great power (see Chapter 2) – has been to 'to accommodate itself to US power and to seek coincidences of interest . . . counterbalanced by a broadening range of stances designed . . . to retain flexibility if relations with Washington should deteriorate' (Hurrell, 2006: 14). Equally pragmatic, this search for win-win scenarios has been fortified by focusing upon the role of international organizations (see Chapter 6), conjoining interests in international trade and investment. In these ways, Beijing presents itself as a supporter of responsible and 'constructive-stakeholding' (*fu zeren daguo*). Such efforts are bolstered by China's refusal to build alliances with other states so as to counteract/balance US power, which is in concordance with its embedded norms of peace, equality and anti-hegemony. Despite US policy efforts at engagement, 'where China has made its greatest advances, it has done so "through working within the existing frameworks and norms" and has been successful because of the order, not despite it' (Clark, 2011: 25), utilizing such interactions to accomplish its wider domestic development, modernization and (for the CCP) legitimacy aims.

Increasing engagement between Washington and Beijing became most apparent after the terrorist attacks of September 11, 2001 (9/11), which improved relations between the two in the form of information-sharing, support of the US-led invasion of Afghanistan (although ambivalent concerning that of Iraq) and cooperation on terrorism and weapons of mass destruction. As a result, the PRC became a 'constructive partner' not a 'strategic competitor', and the 'international terror threat' replaced the 'China threat', as President George W. Bush remarked that 'the world's great powers find ourselves on the same side – united by common dangers of terrorist violence and chaos' (2002: 4). Both sides also began to work together concerning North Korea's nuclear programme, with US officials noting that 'we have been able to harmonize with the Chinese [concerning] not only the goals of this process . . . [but also] our strategy for achieving these goals' (Hill, 2007: 62). High levels of inter-state trade (see below) and agreements on energy efficiency, clean coal technologies and clean vehicles further boosted these positive ties, leading Beijing and Washington's elites to pledge to build 'positive and cooperative relations' (White House, 2013).

Despite such positive interactions, it is still the fear of China's rise that most stimulates tension and upheaval in relations with the United States, leading to a variety of issues within their broad engagement (as detailed below). As the scope of Beijing's international, regional and multilateral interests has expanded and these have become inextricably tied to its domestic/global legitimacy and modernization aims, these ideational-driven pressures – despite the positive contemporary hue of most Sino-US interactions – have adversely impacted their ties. Acknowledging Washington's current hard and soft power preponderance (including unrivalled power projection capabilities), observers note a consensus among CCP elites 'that a confrontational policy toward the US . . . would be counterproductive and should be avoided' (Godwin, 2004: 92). China still desires a peaceful international environment to realize its developmental goals, preferring a multipolar world order rather than hegemony. US elites remain sensitive to Beijing's surging economic clout and military expenditure, primarily through the heavy realist mindset of their leaders, which (historically) portrays such trends as threatening. Notably, policies and their positive-sum or zero-sum outcomes are ultimately dependent upon the perceptions of elites towards them. It is on this basis that scholars note that 'whether China is a threat in the twenty-first century is a matter of perception' (Yee & Feng, 2002: 37), rather than solely deriving from Beijing's relative accumulation of material, coercive or normative power vis-à-vis others (here the United States).

For the United States and India, the end of the Cold War removed a significant 'conditioning reality' (Ogden, 2014b: 143) in their relations. With the elimination of Cold War bipolarity, and a heightening emphasis on economic linkages within the atmosphere of burgeoning globalization, 'New Delhi and Washington [gained] the flexibility to pursue their bilateral relationship unencumbered by strategic, structural dictates' (Shambaugh, 2009: 153). Overcoming past animosities was, however, not immediately achieved, with New Delhi harbouring entrenched negative perceptions towards Washington, particularly in terms of residual distrust concerning any great power machinations that the latter intended towards it. These misgivings related to Western-led anti-nuclear proliferation regimes (primarily the NPT but also the CTBT), US encroachment into the IOR and efforts to reduce India's unaligned status in global politics – all policies that threatened key norms within New Delhi's strategic outlook (see Chapters 3 and 5). Although US officials displayed a general disinterest in South Asia after the Soviet withdrawal from Afghanistan in 1988–9, the two sides pursued closer military ties (via the Kickleighter Proposals of 1991, and joint military and naval exercises from 1992), and enjoyed warmer economic relations as mutual trade increased, with India being named a Big Emerging Market in 1993.

India's multiple nuclear weapons tests of May 1998 served to effectively push New Delhi back into the mainstream of international affairs. The tests fundamentally gained the United States' attention, and after Pakistan quickly retaliated with its own nuclear tests, Washington was forced to engage with South Asia. Cloaked in secrecy after previous attempts by Washington to dissuade New Delhi from testing, the tests openly defied US-led nuclear regimes, and marked the rise of a pragmatic mindset within Indian strategic thinking (see Chapter 2). Although immediately attracting US opprobrium, sanctions (from US partners, such as Japan, but not from major European powers) and a UN Resolution, the tests also catalysed the longest sustained dialogue in Indo-US relations since 1963. Gradually, Indo–US interaction improved, with the former gaining respect for displaying restraint in the 1999 Kargil conflict, during which the latter intervened for the first time against Pakistan, and which evidenced the beginning of India's de-hyphenation from Pakistan in US elite thinking.

Commonalities between the two states also rose to the fore, marking a strategic confluence concerning India's emergent economic prowess (and a growing middle-class market), its indigenously gained nuclear capabilities and its possession of a stable political system based upon 'democracy, pluralism and the rule of law' (Kronstadt et al., 2011: 1).

These material and ideational elements were attractive to a United States that now saw greater cohesion with India, and to an India that by the 1990s had accepted the benefits of enhanced global liberal capitalist interaction so as to achieve its development, moderniza- tion and (great power) status goals (see Chapters 4 and 6). India was now also acknowledged by Washington as the most viable partner for achieving stability in South Asia, whilst US elites recognized and accepted India's great power potential. It was on this basis that the United States, through its own superior positioning in the interna- tional system, acted as a 'sponsor' and initiated New Delhi's great power 'co-option' (Modelski, 1974: 150). Apart from displaying agency via an ability to change its global strategic positioning, India embraced the opportunity to forge beneficial ties with the United States, thus demonstrating a great power proclivity for role-taking and role-making. Notwithstanding Cold War period angsts, the United States and India declared themselves to be 'natural allies' and in 2000 pledged 'to create a closer and qualitatively new relationship' (quoted in Ogden, 2014b: 146).

Bolstered by an array of mutual visits (including the first to India by a sitting US President in twenty-two years when Bill Clinton travelled there in 2000), collaboration quickly deepened to include dialogues on terrorism, Asian security, technology, trade and the promotion of democracy. Although the United States still insisted upon India joining the NPT and CTBT, these demands were dropped after the 9/11 attacks as India became strategically relevant owing to its geo- political location between the Middle East and China, its democratic credentials and its own longstanding experience of terrorism. Just as US policy appeared to reverse Cold War understandings, others declared Indian policy to be a 'breathtaking departure' (Mohan, 2004: 49) from Nehruvian non-alignment, as the two sides were drawn together by a potent mélange of mutual attraction, structural dynamics and interdependence. New Delhi's offer of assistance to the United States after 9/11, including even proposing to host US forces (later rejected by the Indian Parliament), underscored how 'India viewed its national interests as congruent with those of the US' (Blackwill et al., 2011: 4). On this material and ideational basis, in 2002 President George W. Bush vitally declared that 'today we start

154

with a view of India as a growing world power with which we have common strategic interests' (quoted in Chiriyankandath, 2004: 208).

Such events confirmed the ever-evolving nature of international affairs, as relative threats, interests and power balances are in constant flux, rearranging the basis of global politics and – as such – the essence and volition of great power interaction itself. In this atmosphere, Indo-US ties continued to deepen at the beginning of the twenty-first century, with US officials stating that 'India is emerging not as just a regional power but as a global power. . . . I think there are many more opportunities – economic, in terms of security, in terms of energy cooperation – that we can pursue with India' (Condoleezza Rice quoted in A.K. Gupta, 2006: 5). Heightened interpersonal connections, summits and visits strengthened these linkages, confirming US desires to cooperate with what it perceived to be a future great power. In this regard, the visit of President Bush in 2006 was akin to that of Nixon's to Beijing in 1972, acting as a prescient acknowledgement of India's impending international stature, which again bestowed recognition on New Delhi and heightened India's profile. Clear mutual 'win-win' gains accompanied these more ideational aspects, with trade levels, military-to-military ties (including weapons sales) and counter-terrorism links all significantly expanding (as detailed in the section below). These former two areas were particularly desired by India to bolster her material capabilities and regional control (see Chapters 3, 4 and 5).

US officials also displayed greater sensitivity concerning India's regional standing, with New Delhi being regarded as 'a force for stability, prosperity, democracy, and the rule of law in a very dangerous neighbourhood' (CFR, 2011: 3) and as a strategic flank against an increasingly restive Pakistan and Afghanistan, although this was tempered by Washington's wider strategic needs. The acceptance of India's nuclear weapons status (see below) further strengthened relations, and during a 2010 visit President Obama stated that 'India has already risen' (quoted in Corbridge et al., 2012: 305) as a great power, effectively announcing India's perceived status to the world. A visible and highly educated Indian middle class in the United States, and India's largely English-speaking and Western-orientated upper and middle classes, complemented these dynamics. The newfound synergy of post-Cold War Indo-US relations was summed up by President Obama, who stated that 'we are two strong democracies, . . . we are two great republics dedicated to the liberty and justice and equality of all people, . . . and we are two free market economies; . . . that's why I believe that India and America are indispensable partners in meeting the challenges of our time' (White House, 2010).

Engagement and Issues

The enhancement of both Sino-US and Indo-US ties confirms the viewpoint among US officials of the rising centrality of Asia, which is reflected in a policy whereby 'working closely with our network of allies and partners, we will continue to promote a rules-based international order that ensures underlying stability and encourages the peaceful rise of new powers, economic dynamism, and constructive defense cooperation' (Department of Defense, 2012). As shown in the section above, such linkages rest upon the assertion that not only do states have variable short-, medium- and long-term interests, but that these also converge/diverge with those of other actors. Therefore, mutual gain, mutual power acquisition and mutual increased global influence critically underpin how New Delhi and Beijing interact with Washington. Whilst both states have witnessed dramatic and fundamental attitudinal shifts in how they deal with the system's largest player, the core norms and values structuring their identities and strategic cultures have remained – albeit in a rearranged fashion that prioritizes some interests over others. Hence, we can see how both entities have downplayed (for instance) anti-imperialist and anti-colonial sentiments but still emphasize status, equality, peaceful development and multipolarity. Their myriad realms of engagement, and the various issues affecting them, highlight these factors.

It is along core material parameters that Indo-US relations have been most strikingly improved, and provide clear incentives for great power cooperation and interdependence between them. Mounting hard power benefits – primarily economic and military – led Prime Minister Manmohan Singh to proclaim in 2008 that India's 'relationship with the US has never been in such good shape as it is today. . . . [I]t is the intention of my government [that] India and the United States must stand tall, stand shoulder to shoulder' (quoted in Mohan, 2008: 151). Echoing their ever-closer relationship, trade between the two states had increased exponentially, based upon software, gems, textiles, chemicals, pharmaceuticals, aircraft, machinery and personnel exchanges. Amounting to $3.9 billion in goods in 1985, this figure rose to $9.0 billion in 1995, to $26.7 billion in 2005 and to $66.3 billion by 2015 (US Census Board, 2016b). Of note is that since 1985, the United States has always been in deficit in this relationship, importing more than it exports, which amounted to 35 per cent of total trade in 2015 (US Census Board, 2016b). In 2012, US FDI to India was $28.4 billion and that from India to the United

States stood at $5.2 billion (OUSTP, 2016b), and in 2014, President Obama and Prime Minister Modi set a target to boost mutual trade to $500 billion (V. Mishra, 2014: 2). The United States' sizeable Indian diaspora as represented by business and friendship councils, as well as political caucuses (including the highly active US India Political Action Committee) has aided these ties, which President Clinton collectively credited with 'playing a major role in reversing almost forty years of distrust in India–US relations' (quoted in Ayres & Oldenburg, 2005: 115).

Dating from the 'Agreed Minutes' of 1995, over the last twenty years India and the United States have witnessed a sea change in their military-to-military interactions, including increasing arms sales between the two states. Major US weapons imports to India include transport and anti-submarine aircraft, helicopters, anti-ship and anti-tank missiles, guided bombs and radar systems, as well as the production of some of their components in India (SIPRI, 2016a). Military ties have included various working groups and agreements relating to all aspects of military cooperation, counter-terrorism and research and development. Both sides have also participated in numerous joint exercises and exchanges (army, navy, air), multinational operations (including in the IOR) and peacekeeping operations. Such efforts encompass shared regional stability, energy security and trade security concerns, and include counter-terrorist exercises and information-sharing, which greatly benefit from India's high degree of experience and expertise (see Chapter 3). These links currently culminate in a second ten-year 'Defence Framework Agreement' between the two states signed in June 2015, which noted 'a wide-ranging, strategic partnership that reflects their common principles, democratic traditions, long-term strategic convergence, and shared national interests' (quoted in *India Strategic*, 2015). Envisioning India as a regional security provider, US Defense Secretary Ashton Carter highlighted an 'everybody wins and everybody rises' (quoted in Garamone, 2015) quality to these interactions.

Apart from improved Indo-US ties enhancing New Delhi's hard economic and military power quotients, it has been able to gain legitimacy concerning its nuclear capabilities. As such, the 'Next Steps in Strategic Partnership' initiated in 2004 in part focused upon India's civilian nuclear programme, and led to the 2005 'US–India Civilian Nuclear Cooperation' announcement, through which New Delhi agreed to separate its civilian and military nuclear facilities. Giving India *de facto* nuclear recognition, it fulfilled a wider US strategic aim whereby 'India can make a major contribution to Asia and the world if

157

it is co-opted into the non-proliferation regime instead of being treated with hostility as an outsider' (Henry Kissinger quoted in B. Mishra, 2005: 95). After gaining a waiver from the Nuclear Suppliers Group and approval from the International Atomic Energy Agency, via unprecedented US lobbying that effectively allowed India to sidestep the NPT, Washington legislated its position in the 2008 "US–Indian Nuclear Cooperation Approval and Nonproliferation Enhancement Act'. Ending all post-1974 sanctions, the Act 'symbolized a turning point in US–India relations with the two nations deciding to leave their suspicion-ridden past behind and enter into . . . a "strategic partnership"' (Pant, 2009b: 273). For contemporary Indian leaders, there is accord that 'the agreement was the centrepiece of our transformed relationship, which demonstrated new trust' (Narendra Modi quoted in N. Singh, 2015).

These events also served effectively to conjoin important material and ideational aspects within New Delhi's great power calculus. Thus, not only did India safeguard its nuclear capacity, but it was also granted exceptional recognition by the system's hegemon to possess such facilities, despite appearing to break aspects of established international anti-proliferation regimes. Only the primacy of the United States, along with other great powers, could facilitate such a process, and this was underpinned by Washington seeing New Delhi's expected future trajectory, and desiring to guide (and benefit from) it. Such actions set a precedent for a number of India's other global relationships (most notably with key US allies such as Japan and Israel – see Ogden, 2014b: 135–8, 163–6), with the United States essentially inaugurating its (future) international status, regardless of any material limitations. Given that '"recognition" is an equally important goal as "security" for the Indian state' (S. Singh, 2014: 191), and represents a major step *en route* to New Delhi achieving its great power ambitions, Indo-US ties have become part of the bedrock of its global affairs.

Despite all of these positive exchanges, observers note how 'lingering legacies of past prejudices still sometimes come in the way of the great services each side should now be rendering the other' (Blackwill et al., 2011: 11). Many of these issues relate to deep-seated norms held by New Delhi favouring the maintenance of Indian self-sufficiency in all areas, whilst wishing to be treated equally and with admiration by other states – elements that 'continue to permeate the elite, bureaucratic and public consciousness' (Ogden, 2014b: 156). Typical of such sensitivities was the arrest in December 2013 of an Indian diplomat, Devyani Khobragade, for visa fraud, which nearly derailed Indo-US relations, with officials feeling that Washington was disrespecting them. More significantly, New Delhi is wary of continued US–Pakistan ties (including the ongoing provision of military aid to Islamabad), noting the previous negative long-term impacts of short-term US interests on the region, most notably the rise of the Taliban and the Kashmir insurgency as a side-effect of Washington's efforts to oust Moscow from Afghanistan in the 1980s. At its heart, for New Delhi, US support of Pakistan undercuts India's regional influence, hence reducing its strategic autonomy, and thus essentially limits the speed of its expected great power ascent. The two sides also disagree in the WTO concerning the rate of India's economic liberalization, although notably in November 2014 they found accord on food security issues.

Whilst Washington has been supportive of India's UN Security Council ambitions, such reform appears unlikely as it would reduce the US's own global standing, whilst New Delhi refuses to sign the NPT and CTBT, which lessens the legitimacy of US-conceived global nuclear regimes. Such examples point to ongoing fundamental differences in how each state perceives the world order. On this basis, officials in India also ask whether Indo-US relations are truly reciprocal or if they are driven by a purely economic/new market need or as a reaction to broader system dynamics – primarily the US's need to counteract China's rapid rise on the Asian and global stages. The more cynical of these note that the Indo-US strategic partnership only emerged once China was designated a strategic competitor by Washington. More fundamentally, some fear that the US belief in India's imminent rise to China-type proportions is 'a Western construct, which has unrealistically raised expectations for both Indian growth and the country's international commitments' (Miller, 2013: 15). Nevertheless, while such fears sustain a level of distrust in Indo-US relations that is historically engrained, heart-felt and persistent, they are being tempered by the clear gains New Delhi enjoys via the recent revolution across the full range of its interaction.

For Sino-US relations, similarly embedded misgivings punctuate the ties between the two states and are magnified by varying perceptions concerning great power/hegemonic competition, with observers noting that 'lasting progress will remain elusive . . . until the underlying sources of mistrust and resentment are addressed' (Shepperd, 2013: 175–6). On an official level, Xi Jinping has recognized such 'strategic distrust and miscalculations' (quoted in *Global Times*, 2015) as being the central concern amid increases in the scope, weight and significance of their relations. The most combustible area of tension rests on Chinese nationalism, primarily directed towards the United States, Japan and the broader Western-led international system. Numerous incidents epitomize such tensions, such as US carrier groups conducting operations close to the Taiwan Straits in 1996, the NATO (US-led) bombing of the Chinese embassy in Belgrade in May 1999 and the April 2001 Hainan spy plane incident. More recently, amid US criticism of Beijing's perceived expansionist policies in the South China Sea (see Chapter 5), both sides have accused the other of 'militarization' (BBC, 2016) and therefore heightening regional tensions. Taiwan also remains as another trigger point in Sino-US dynamics, with Washington persisting in selling arms to Taipei in an effort to maintain its influence, whilst for Beijing the island represents an unresolved ideational issue that resurrects negative imperial experiences and signals China's yet-to-be-achieved territorial integrity.

Esteem, respect and perception underscore these exchanges, and core differences further inform such observations, especially concerning the perceived intent of one state vis-à-vis the other and the meaning ascribed to different power sources, especially military capabilities. This being the case and again maybe reflecting the engrained influence of mainly Western-derived realist understandings about international politics, US officials commonly note that 'China's rapid military modernization and increases in capabilities raise questions about the purposes of this buildup and China's lack of transparency' (Zoellick, 2015: 8). Such fears occur despite China being far behind US capabilities (see Chapter 3). On this basis, and when combined with ideational sources – such as fraught histories, unresolved traumas and as-yet-unfulfilled aspirations –, nationalism remains as an uncertain, volatile and reactionary element in Sino-US relations. Moreover, observers note how 'rising nationalism coupled with generations of propaganda about the unity of China could compel Chinese leaders to take actions contrary to China's larger strategic interest' (Garrett, 2006: 403), as elites respond to their population's emotional needs. Such a resource may be useful to deflect criticism away from the CCP, particularly in the event of a serious crisis (such as a major economic downturn), but could also be a powerful variable that is difficult to control. Ideological differences and different conceptions of how the world ought to be ordered (see Chapter 6) feed into these nationalist accounts, also indicating that 'China's soft power is a threat to the west' (Follath, 2010).

Confirming the multi-layered essence of international relations, as well as their positioning as two of the most important states in the current globalized environment, China and the United States are also

160

bound together economically. This mutually indispensable symbiosis is premised upon China traditionally providing cheap manufactured goods and the United States having a stable export market, and is primarily based upon the sale of aircraft, machinery, vehicles, furniture, toys and footwear. For liberalists, such economic interdependence will 'continue to draw them together, constraining and damping any tendencies towards conflicts' (Friedburg, 2005: 13). Amounting to $7.7 billion in goods in 1985, trade rose to $57.3 billion in 1995, to $284.7 billion in 2005 and to $598.1 billion by 2015 (US Census Board, 2016a). Of note is that since 1985, the United States has always been in deficit in this relationship, importing more than it exports, which amounted to 61 per cent of total trade in 2015 (US Census Board, 2016a). In 2012, US FDI to China amounted to $51.4 billion and from China to the US stood at $5.2 billion (OUSTP, 2016a), further linking together the two major economies. Despite such mutual benefits, Beijing has been criticized for gaining unfair trade advantages by undervaluing its currency, disrespecting trade regulations and having weak labour/environmental laws. China is also accused of carrying out cyber-warfare and cyber-espionage attacks against the United States – claims fortified by perceptions that the Chinese state and Chinese industries are 'one and the same'. The purchase of US corporations by Chinese companies has therefore been blocked by US elites. Notably, the US's cyber capabilities far exceed those of Beijing (Lindsay, 2014/15), whilst in 2015 Xi Jinping called for 'cyber sovereignty' of state-specific internet networks (BBC, 2015b).

Beijing continues to criticize the neo-imperialism of US corporations, while China trades in a largely non-ideological manner across the Middle East, Central Asia and Africa, particularly concerning access to energy resources (see Chapter 4) – which draws the two sides into ideational competition over their diplomatic links with pariah states. In turn, Beijing officials have perceived US climate change initiatives as 'retard[ing] China's growth' (Holloway & Lei, 2014: 143). Thus, even though CCP elites have noted that 'the US and China are in a win-win, lose-lose symbiotic economic-strategic relationship' (Jiang Zemin quoted in Garrett, 2006: 395), their mutual economic and trade success increases their mutual diplomatic and political power, which leads to almost inevitable eventual competition in some areas. Chinese holdings of US debt (the world's highest, at $1.24 trillion or 20 per cent of the total, in May 2016 – USDT, 2016), along with Beijing's enormous foreign exchange reserves, have led US officials to ask, 'How do you get tough on your banker?' (Hillary

Clinton quoted in Curry, 2007). However, given their close links and geo-central economies, any global crisis will affect both sides, and hence Washington favours an economically strong, stable and peaceful China, and Beijing desires relations 'beneficial to [the] peace, stability and prosperity of the Asia-Pacific region, and the world at large' (Hu Jintao quoted in *Xinhua*, 2009). Nevertheless, for Beijing, the 2008 credit crunch was a crisis of a specific form of 'Western' liberal capitalism (X. Wu, 2010), and any repeat may augur efforts by China to assert the role (and norms) of the NDB and the AIIB (see Chapter 6), and to create a 'super-sovereign reserve currency' that is 'disconnected from individual nations and is able to remain stable in the long run' (Zhou Xiaochuan quoted in D. Roberts, 2013).

Underpinning all of these tensions is the striving of both states for status, recognition and positioning in East Asia, whereby 'the US is unwilling to accept China's push for regional hegemony' (Pant, 2012: 243), which runs contrary to Beijing's self-image (see Chapter 5). Thus, Washington's 'Asian rebalancing strategy' or pivot of 2012 aimed to increase its presence in the region. In response, Chinese elites retorted that 'a "certain country" . . . has strengthened its Asia-Pacific military alliances, expanded its military presence in the region, and frequently makes the situation there tenser' (IOSC, 2013). Such concerns include the growth of US theatre missile defence efforts in Taiwan, South Korea and Japan. Beijing's military modernization, in particular its anti-ship ballistic missiles (see Chapter 3), is hence partially aimed at countering any US threat if it were to arise. Regardless, with the structural centrality of the two states, observers have long realized that 'few developments could cause greater instability in Asia than a breakdown of relations between the US and China' (Jerry Leach quoted in Kornberg, 1996: 14). Ultimately, it is perceptions in Sino-US relations that will dictate outcomes, for, in the words of one American observer, 'the greatest danger we have is overestimating China and China overestimating itself' – a state of affairs that overlooks the reality that 'China is nowhere near close to the US', and so creates unwarranted 'fear in the US and hubris in China' (Joseph S. Nye quoted in Shambaugh, 2002: 311).

Dominance, Interaction and Evolution

While US dominance appears as an undeniable reality within the current international system, such hegemony – both as a material or ideational fact, or as the critical reference point for international affairs itself – is increasingly at odds with elite perspectives in China and India. With hegemony being seen to combine elements of '"benignancy" and coercion' (Schoeman, 2007: 77), the emphasis of Asia's emergent greater powers is very much more on the former. Therefore, although 'hegemonic power is now exercised in an international society with a highly developed sense of shared interest in a stable international order' (L.R. Lee, 2010: 157), the very emergence of New Delhi and Beijing as global power centres is altering the relative balance of power with Washington, in terms of both the projection and the actualization of their particular worldviews. Thus, despite both Sino-US and Indo-US relations being premised upon closer economic cooperation as per the liberal capitalist nature of the present system, this innate difference leads to competition between India's and China's and Washington's desired world orders, concerning multipolarity and hegemony, respectively. This divergence is fuelled in part by the centre of the world economy (and military spending) shifting to Asia, which will give Beijing and New Delhi a greater say in how that world functions (see Chapters 4 and 6). More fundamentally, their own identities, norms and cultures, as derived from elite experience, history and memory, show how 'images of the world created by ideas very often serve as switches determining the tracks on which the dynamism of interests kept actions moving' (Max Weber quoted in Morgenthau, 1973: 17).

Within these dynamics, Sino-US ties are 'the most important relationship that the US maintains . . . [and] the most consequential for global stability' (Pant, 2012: 248). The importance of self/other perceptions dictates the nature of these relations concerning how elites in both states view each other and their relative intentions. Thus, if seen in a negative light, Beijing's foreign policy will take on an expansive and aggressive realist tone as it seeks material resources to extend its economic and military clout, inexorably bringing it into competition with the United States. If seen positively, China's increasing political, economic and systemic interdependence will bring increased common ground, leading to cooperation premised upon a liberalist Chinese foreign policy whose peaceful rise is accepted by others, including the United States. In the latter formulation, US hegemony will not be openly challenged, and in the former it will – eventualities wholly dependent upon how elites in Washington and Beijing decide to engage with other and how they evaluate different power quotients. These assertions highlight the interactional, co-constitutive and evolving nature of great power politics, which is dependent upon material *and* ideational sources. Trauma, mistrust and suspicion have the potential to affect such interplays, and to create unrepresentative false images or *pareidolia* – the perception of a familiar pattern or meaning where none actually exists.

Such assertions are equally relevant to the Indo-US relationship, which has similarly oscillated between negativity (during the Cold War) and positivity (from the late 1990s onwards). Thus, elements of distrust and anti-imperialism have contemporarily been largely over-taken by complementary interests – such as trade, counter-terrorism and shared political values – as part of 'a strong, vibrant, ever-deepen-ing US–India relationship [that] furthers the vital national interests of both countries' (CFR, 2011: 1). Changing US interests and structural dynamics have aided this positive change, in much the same way as US attitudes towards Beijing negatively hardened after the end of the Cold War. Of particular note here is the observation that 'India is not subordinating itself to another power or seeking to be a junior partner in any coalition; rather it is pursuing its own agenda as an emerging great power, whose interests presently coincide with those of the United States and its regional allies' (Ladwig, 2009: 106). As such, Indo-US relations also have scope to change and evolve *over time* in line with their relative material and ideational power sources, and in terms of how these sources are intersubjectively perceived by their leaders and elites *at any future juncture*. It is for this reason that Washington and New Delhi may also emerge as rivals, particu-larly if India overtakes China on key material power measures (see Chapters 3 and 4). Such an evolution in perception could also be present if China–India bipolarity were ever to exist.

CONCLUSIONS: EVALUATION AND FUTURE POSITIONING

Great power is multifaceted, interweaving a combination of aggregate material and ideational, tangible and intangible, and objective and subjective elements. Reflecting this interplay, and as the Introduction stated, each of this volume's chapters has interrogated and expanded upon some aspect of Nayar and Paul's 'Ten Virtues'. On this basis, Chapters 3 and 4 focused upon 'hard' power quotients concerning military and nuclear capabilities, and economic strength, respectively, while considering the role of technological advancement and demographics. Other chapters investigated 'soft' characteristics: domestic determinants (Chapter 1), strategic cultures (Chapter 2) and multilateralism (Chapter 6), and thus encompassed discussions relating to norms, culture, leadership of international forums, state capacity, strategy and diplomacy, and national leadership. The remaining chapters extended these analytical foci to additionally consider circumstantial and relative factors concerning peripheral relations (Chapter 5), and engaging with hegemony (Chapter 7). Those states that collectively possess superiority, if not supremacy, within and across these virtues can be indentified as great powers. These virtues are also co-constitutive, drawing together the domestic and international spheres – a central premise of constructivism. As shown in our analysis, these virtues possess a dynamic chemistry – they are 'concordant, in the sense that a nation that ranks high on one dimension has a tendency to also to rank high on other dimensions' (Johan Galtung quoted in Modelski, 1974: 176).

In a process of constant flux, we have seen how these factors affect and interact with each other, with our understanding of great power morphing after the end of the Cold War and the advent of the globalized age. It has also broadened beyond any single major factor, as state interests have concurrently become more non-traditional and comprehensive in nature. The power quotients related in this book therefore represent a continually changing menu, with certain factors being variously prioritized/de-prioritized, and fluctuating over time. This fluid variability is ably summed up by Baldwin's five key dimensions: '*scope* . . . that an actor's power may vary from one issue to another; *domain* . . . the actor(s) subjected to the influence of one actor; *weight* . . . the likelihood of one actor affecting the behavior of (an)other actor(s); *costs* . . . how costly or cheap it is for (one) actor(s) to comply with the demands of (an)other actor(s); (and) *means* . . . the variety of different means of exercising influence' (2003: 278–9). Such considerations confirm our key analytical aspects, namely that international relations are interactional and relative as formulated by the building blocks of experience, state identity and peer recognition. Moreover, ideational volition and intent critically inform the relationship between resources and behaviour, with the former transforming material capabilities into foreign policy tools, actions and behaviours.

These processes become apparent over time and it is therefore formative interaction that shapes international history, providing the defining inference points of what states are, whilst acting as a potential projector of future behaviour. The formation of longstanding attitudes is part of such a process, leading into state-specific histories that are 'built not merely of events but of varying perceptions of them' (Gong, 2001: 3) – an observation which accounts for China's and India's different understandings of the world. Thus, history (and its recollection) is the kinetic force behind ideational continuity and change, and the resultant values, norms and identities that it helps to craft act as 'a process of change that leaves an imprint on state identity' (Katzenstein, 1996: 23), and thus on security policy. By recording shared meanings, values and dispositions, history-contingent frameworks of identity produce anticipated social and interactive inclinations, as elucidated by India's and China's particular identities. Precedents, experiential limits and the lessons of previous interaction – along with its recollection and memory – thus provide an ideational trail of how particular states (and the leaders and political groupings which lead them) are recurrently interpreting and reinterpreting their place in the world.

It is on this basis that 'the meaning of material structure is ultimately contingent upon ideas' (Wendt, 1992: 394–5), confirming the interaction between material and ideational factors within (in this case, China and India's) international relations. Self-image, ego, desire and ambition vitally sustain such arguments, along with a great power pro-activeness concerning role-giving, role-taking and role-making, and the (perceived) status, value and esteem assumed to be inherent in particular material resources – all of which are elements that we have seen consistently displayed throughout the various chapters of this book. How other states regard these behaviours, and whether or not they recognize other states as being great, also adds a further interactional and intersubjective element to this perspective. In these ways, 'ideas and material capabilities are always bound together, mutually reinforcing one another, and not reducible one to the other' (Robert Cox quoted in Payne, 1994: 153) – an interrelational dynamism that further points to some realization of what might be considered to be a hybrid form of 'materiational' power.

Appraising the Four Prisms

Interconnection

For both states an element of synergy is evident with regard to the many factors discussed in this volume. Beijing's great power desire rests upon restoring its previous status in the international system, hence intimately connecting its experiential past to its contemporary behaviour. Key attitudinal perspectives bolster such an ambition, as exemplified by China's strategic culture, which rests upon (for instance) central principles relating to anti-imperialism, non-intervention and multipolarity. Such perspectives are also vital mainstays of legitimation for the ruling CCP within China's domestic context, which themselves radiate outwards into its international policies. Such understandings in turn inform its use of military force, which has undulated between being seen as an offensive (under Mao) and as a defensive (post-Mao) means with which to augment its comprehensive national strength. In the last few decades, the rate of China's military modernization has been fuelled by its growing economic prowess, which has then consequently sustained its mounting trade and energy security needs. In turn, these elements are further conjoined within its peripheral relations as either an initial means of realist (military) defence/assertion or a demonstration of contemporary liberal (economic) interdependence. Historically derived ideational considerations relating to the workings of the international system, desired territorial make-up and regional competition with Japan additionally feed into these dimensions. Moreover, domestic, strategic, military, economic and peripheral concerns all coalesce

167

into Beijing's interaction with – and attitude towards – multilateral and regional institutions. In much the same way, these ideational and material factors have informed its fluctuating relations with the United States, which have variously emphasized different (competing) power interactions over time.

New Delhi's great power ambitions also act as the crucible in which a mixture of different power sources has been amalgamated. Domestic determinants relating to status, modernization and development have thus conjoined particular principles relating to asserting India's self-reliance, preferred territorial imagining and international positioning, in accordance with its strategic culture. These elements in turn inform its attitude towards the use of military force, which, through its interaction with other states, switched from being seen as unnecessary (pre-1962) to essential, including the acquisition of nuclear weapons. As with Beijing, growing economic prowess has enabled New Delhi's military strength to increase in a largely co-dependent manner, whilst self-reliance (pre-1991) gave way to great power aspiration (post-1991), leading to its embrace of liberalized trade. The mutual stimuli of these two elements underpin New Delhi's military modernization and high volume of weapons imports, and bolsters its growing ability to protect trade and energy security interests. Regionally, India's self-image as the dominant state in South Asia has informed its varied material interactions with its smaller neighbours, while contestation with Pakistan has been driven by an interplay across mainly ideational schisms interconnected with military capabilities. During the Cold War, ideational linkages were highly evident in New Delhi's relations with multilateral institutions, most notably with the NAM, which linked India's domestic identity with the wider international system. In the post-Cold War period, however, these were superseded to a degree by a deeper correlation with economic interlinkages. Regarding Indo-US relations, the entire gamut of India's ideational and material precepts has continued to inform the basis of the two states' affairs and, as for Beijing, serves to characterize these precepts' grand intermingling and union.

Perception

Perceptions towards and between states, and concerning the basis of great power itself, have also been prominent in our analysis. For India, its leaders' understandings of the international system, as indicative of its particular material and ideational needs, have been formed via New Delhi's historical international interaction. Here, there has been a critical deep-seated distrust and suspicion of other major powers' intentions, premised upon negative colonial experiences. Serving to create an intersubjective basis for its foreign power behaviour, these perceptions also entail its desired self-image to be a great power, and have been evident across the full range of its interactions. Within its strategic culture, conceptions of how the world ought to be have driven forward anti-imperialist, non-interventionist and multi-polarity strands in its elites' thinking, which in turn have directly impacted upon how they have regarded the role to be played by material power measures, such as military prowess and economic strength. Perceptions of benignancy, Third World leadership and the avoidance of great power competition dictated the non-acquisition of military power before the 1962 war with China, but India's defeat in that conflict replaced this precept with an understanding that military means were now necessary. Equally, until the 1990s, a reading of the global economic system as threatening and coercive led to minimal engagement, but this was then supplanted (not replaced) by a perception of the benefits of such interaction after 1991. Perceptions of dominance also influenced India's desired position in South Asia. New Delhi's multilateral engagement has equally been determined by a shifting mélange of these same perceptions of benefit or threat, as have Indo-US ties, such that fluctuations between divergence and convergence have been based upon their inter-perceptual interaction.

With regard to China, the perception of an aggressive and coercive international system was fomented through Beijing's negative experiences during the Century of Humiliation, the narrative of which had a significant impact upon the guiding structure of its domestic and foreign policy. As with India, this perception would serve as an intervening variable influencing elites' perceptions concerning the fundamental principles dictating how they viewed the world, as enshrined within China's strategic culture. The use and efficacy of material power were vitally influenced by such perceptions (and indeed buoyed by direct experience), with military power regarded as a necessary tool both during (offensively) and after (defensively) the Cold War. Such perceptions were also reflected in Beijing's attitude towards economics, with the benefits of engagement outweighing risks from the 1980s onwards. The belief in such advantages then further influenced the conduct of its foreign policy across its periphery. Notably here, entrenched threat perceptions emanating from toxic, unresolved and status-driven contestation continued to be the hallmark of relations with Japan, dominating the ties between the two states – a situation echoed in India–Pakistan affairs. Further

169

displaying how ideational forces (perceptions) can influence attitudes towards a particular power source, China's multilateral engagement has also developed owing to the changing perceptions of its leaders concerning its overall usefulness, especially when intertwined with a central desire to maximize its material power quotients. Most conspicuously, it is within Beijing's relations with the United States that perceptions have the most saliency – with negative perceptions between the two entities seemingly acting as triggers for conflict, and positive perceptions acting as potential foundations for peaceful collaboration.

Evolution

Change, learning and progression have, furthermore, been recogniz-able parameters within the ascent of Asia's largest states. These ele-ments are also evident throughout our discussion of the definition of great power. For Beijing, its elites' perception of the world evolved from initial high levels of suspicion (leading to China's isolationist proclivities) to a gradual acclimatization towards the benefits of deeper involvement. On this basis, the ideologically charged view of the Mao era gave way to the pragmatism of his successors – a change informed by Beijing's heightened engagement across all spheres. Elements in China's strategic culture reflected these dynam-ics, along with shifting understandings relating to the use of military force – from total war to a more local focus. Fundamental policy moves were also discernible within economics, as again elite think-ing informed the basis and realization of China's trade relations with other states, whose cost–benefit equation transformed from being regarded as highly negative to positive. This progression was also evident in evolving considerations of both different possible inter-connections between various kinds of power and the perceptions underlying these understandings. Regionally, Beijing's self-awareness of its own rising stature, along with the need for a peaceful environ-ment to better harness economic stability, led to a further change in focus. Equally, China's initial reluctance and caution with regard to multilateral involvement was replaced by confidence and innova-tion, as shown by its creation of groupings such as the SCO. Finally, relations between China and the United States have reflected these multiple areas of evolution, as witnessed by increased trade and multilateral and regional linkages, although these are still beset by distrust and rivalry.

India's foreign policy behaviour has also witnessed a range of transformations over the last sixty years, the result of its greater learning from – and interaction with – the international system and its constituent states. Although still wary of other states' intentions towards her, India's elites gradually shifted their predominant world-views from being wholly idealist (under Nehru) to being much more realistic in orientation. Key interactions often played into this change, most notably the 1962 war with China, which served to socialize India into the necessity of having a hard military capacity, and its embrace of *realpolitik* prior to the 1971 East Pakistan War. Elite attitudes towards nuclear weapons would also gradually gestate, allowing for their attainment in 1998. With regard to economics, it took a crisis (in 1991) to accelerate India's economic liberalization and to appreciate the virtue of global engagement. The evolution of the international structure away from Cold War bipolarity further supported this prism of analysis, and blended with New Delhi's own learning. Such considerations (and the decline of the Soviet Union) also influenced India's regional outlook (although not its underlying expectation of its own superiority), and led to an approach towards most of its neighbours that was more benevolent than coercive. Regarding mul-tilateral institutions, there was less evidence of explicit evolution as India supported the NAM in the 1950s along with the creation of the United Nations. Instead, it was the scope of New Delhi's involvement with the UN that changed, as it gradually demanded a permanent veto seat. The greatest transformation has been in Indo-US relations, which evolved from a linkage beset by tension and divergence to one that encapsulated India's growing global power across all spheres.

Commonality

This volume has sought not only to compare the emergence of China and India as great powers but also to highlight ways in which their rise has displayed elements of congruence. In terms of their modern incarnations, the two states emerged at the same time and within a post-colonial and post-imperial context whereby they had both suf-fered from external aggression, domination and (in the case of India, full) occupation. Such a context entrenched a common and sustained distrust of the international system and the intentions of its major powers towards them (especially in Western-derived multilateral institutions), along with a shared desire for self-reliance and auton-omy. Both states were also initially deeply impoverished entities, which would form the motive for their desired long-term achievement of common development and modernization goals – aims magnified

171

by both having gigantic and world-leading populations. The restoration of past status – primarily to re-become, and to be recognized by others as, great powers – also acted as a shared ambition that would consistently drive forward the domestic and foreign policy behaviours of each state. With regard to the international system, Beijing and New Delhi would further adhere to the same set of core ideals: the 'Five Principles of Peaceful Co-existence' that emerged in the 1950s concerned respect for territorial integrity and sovereignty; non-aggression; non-interference in another state's internal affairs; equality and cooperation for mutual benefit; and peaceful coexistence. These principles would continue to define the underlying essence of their international affairs (with some caveats), as they both began to increase their comprehensive national strength. Improving the position of Asian states, and seeking to lead the non-Western world, furthermore acted as vital sources of inspiration for generations of elites in both Beijing and New Delhi.

Militarily, both sides are increasing their capabilities, as part of shared modernizing drives but also as a means to protect their borders, along with vital trade and energy security routes, which demand an expansion of their capabilities in terms of physical reach and presence. Such expansions are leading to heightening tensions with their neighbours (more so for Beijing), as well as with each other, and they both face significant internal security threats via separatists, insurgents and terrorism, although this factor is far worse for New Delhi. Amassing economic prowess is also a shared common element whose necessity has now been embraced by both sets of elites and populations, and whose trade tactics are equally marked by a common non-ideological approach to finding new markets, investment and energy supplies. Mutual transitions towards significant global economic status have, furthermore, brought shared domestic problems relating to corruption, inequality and high levels of environmental degradation – solutions for which are not immediately apparent. Within their regions, Beijing and New Delhi also each face a key contestation (with Japan and Pakistan, respectively) premised upon historically embedded animosities and conflicting status/recognition issues, and which appear to prevent either of them from gaining hegemony. Notably, in addition, they have a considerable unresolved territorial dispute with each other. With regard to the basis of the international system, India and China subscribe to a multipolar vision that eschews global hegemony, and seeks a greater voice for developing states either in existing multilateral institutions or by devising new competitor regimes of their own making. Finally, both New Delhi and

CONCLUSIONS

Beijing have improved their ideational and material relations with Washington, but neither side has allied with it – indeed, China is now openly feared by the United States.

Global Reckoning

Notwithstanding the pitfalls highlighted within this volume concerning the comparison of states with each other – and the impact that perceptual factors have upon material measures –, a cursory grouping of states along key indicators reveals some central perspectives concerning the relative positioning of China and India within the echelons of great power. Regarding economic prowess, which we can see as the most translatable and indicatory source of great power, both of our target states ranked very high in terms of their GDP in PPP terms in 2015, as shown by Table 2. Further accounting for significant shares of the global total, having such a status is something shared by all other major powers (including all the P5 members of the UN Security Council, along with other commonly attributed candidate great powers such as Germany and Japan, and the wider EU bloc). Overall, India and China are ranked fourth and first, respectively, but each has a relative stage of development (in terms of GDP per capita) that is still vastly behind their peers, particularly in the case of New Delhi.

Beyond this contemporary snapshot, looking back over the last five

Table 2   GDP (purchasing price parity US$) (2015)

	GDP (PPP) (US$) (2015)			
	Total (tr)	% (world)	Ranking	Per capita
China	19.51	17.15	1	14,300
France	2.65	2.33	11	41,400
Russia	3.47	3.05	7	23,700
UK	2.66	2.34	10	41,200
US	17.97	15.80	3	56,300
EU	19.18	16.86	2	37,800
Germany	3.84	3.38	6	47,400
India	8.03	7.06	4	6,300
Japan	4.66	4.10	5	38,200
World	113.77	100.00	–	15,800

Source: CIA, 2016d.

Table 3   Average annual GDP growth (%) (1960–2015)

	Average annual GDP growth (%)						
	1960s	1970s	1980s	1990s	2000s	2010–15	2015
China	3.38	7.46	9.78	10.01	10.30	8.30	6.90
France	5.55	4.05	2.36	2.01	1.42	1.07	1.20
Russia	–	–	–	–4.91	5.48	1.77	–3.70
UK	2.90	2.63	2.62	2.36	1.85	2.02	2.30
US	4.65	3.54	3.14	3.23	1.82	2.10	2.40
EU	4.94	3.50	2.34	2.22	1.59	0.85	1.70
Germany	–	3.08	1.96	2.22	0.82	1.97	1.70
India	3.91	2.93	5.69	5.77	6.90	7.32	7.60
Japan	10.44	4.11	4.37	1.47	0.56	1.30	0.50
World	5.48	3.99	3.06	2.70	2.61	2.90	2.50

Source: World Bank, 2016c.

or so decades, we can also see that India and China have been consistently outstripping other great power states in terms of their average annual GDP growth (as detailed in Table 3). For Beijing, this began in the 1970s and for New Delhi in the 1980s, with the former's growth percentage rising decade on decade until 2010–15, and for the latter increasing incrementally throughout the last half-century.

Such figures not only confirm that China and India's emergence as great powers has been taking place for some time (and that it is an embedded contemporary dynamic within international relations), but they also form the basis for their continued rise and future pre-eminence, if such trajectories can be maintained. The fact that their annual GDP growth rates are so high furthermore serves to accelerate their accumulation of this economic power over time, providing a key momentum whereby power begets power. This interconnection affirms Paul Kennedy's (1988) assertion concerning a 'time lag' between gaining economic power and its conversion to other power types (such as military, as shown below). Overall, both Beijing and New Delhi are transitioning from being developing to developed states, with India trailing ten to twenty years behind China, which again points to the importance of relative status concerning industrialization, modernization and infrastructure/living standards.

Having world-leading populations and landmasses further harnesses India and China's economic strength, and both states rank very

Table 4   Landmass and population size (2015)

	Land (km^2)	Ranking	Population (m)	Ranking
China	9,596,960	4	1,367.49	1
France	643,801	44	66.55	22
Russia	17,098,242	1	142.42	10
UK	243,610	81	64.09	23
US	9,826,675	3	321.37	4
EU	4,324,782	7	513.95	3
Germany	357,022	64	80.85	18
India	3,287,263	8	1,251.70	2
Japan	377,915	63	126.92	11
World	510,072,000	–	7,256.49	–

Source: CIA, 2016a, 2016e.

high on these quotients (see Table 4) – a commonality shared with the EU, Russia and the United States. These elements are not inevitably a defining characteristic of great power, as not all major listed states rank very highly on them. Instead, they act as potentially potent resources on which great powers can draw, but these must be fully enabled through their interaction with other factors, most notably economic development.

Furthermore, if we recall how a large working population can hypothetically realize greater levels of economic growth (see Introduction), wider demographic trends underpinning China and India's vast populations provide further insights regarding their future trajectory. As can be seen from Table 5 below, China's population is older and growing comparatively slowly, leading to slower growth and hence potentially lower productivity, while India's population is relatively younger and growing more quickly (than China, the United States and the EU), leading to a much larger working population, although these surpluses are somewhat offset by lower life expectancy and much higher rates of infant mortality. In the longer term, China's population is projected to decline (from 1,415.5 million in 2030, to 1,348.1 million in 2050, to 1,004.4 million by 2100), whilst India's will grow (from 1,527.7 million, to 1,705.3 million, to 1,659.8 million across the same periods) (UN, 2015: 18–22). Courtesy of these gigantic populations, both Beijing (sooner) and New Delhi (later) will face the mounting healthcare, education, housing, employment and pension costs associated with them.

Whilst the broad veracity of these observations appears to be

Table 5 Demographic trends (2015)

	Annual growth (%)	Age structure (%)				Life expectancy	Infant mortality
		0–14	15–64	65+	Median		
China	0.45	17.1	72.9	10.0	36.8	75.4	12.4/1,000
EU	0.25	15.5	65.7	18.8	42.5	80.2	4.0/1,000
India	1.22	28.1	66.0	5.9	27.3	68.1	41.8/1,000
US	0.78	19.0	66.1	14.9	37.8	79.7	5.9/1,000
World	1.08	25.6	65.9	8.5	29.9	68.7	35.4/1,000

Source: CIA, 2015a, 2015b, 2016b, 2016g, 2016h.

self-evident, issues concerning the use of GDP as a truly reliable measurement of economic growth serve to reduce its potency. First, not all measures are comparable, pointing to an element of imprecision in their usage. As such, there is a marked contrast between figures based upon GDP in current US dollars (as used by the World Bank, and for the figures detailed in Chapter 4) and those in PPP US dollars (as detailed above) – a measure which is designed to achieve greater equivalence in state-to-state comparisons. Thus, in 2015, the former measure produced figures of $10.87 billion (for China), $2.07 billion (for India) and $17.95 billion (for the United States) (World Bank, 2016b), while the latter indicated $19.51 billion (China), $8.03 billion (India) and $17.97 billion (the United States) (CIA, 2016d). Taken in isolation, such contrasts point to very different dynamics, particularly if states are ranked upon such measures. On the latter scale, if these powers were to maintain their 2015 GDP growth percentages (as per Table 3), China and India will rank as the world's top two economies by 2032 but many decades later if the former gauge is used. A similar comparison concerning GDP per capita reveals a parallel disconnect, with current US dollars in 2015 standing at $7,925 (for China), $1,582 (for India) and $55,837 (for the United States) (World Bank, 2016d), versus $14,100 (China), $6,200 (India) and $55,800 (the United States) in PPP terms across the same period (CIA, 2016c).

These figures further show the advantages of a state's currency being the base currency in any such calculations, and the relative ranking that this produces, along with the wider importance of gaining and sustaining such a declaratory position (as in the case of the United States). In turn, relative levels of investment, poverty and indeed any numerically based factors are also all prone to such differences/biases, which reduce their effectiveness for cross-comparison,

Table 6   Total GDP (current US$) – by decade (1960–2015)

	Total GDP (current US $s, trillion)						
	1960s	1970s	1980s	1990s	2000s	2010–15	1960–2015
China	0.63	1.39	2.61	6.84	25.73	52.71	89.91
France	0.99	3.34	7.32	14.39	21.03	16.25	63.33
Russia	–	–	0.51	3.98	7.87	10.71	23.08
UK	0.94	2.36	6.24	12.71	22.10	16.15	60.53
US	7.42	17.14	41.81	76.00	126.23	98.78	367.40
EU	5.45	18.44	41.77	87.55	136.41	100.56	390.18
Germany	–	4.82	9.86	21.78	27.77	21.69	85.93
India	0.50	1.02	2.41	3.60	8.45	11.36	27.32
Japan	0.95	5.49	17.87	42.47	45.00	31.00	142.77
World	19.24	57.80	141.42	281.70	461.43	439.93	1,401.51

Source: World Bank, 2016b.

and inject ambiguity into their overall reliability. On this basis, it may be of use to note the culminative acquisition of material resources over time, as detailed in Table 6. Such a perspective is realist and liberalist, in terms of highlighting how states aim to amass more material resources than each other. Although presaging the importance of economic strength over other factors, such a longer-term and compound perspective (despite differences in the costs of production, wages, infrastructure, benefits and so on in each state) does highlight the residual latent power of each state, as well as the temporal extent of this relative superiority/inferiority as per specific historical periods. Thus, the figures underscore the US's current deep-seated fiscal dominance, and that of the EU, as well as China's rapid raise to parity with many other states, along with India's relative historical power dearth. The figures do however share the same haziness regarding their measurement basis, and also question the analytical and temporal scope of any such comparison, particularly if figures for some states (most notably in this example for Russia and Germany) are not consistently available.

Beyond these issues relating to measurement, comparison and their appraisal over time, both China and India have faced criticism concerning how they calculate their GDP levels – debates that highlight the ongoing importance of values and perceptions. Critically, in 2015, New Delhi revised its formula to calculate India's annual GDP, leading to the figure for 2014–15 being raised from 4.7 to

7.4 per cent (BBC, 2015e). Such moves questioned the accuracy of India's prior and future GDP calculations, as observers noted that 'either the government was getting it wrong all these years or they are presenting a far sunnier picture of the economy than it actually is' (Paranjoy Guha Thakurta quoted in Biswas, 2015). In a similar vein, Beijing has been repeatedly accused of manipulating and inflating its GDP figures, and in 2007 future Premier Li Keqiang 'described regional GDP data as "man-made" and unreliable' (quoted in Illmer, 2016). For these reasons, regardless of how states deploy such economic measures, they lose their objectivity through the meaning and value attributed to them by others (singularly or collectively) – an observation apparent concerning the varying historical importance of some commodities over others (currently gold and oil, but, say, tulips in the seventeenth century). More broadly, (economic) meaning is based upon perceptions, as exemplified, for instance, by the *en masse* perspectives of stock markets and their associated bull, bear and herd behaviour. As such, whilst undoubtedly interrelated, the perception underlying a particular material resource remains paramount, again pointing to a materiational emphasis that goes beyond the dualistic exclusivity of either material *or* ideational factors, and which thus critically prioritizes the belief in what the material measure *itself* represents or equals.

These arguments are also applicable to military expenditure, in terms not only of raw data but also of the perceived meaning of such data, which again is highly state-specific in designation. Table 7 shows average annual military expenditure, with China ranking second (both in 2015, and in total from 1990 to 2015) and India sixth (in 2015) and last (from 1990 to 2015) – a status thus of greater significance for the former than the latter. While the United States accounted for 34.25 per cent of all global military expenditure in 2015 (SIPRI, 2016b), if the United States and China continue to expand their spending at the same rate as they did between the 1990s and the 2000s, Beijing will have the world's largest military budget by 2030. While this overtaking provides some context for US fears over China's rise, Washington's military spending from 1990 to 2015 was over six times that of Beijing and seventeen times that of New Delhi, suggesting a different (realist) emphasis upon the utility (and necessity) of possessing military force, as also borne out by a higher GDP percentage. On a wider scale, vis-à-vis total military spending from 1949 to 2007, the US spent $10.50 trillion compared with $1.35 trillion by China and $0.37 trillion by India (Sarkees & Wayman, 2010). Again, such observations point to the residual military power of states over time, and

Table 7 Military expenditure (constant 2014 US$) (1990–2015)

	Average annual expenditure (US$ billion)				Total	% GDP
	1990s	2000s	2010–15	2015	1990–2015	(2015)
China	28.18	82.10	177.78	214.49	2,169.42	1.9
France	65.37	63.91	63.16	60.75	1,671.73	2.1
Russia	62.12	42.77	76.03	91.08	1,442.94	5.4
UK	56.63	62.68	63.10	59.73	1,571.74	2.0
US	455.27	570.56	678.03	595.47	14,326.47	3.3
Germany	57.32	48.08	47.67	47.05	1,340.06	1.2
India	19.99	34.25	49.44	51.12	838.93	2.3
Japan	44.96	46.73	46.48	46.35	1,195.70	1.0

Source: SIPRI, 2016b.

must be tempered by their relative stages of development, modernization, inflation and state-specific costs.

Further comparisons concerning the possession of different kinds of military capabilities are also feasible. Significantly, both India and China currently rank in the world's top four states concerning troop, tank, artillery, aircraft and submarine numbers but have power projection means that are drastically behind those of the United States (*Military Balance*, 2016: 22–3). Asia's emergent great powers are also two of eight proven nuclear weapons states in the world (alongside France, North Korea, Russia, Pakistan, the United Kingdom and the United States) and both possess a nuclear triad, which is only shared by Moscow and Washington. China is also the world's fifth highest arms exporter, whilst India's activities in this regard are negligible (SIPRI, 2016a). Again, the deeper value of such comparisons is heavily dependent upon the (constructivist) meaning ascribed to them, and as such differing (realist) perspectives will place varying weight upon varying quotients as per whether they are regarded as offensive or defensive. Such meanings are essentially intersubjective as they are dependent – in this example – upon perceptions of threat and fear, and an expectation that high military expenditure is a prerequisite to be a great power. Direct experience of war may be a significant factor here, in terms of creating precedents concerning its efficacy or not, but will ultimately be seen in either a largely positive or negative manner regarding its deeper efficacy – itself an observation that is therefore constructed and value-laden (see Singer & Small, 1972: 282).

Similar hybridity between material and ideational influences is also arguably applicable to the basis of a state's political functioning. Although political similarity and difference in terms of governing systems can affect how states interact with each other, in terms of being a great power the stability and competence of a state's elites appear to be more critical than their actual type of government, with other (particularly economic) interests typically overriding any such differences (as evidenced by India and China's myriad international relations throughout this volume). Wider acceptance and recognition are instead more appreciable founts of legitimation, an assertion that is most apparent in major multilateral groupings. As has been discussed at length, this recognition is based upon the interplay of perceptions, which are importantly determined by a state's domestic context and the prevailing worldviews of its leaders. Such perceptions interconnect with the meaning that different states give specific principles and values, as well as material factors, and which collectively evolve and fluctuate in their importance across time. In this regard, China currently enjoys the positional advantages of a permanent veto in the UN Security Council (along with France, Russia, the United Kingdom and the United States), whilst India is outside such a key institutional stronghold. As long as the UN remains of critical international importance, so will having such a position, but this particularity can change if belief in that regime falters or is surmounted by another grouping, which again underlines how the value given to any factor is ultimately perception-dependent.

Alchemy, Perception and Authoring

There is no single factor that can determine whether or not a state is a great power. Rather than solely economic strength or high military spending or a hefty population or a loud international voice, or even simply national belief and ambition, it is the amalgamation and mixture of different elements that produces the composite, complex and dynamic alchemy of great power. The material and the ideational mix and merge with each other, whereby the value and meaning attributed to different power quotients become of paramount importance between the states making these evaluations. The self/other nexus of co-constitutive and intersubjective interaction lies at the heart of this equation, with perceptions acting as the key enabling factor that converts varying types of material, ideational and institutional power into indicators of great power. Recognition, legitimation and acceptance all reside within this mélange, and combine with the dominant

180

consensuses of the dominant states (and their often self-imagined regimes) concerning what is the international system's agreed *lingua franca*, as do acts of role-giving, role-taking and role-making – by states towards others and themselves. Such elements, and their hierarchical importance, change over time, as material and ideational balances rise, fall and evolve – processes that serve to constantly prioritize, de-prioritize and re-prioritize certain factors over others. Within this dynamism, those whom we regard as great powers are also subject to change – a status historically epitomized by various states, and by the current re-emergence of Asia's giants, China and India.

On this basis, it is the ability of a state to decide the terms of reference for these processes that is of utmost importance, so as to influence and control the narrative of what is (or is not) a great power. Such authoring is engendered through gaining primacy within any given power quotient(s), whereby a state gains a critical voice in the international system – something we have seen most clearly for India and China concerning their growing (if varying) economic prowess. On this basis, a state can start to determine key parameters concerning how the international system functions – from the substance of global finance to the working of multilateral institutions to the fundamental essences of the system itself. Garnering approval from other states legitimizes such narratives – and their accompanying norms, principles and values – in the form of alliances (such as by the United States with the EU, Japan and Israel, among others), strategic partnerships (as contemporarily pursued by both China and India) or existing great power sponsorship. Such linkages – themselves acts of mutually reinforcing (if accepted) or mutually dichotomizing (if rejected) co-authorship – provide the basis for a state to actively manage these narratives, and their use as a vehicle to exert power through the projection and enhancement of the proclivities, aims and interests of its elites. This process is not simply the product of interaction, experience and learning but is an unending act of construction – the doing of being that is constant, embryonic and adaptive. It applies not only to a great power's foreign policy behaviour but also to how other actors/states/institutions in the international system respond to it, along with (more broadly) how scholars, analysts, observers and populations choose to report on, write about, debate about and perceive it. At its most innate, this process includes the writing of this sentence by the author and its comprehension by the reader.

It is for these reasons that 'the facts speak only when the historian . . . decides which facts to give the floor, and in what order or context' (Carr, 1961: 11). As we have seen throughout this volume, history – often in its most selective form – has been integral for elites in both Beijing and New Delhi, especially in terms of nationalism and the formation of their specific foreign policy concerns, as mutually constituted by their states' interaction (and its remembrance) with others. India and China are two states who desire to look back and to use the past as a resource for their rise, whereby it becomes a touchstone for the future, pointing to history (and its authorship) as the intervening variable that regulates relations between states. History is also a vital resource for the meaning of great power itself, as past actions, precedent and performance are used to explain the future, especially in the material sphere. This insistence that the past can dictate the future forms the basis for thinking about what kind of powers China and India will be. According to this futurology, they are most commonly depicted either as responsible actors who respect the current status quo, or as revisionist states who will re-craft that status quo towards their own ends. Such a dichotomy is largely set by the current hegemon, the United States, whose (albeit debated) unipolarity as seen through a realist lens pushes it to look for new threats (Waltz, 2000: 28–9). Not only does this underline the problem of applying old measures to new realities, it also indicates how competing state narratives, as influenced by the past and its projection into the future, produce an inter-perceptual push and pull that determines the course and the very quintessence of great power.

As noted by Niall Ferguson concerning US foreign policy, and as a broader critique of realism, these observations highlight the issue of a '*history deficit*: the fact that key decision-makers know almost nothing not just of other countries' pasts but also of their own, . . . worse, they often do not see what is wrong with their ignorance' (quoted in Allison, 2015). This volume has sought to overcome this shortfall by focusing upon the state-specific inclinations of China and India, and then deploying a longitudinal and domestically derived lens to better understand their contemporary pathways towards their mutual acquisition of great power status. Apart from the myriad issues that beset the trajectories of both entities (including environmental damage, economic overheating/mismanagement, inequality, corruption, demographic issues, internal stability problems and overcoming perceptions of past ill treatment by the international system), as the world is being constantly authored by states, the past cannot equal the future. As such, unforeseen economic shocks, military crises or domestic legitimation issues may serve to derail their great power ascents. They may also provide the context to re-craft the system, take control of the narrative and project their visions of the world.

For China and India, such a (common) vision rests upon notions of equality, mutual development, non-intervention and multipolarity, to realize a post-colonial Asian world order. Thus, according to the principle that 'if ideological power is weakened, alternatives become imaginable' (Clemens & Cook, 1999: 458), another significant global financial crisis on the scale of that of 2008 could, for instance, presage the decline of Western-led economics and herald the rise of an Asian-imagined fiscal infrastructure. A critical event similar to 9/11 could also act as such a similarly critical interlude, as it is the repercussions of such events that 'provide the opportunity and set the scene for the exercise of great power authority' (Modelski, 1974: 152).

With these factors in mind, Wight pertinently asserts that 'the truest definition of a great power must be a historical one, which lays down that a great power is a power which has done such and such; . . . a scientific definition, laying down the attributes that a great power may be supposed to possess, will be an abstraction in some degree removed from our complicated and unmanageable political experience' (1979: 48). Thus, at this juncture, and as displayed in this book's analysis, both China and India are undoubtedly rising and emergent great powers with their economic, military, institutional and ideational power quotients all in the ascendant. Moreover, and reflective of their relative levels of residual and latent power (as explicated above), China can be considered to be already great, whilst India is more nascent, as the former's culminative acquisition of – particularly economic and military – power has been far greater/more sustained over the last sixty years. If current trends continue, and its population is utilized, and notwithstanding the caveats noted above, New Delhi will arguably share such a mantle by 2035. Such observations further indicate that an element of mastery is required to be a great power, in terms of how long a state has been playing the great power game using whatever its dominant dynamics may be at any given time (conquest, war, economics, diplomacy, and so on). As a new international state in its modern incarnation, it is unsurprising that New Delhi is deficient in this regard, but this can be ameliorated over time through experience, interaction, learning and increasing global authorship.

Fundamentally, however, and as shown across this volume, perceptions are as much about the future as they are about the past, and have a realizable and self-fulfilling quality to them. As such, just as meanings are ascribed to what different kinds of power and behaviour in international relations signify, and are made 'real' when they are shared by a sufficiently large constituency, the same is true, by extension, for great power status. Consequently, if enough actors (states, institutions, media, experts, and so on) believe that a particular state is a great power, it will become a great power regardless of any apparent material (objective) or ideational (subjective) deficiencies. Once a narrative – either domestically and/or internationally derived – achieves enough widespread acceptance (typically buoyed by its promotion by existing great powers/hegemons), it thus achieves legitimacy, as does that state's ability to then reshape the system's prevailing normative balance. Such a process is arguably at work in relation to modern-day India, which was pulled back into the mainstream by the United States and several other powers after New Delhi's 1998 nuclear tests, and which elites in Washington (and elsewhere) are now consistently categorizing as a great power, despite its clear relative material weaknesses. The consistent historical advertising of India as a great power by its own elites only serves to compound these perspectives, as does a widely held belief in its future economic, military and diplomatic significance. On this ideational basis, great power – by whatever formula it is concocted – may be nothing more than a great perception.

REFERENCES

Adeney, Katharine & Wyatt, Andrew (2010) *Contemporary India*. Basingstoke: Palgrave Macmillan.

Adler, Emmanuel & Barnett, Michael (1998) *Security Communities*. Cambridge: Cambridge University Press.

AIIB (2016) Asian Infrastructure Investment Bank. Available at *http://www.aiib.org/*.

Alagappa, Muthiah (1998a) 'Asian Practice of Security: Key Features and Explanations', in Muthiah Alagappa (ed.), *Asian Security Practice: Material and Ideational Influences*. Stanford: Stanford University Press, pp. 611–76.

Alagappa, Muthiah (1998b) 'International Politics in Asia: The Historical Context', in Muthiah Alagappa (ed.), *Asian Security Practice: Material and Ideational Influences*. Stanford: Stanford University Press, pp. 65–114.

Allison, Graham (2015) 'The Key to Henry Kissinger's Success'. *The Atlantic*, 27 November. Available at *http://www.theatlantic.com/international/archive/2015/11/kissinger-ferguson-applied-history/417846/*.

Anderson, Benedict (1991) *Imagined Communities: Reflections on the Origin and Spread of Nationalism*. London: Verso.

Anderson, Walter (2001) 'Recent Trends in Indian Foreign Policy'. *Asian Survey* 41(5): 765–76.

Appadorai, A. (1981) *The Domestic Roots of Indian Foreign Policy: 1947–1972*. Delhi: Oxford University Press.

Ayoob, M. (1999) 'From Regional System to Regional Society: Exploring Key Variables in the Construction of Regional Order'. *Australian Journal of International Affairs* 53(3): 247–60.

Ayres, Alyssa & Oldenburg, Phillip (2005) *India Briefing: Takeoff at Last?* Armonk, NY: M.E. Sharpe.

Bajpai, Kanti (1998) 'India: Modified Structuralism', in Muthiah Alagappa (ed.), *Asian Security Practice: Material and Ideational Influences*. Stanford: Stanford University Press, pp. 157–97.

Balachandran, Manu & Dutta, Saptarishi (2015) 'Here's How the BJP Surpassed China's Communists to Become the Largest Political Party in the World'. *Quartz India*, 31 March. Available at *http://qz.com/372466/*

185

heres-how-the-bjp-surpassed-chinas-communists-to-become-the-largest-political-party-in-the-world/.

Baldwin, David A. (2003) 'Power and International Relations', in Walter Carlsnaes, Thomas Risse & Beth Simmons (eds), *Handbook of International Relations*. Thousand Oaks, CA: Sage Publications, pp. 273–97.

Barabantseva, Elena (2012) 'Nationalism', in Chris Ogden (ed.), *Handbook of China's Governance and Domestic Politics*. London: Routledge pp. 153–64.

Baral, Lok Raj (2006) 'Cooperation with Realism: The Future of South Asian Regionalism'. *South Asian Survey* 13(2): 265–75.

Barnett, Michael & Duvall, Raymond (2005) 'Power in International Politics'. *International Organization* 59(1): 39–75.

Basrur, Rajesh M. (2001) 'Nuclear Weapons and Indian Strategic Culture'. *Journal of Peace Research* 38(2): 181–98.

BBC (2011) 'China Communist Party "Exceeds 80 Million Members"'. BBC News Online, 24 June. Available at *http://www.bbc.co.uk/news/world-asia-pacific-13901509*.

BBC (2012a) 'CCP Confirms Leadership Change'. BBC News Online, 15 November. Available at *http://www.bbc.co.uk/news/world-asia-china-20338586*.

BBC (2012b) 'China Party Congress Wraps up Ahead of Leadership Unveiling'. BBC News Online, 14 November. Available at *http://www.bbc.co.uk/news/world-asia-china-20321386*.

BBC (2015a) 'Are India's Plans to Celebrate the 1965 War "Victory" in "Bad Taste"?' BBC News Online, 13 August. Available at *http://www.bbc.com/news/world-asia-india-33815204*.

BBC (2015b) 'China Internet: Xi Jinping Calls for "Cyber Sovereignty"'. BBC News Online, 16 December. Available at *http://www.bbc.co.uk/news/world-asia-china-35109453*.

BBC (2015c) 'China Market Slump: Central Bank Cuts Interest Rates'. BBC News Online, 25 August. Available at *http://www.bbc.co.uk/news/uk-34052618*.

BBC (2015d) 'China Military Parade Commemorates WW2 Victory Over Japan'. BBC News Online, 3 September. Available at *http://www.bbc.co.uk/news/world-asia-china-34125418*.

BBC (2015e) 'India Growth Figures Baffle Economists'. BBC News Online, 9 February. Available at *http://www.bbc.co.uk/news/world-asia-india-31294508*.

BBC (2016) 'South China Sea: Beijing Accuses US of Militarisation'. BBC News Online, 15 February. Available at *http://www.bbc.com/news/world-asia-35610809*.

Beckley, Michael (2011) 'China's Century? Why America's Edge Will Endure'. *International Security* 36(3): 41–78.

Beeson, Mark & Li, Fujian (2012) 'Charmed or Alarmed? Reading China's Regional Relations'. *Journal of Contemporary China* 21(73): 35–51.

Benner, Jeffrey (1984) *Structure of Decision: The Indian Foreign Policy Bureaucracy*. New Delhi: South Asia Publishers.

Bisley, Nick (2012) *Great Powers in the Changing International Order*. Boulder, CO: Lynne Rienner.

Biswas, Soutik (2015) 'Is India's Growth Exaggerated?' BBC News Online, 1 June. Available at *http://www.bbc.co.uk/news/world-asia-india-32955124*.

Blackwill, Robert D., Chandra, Naresh & Clary, Christopher (2011) *The United States and India: A Shared Strategic Future*. Aspen Institute India/

Council on Foreign Relations. Available at *http://www.cfr.org/india/united-states-india-shared-strategic-future/p25740*.

Blanchard, Ben & Ruwitch, John (2013) 'China Hikes Defense Budget, to Spend More on Internal Security'. Reuters, 5 March. Available at *http://www.reuters.com/article/2013/03/05/us-china-parliament-defence-idUSBRE92403620130305*.

Blasko, Dennis J. (2012) *The Chinese Army Today: Tradition and Transformation for the 21st Century*. London: Routledge.

Blasko, Dennis J. (2013) 'The Role of the PLA', in Chris Ogden (ed.), *Handbook of China's Governance and Domestic Politics*. London: Routledge, pp. 27–38.

Bo, Zhiyue (2013) 'State Power and Governance Structures', in Chris Ogden (ed.), *Handbook of China's Governance and Domestic Politics*. London: Routledge, pp. 12–26.

Boesche, Roger (2002) *The First Great Political Realist: Kautilya and His Arthashastra*. Lanham, MD: Lexington Books.

Braumoeller, Bear F. (2012) *The Great Powers and the International System: Systemic Theory in Empirical Perspective*. Cambridge: Cambridge University Press.

Braumoeller, Bear F., & Carson, Austin (2011) 'Political Irrelevance, Democracy, and the Limits of Militarized Conflict'. *Journal of Conflict Resolution* 55(2): 292–320.

Brecher, M. (1968) *India and World Politics: Krishna Menon's View of the World*. New Delhi: Praeger.

Breslin, Shaun (2009) 'Understanding China's Regional Rise: Interpretations, Identities and Implications'. *International Affairs* 85(4): 817–35.

Brewster, David (2011) 'Indian Strategic Thinking about East Asia'. *Journal of Strategic Studies* 34(6): 825–52.

Brown, Kerry (2013) 'The CCP and the One-Party State', in Chris Ogden (ed.), *Handbook of China's Governance and Domestic Politics*. London: Routledge, pp. 3–11.

Bull, Hedley (1977) *The Anarchical Society*. New York: Palgrave Macmillan.

Bush, George W. (2002) *The National Security Strategy of the United States of America*. Washington, DC: The White House. Available at *http://www.au.af.mil/au/awc/awcgate/nss/nss_sep2002.pdf*.

Buzan, Barry (2004) *The United States and the Great Powers*. Cambridge: Polity.

Calder, Kent & Ye, Min (2010) *The Making of Northeast Asia*. Stanford: Stanford University Press.

Callahan, William A. (2006) 'History, Identity and Security: Producing and Consuming Nationalism in China'. *Critical Asian Studies* 38(2): 179–208.

Campbell, David (1992) *Writing Security: United States Foreign Policy and the Politics of Identity*. Minneapolis: University of Minnesota Press.

Carey, Roger (2008) 'Power', in Mark Imber & Trevor Salmon (eds), *Issues in International Relations*. London: Routledge, pp. 61–73.

Carr, E.H. (1961) *What Is History?* London: Penguin.

CDIAC (2015) 'Ranking of the World's Countries by 2011 Total CO^2 Emissions'. Carbon Dioxide Information Analysis Center (CDIAC). Available at *http://cdiac.ornl.gov/trends/emis/top2011.tot*.

Census of India (2011) 'Distribution of Population by Religions'. Drop-in-Article on Census, 4. New Delhi: Census of India, Ministry of Home Affairs. Available at *http://censusindia.gov.in/Ad_Campaign/drop_in_articles/04-Distribution_by_Religion.pdf*.

CFR (2011) *The United States and India: A Shared Strategic Future*. New York: Council on Foreign Relations.

Chan, Steve (2004) 'Exploring Puzzles in Power-Transition Theory: Implications for Sino-American Relations'. *Security Studies* 13(3): 103–41.

Chaturvedi, Sanjay (2000) 'Representing Post-Colonial India: Inclusive/ Exclusive Geopolitical Imaginations', in Klaus Dodds and David Atkinson (eds), *Geopolitical Traditions: A Century of Geopolitical Thought*. London: Routledge, pp. 210–24.

Chaudhuri, Joyotpaul (1993) 'Federalism and the Siamese Twins: Diversity and Entropy in India's Domestic and Foreign Policy'. *International Journal* 48(3): 419–84.

Chaudhuri, Rudra (2012) 'The Limits of Executive Power: Domestic Politics and Alliance Behavior in Nehru's India'. *India Review* 11(2): 95–115.

Chaulia, Sreeram (2002) 'The BJP, India's Foreign Policy and the "Realist Alternative" to the Nehruvian Tradition'. *International Politics* 39: 215–34.

Chaulia, Sreeram (2011a) 'India and the United Nations', in David Scott (ed.), *Handbook of India's International Relations*. London: Routledge, pp. 277–88.

Chaulia, Sreeram (2011b) 'India's "Power" Attributes', in David Scott (ed.), *Handbook of India's International Relations*. London: Routledge, pp. 23–34.

Chen, Dongxiao (2003) 'Constructivist Challenge to Debate on East Asian Security in the New Century', in David W. Lovell (ed.), *Asia-Pacific Security: Policy Challenges*. Singapore: Institute of Southeast Asian Studies, pp. 165–76.

Chen, Meina (2014) 'CASS Issues China's First Report on National Security'. Chinanews.com, 12 May. Available at *http://english.cssn.cn/research/politics/201405/t20140512_1156064.shtml*.

Chidambaram, P. (2007) *A View from the Outside: Why Good Economics Works for Everyone*. New Delhi: Penguin Books.

Chin, Gregory (2010) 'China's Rising Institutional Influence', in Alan S. Alexandroff & Andrew F. Cooper (eds), *Rising States, Rising Institutions: Challenges for Global Governance*. Waterloo, Ont.: The Centre for International Governance Innovation, pp. 83–104.

China Gov (2005) 'China Pledges to Pursue Peaceful Development Road'. Chinese Government's Official Web Portal, 22 December. Available at *http://www.gov.cn/english/2005-12/22/content_134226.htm*.

China's National Defense (2004) 'China's National Defense'. Embassy of China, Vienna, 13 May. Available at *http://www.chinaembassy.at/det/js/t104684.htm*.

China's National Defense (2010) 'Full Text: China's National Defense in 2010'. Information Office of the State Council, Beijing, 31 March. Available at *http://news.xinhuanet.com/english2010/china/2011-03/31/c_13806851.htm*,.

Chiriyankandath, James (2004) 'Realigning India: Indian Foreign Policy after the Cold War'. *The Round Table* 93(374): 199–211.

Christensen, Thomas (1996) 'Chinese Realpolitik: Reading Beijing's Worldview'. *Foreign Affairs* 75(5): 37–52.

CIA (2015a) 'China', *CIA World Factbook*. Available at *https://www.cia.gov/library/publications/the-world-factbook/geos/ch.html*.

CIA (2015b) 'India', *CIA World Factbook*. Available at *https://www.cia.gov/library/publications/the-world-factbook/geos/in.html*.

CIA (2016a) 'Area', *CIA World Factbook*. Available at *https://www.cia.gov/library/publications/the-world-factbook/rankorder/2147rank.html*.

CIA (2016b) 'European Union', *CIA World Factbook*. Available at *https://www. cia.gov/library/publications/the-world-factbook/geos/ee.html*.

CIA (2016c) 'GDP Per Capita (Purchasing Power Parity)', *CIA World Factbook*. Available at *https://www.cia.gov/library/publications/the-world-factbook/rank order/2004rank.html*.

CIA (2016d) 'GDP (Purchasing Power Parity)', *CIA World Factbook*. Available at *https://www.cia.gov/library/publications/the-world-factbook/ rankorder/2001rank.html*.

CIA (2016e) 'Population', *CIA World Factbook*. Available at *https://www.cia. gov/library/publications/the-world-factbook/rankorder/2119rank.html*.

CIA (2016f) 'Reserves of Foreign Exchange and Gold', *CIA World Factbook*. Available at *https://www.cia.gov/library/publications/the-world-factbook/ rankorder/2188rank.html*.

CIA (2016g) 'United States', *CIA World Factbook*. Available at *https://www.cia. gov/library/publications/the-world-factbook/geos/us.html*.

CIA (2016h) 'World', *CIA World Factbook*. Available at *https://www.cia.gov/ library/publications/the-world-factbook/geos/xx.html*.

Ciorciari, John D. (2011) 'India's Approach to Great-Power Status'. *The Fletcher Forum of World Affairs* 35(1): 61–89.

Clark, Ian (2011) 'China and the United States: A Succession of Hegemonies?' *International Affairs* 87(1): 13–28.

Clarke, Michael E. (2013) 'Separatism', in Chris Ogden (ed.), *Handbook of China's Governance and Domestic Politics*. London: Routledge, pp. 221–32.

Clemens, Elisabeth S. & Cook, James M. (1999) 'Politics and Institutionalism: Explaining Durability and Change'. *Annual Review of Sociology* 25: 441–66.

Cohen, Jerome A. (1973) 'China and Intervention: Theory and Practice'. *Harvard Law School: Studies in East Asian Law (China)* 21(X): 471–505.

Cohen, Stephen P. (2002) *India: Emergent Power*. Oxford: Oxford University Press.

Contessi, Nicola P. (2010) 'Multilateralism, Intervention and Norm Contestation: China's Stance on Darfur in the UN Security Council'. *Security Dialogue* 41(3): 323–44.

Copeland, Dale C. (2006) 'The Constructivist Challenge to Structural Realism: A Review Essay', in Stefano Guzzini & Anna Leander (eds), *Constructivism and International Relations: Wendt and His Critics*. London: Routledge, pp. 1–20.

Corbridge, Stuart, Harriss, John & Jeffrey, Craig (2012) *India Today: Economy, Politics and Society*. Cambridge: Polity.

CPDA (2015) 'Introduction'. China Public Diplomacy Association. Accessible at *http://www.chinapda.org.cn/eng/xhgk/xhjj/*.

Curry, Tom (2007) 'Clinton Sounds the China Alarm as '08 Issue'. NBC News, 2 March. *Available at http://www.nbcnews.com/id/17403964/ns/politics-decision_08/t/clinton-sounds-china-alarm-issue/#.VtQ_bhyQEy4*.

Danilovic, Vesna (2002) *When the Stakes Are High: Deterrence and Conflict Among Major Powers*. Ann Arbor: University of Michigan Press.

Dash, Kishore (2001) 'The Challenge of Regionalism in South Asia'. *International Politics* 38(2): 201–28.

Datta, A. (2005) *Indian Non-Alignment and National Interest: From Jawaharlal Nehru to Indira Gandhi*. Kolkata: Sujan.

Deng, Yong (2008) *China's Struggle for Status: The Realignment of International Relations*. New York: Cambridge University Press.

189

Deng, Yong & Wang, Fei-Ling (1999) 'Introduction: Toward an Understanding of China's Worldview', in Yong Deng & Fei-Ling Wang (eds), *In the Eyes of the Dragon: China Views the World*. Lanham, MD: Rowman & Littlefield Publishers, pp. 1–20.

Department of Defense (2010) *Quadrennial Defense Review (QDR)*. Washington, DC: Department of Defense.

Department of Defense (2012) *Sustaining US Global Leadership: Priorities for 21st Century Defense*. Washington, DC: Department of Defense. Available at *http://www.defense.gov/news/defense_strategic_guidance.pdf*.

Destradi, Sandra (2012) *Indian Foreign and Security Policy in South Asia: Regional Power Strategies*. London: Routledge.

Devotta, Neil (2003) 'Is India Over-Extended? When Domestic Disorder Precludes Regional Intervention'. *Contemporary South Asia* 12(3): 365–80.

Dittmer, Lowell (2004) 'Taiwan and the Issue of National Identity'. *Asian Survey* 44(4): 475–83.

Dixit, J.N. (2004) *Makers of India's Foreign Policy: From Raja Ram Mohun Roy to Yashwant Sinha*. New Delhi: HarperCollins.

Dombrowski, Peter & Demchak, Chris C. (2014) 'Cyber War, Cybered Conflict, and the Maritime Domain'. *Naval War College Review* 67(2): 71–97.

Domke, William K. (1989) 'Power, Political Capacity, and Security in the International System', in Richard J. Stoll & Michael D. Ward (eds), *Power in World Politics*. Boulder, CO: Lynne Rienner, pp. 159–74.

Doniger, Wendy (2009) *The Hindus: An Alternative History*. Oxford: Oxford University Press.

ECI (2015) 'Election Results – Full Statistical Results'. Electoral Commission of India. Available at *http://eci.nic.in/eci_main1/ElectionStatistics.aspx*.

Fair, Christine (2012) 'Prospects for Effective Internal Security Reforms in India'. *Commonwealth & Comparative Politics* 50(2): 145–70.

Farnham, Barbara (2004) 'Impact of the Political Context on Foreign Policy Decision Making'. *Political Psychology* 25(3): 441–63.

Ferguson, Niall (2004) *Colossus: The Price of America's Empire*. New York: Penguin Press.

Fierke, Karin (2007) *Critical Approaches to International Security*. Cambridge: Polity.

Finnemore, Martha & Sikkink, Kathryn (1998) 'International Norm Dynamics and Political Change'. *International Organization* 52(4): 887–917.

FMPRC (1996) 'China's Position Paper on the New Security Concept'. Ministry of Foreign Affairs of the People's Republic of China. Available at *http://www.fmprc.gov.cn/ce/ceun/eng/xw/t27742.htm*.

Follath, Erich (2010) 'The Dragon's Embrace: China's Soft Power Is a Threat to the West'. *Spiegel Online*, 28 July. Available at *http://www.spiegel.de/international/world/the-dragon-s-embrace-china-s-soft-power-is-a-threat-to-the-west-a-708645.html*.

FP (2016) 'Foreign Policy Fragile States Index'. *Foreign Policy*. Available at *http://foreignpolicy.com/fragile-states-index-2016-brexit-syria-refugee-europe-anti-migrant-boko-haram/*.

Fravel, M. Taylor (2008) 'China's Search for Military Power'. *The Washington Quarterly* 31(3): 125–41.

Fravel, M. Taylor & Medeiros, Evan (2010) 'China's Search for Assured

Retaliation: The Evolution of Chinese Nuclear Strategy and Force Structure'. *International Security* 35(2): 48–87.

Friedburg, Aaron L. (2005) 'The Future of US–China Relations: Is Conflict Inevitable?' *International Security* 30(2): 7–45.

Friedburg, Aaron L. (2006) *'Going Out': China's Pursuit of Natural Resources and Implications for the PRC's Grand Strategy.* Washington, DC: NBR Analysis.

Gandhi, Indira (1975) *India: The Speeches and Reminiscences of Indira Gandhi.* New Delhi: Rupa.

Gandhi, Rajiv (1985) *Seventh Five Year Plan (Volume 1).* Delhi: Government of India, Planning Commission.

Ganguly, Sumit (2010) 'Structure and Agency in the Making of Indian Foreign Policy'. *ISAS Working Paper (Singapore)* 116 (21 November).

Ganguly, Sumit & Pardesi, Manjeet S. (2009) 'Explaining Sixty Years of India's Foreign Policy'. *India Review* 8(1): 4–19.

Gao, Helen (2013) 'With Friends Like These ...'. *Foreign Policy,* 9 April. Available at *http://www.foreignpolicy.com/articles/2013/04/09/with_friends_ like_these_china_north_korea.*

Garamone, Jim (2015) 'US, India Sign 10-Year Defense Framework Agreement'. US Department of Defense, 4 June. Available at *http://www.defense.gov/ News-Article-View/Article/604775.*

Garofalo, Pat (2012) 'China's Richest 1 Percent Hold 70 Percent of Their Nation's Private Wealth'. *Think Progress,* 17 August. Available at *http://think-progress.org/economy/2012/08/17/708521/china-1-percent/.*

Garrett, Banning (2006) 'US–China Relations in the Era of Globalization and Terror: A Framework for Analysis'. *Journal of Contemporary China* 15(48): 389–415.

Garver, John (1992) *Foreign Relations of the People's Republic of China.* Englewood Cliffs, NJ: Prentice Hall.

Gautam, P.K. (2013) 'Relevance of Kautilya's Arthasastra'. *Strategic Analysis* 37(1): 21–8.

Geller, Daniel S. & Singer, J. David (1998) *Nations at War: A Scientific Study of International Conflict.* Cambridge: Cambridge University Press.

Genest, Marc A. (2004) *Conflict and Cooperation: Evolving Theories of International Relations.* Belmont, CA: Thomson/Wadsworth.

Gilboy, George & Heginbotham, Eric (2012) *Chinese and Indian Strategic Behaviour: Growing Power and Alarm.* Cambridge: Cambridge University Press.

Gill, Stephen (1997) 'Global Structural Change and Multilateralism', in Stephen Gill (ed.), *Globalization, Democratization and Multilateralism.* Tokyo: United Nations University Press, 1–17.

Gilpin, Robert (1981) *War and Change in World Politics.* Cambridge: Cambridge University Press.

Giridharadas, Anand (2008) 'Land of Gandhi Asserts Itself as Global Military Power'. *The New York Times,* 21 September.

Glaser, Bonnie S. (2012) 'Armed Clash in the South China Sea'. Contingency Planning Memorandum, 14, April (Washington: Council on Foreign Relations). Available at *http://www.cfr.org/world/armed-clash-south-china-sea/p27883.*

Glaser, Bonnie S. & Medeiros, Evan S. (2007) 'The Changing Ecology of Foreign Policy Making in China: The Ascension and Demise of the Theory of "Peaceful Rise"'. *The China Quarterly* 190: 291–310.

Glaser, Bonnie S. & Saunders, Philip (2012) 'Chinese Civilian Foreign Policy Research Institutes: Evolving Roles and Increasing Influence'. *The China Quarterly* 171: 597–616.

Global Times (2015) 'Xi–Obama Meet Can Set Template for Future'. *Global Times*, 24 September. Available at *http://www.globaltimes.cn/content/944137.shtml*.

Godwin, Paul H. (2004) 'China as Regional Hegemon?', in Jim Rolfe (ed.), *The Asia-Pacific: A Region in Transition*. Honolulu: Asia-Pacific Center for Security Studies, pp. 81–101.

Goldstein, Avery (2001) 'The Diplomatic Face of China's Grand Strategy: A Rising Power's Emerging Choice'. *The China Quarterly* 168: 835–64.

Goldstein, Avery (2005) *Rising to the Challenge: China's Grand Strategy and International Security*. Stanford: Stanford University Press.

Golwalkar, M.S. (2000) *Bunch of Thoughts*. Bangalore: Jagarana Prakashana.

Gong, Gerrit W. (2001) *Memory and History in East and Southeast Asia: Issues of Identity in International Relations*. Washington, DC: CSIS Press.

Gordon, Sandy (2014) *India's Rise as an Asian Power: Nation, Neighborhood, and Region*. Washington, DC: Georgetown University Press.

Government of India (1973) *The Years of Challenge: Selected Speeches of Indira Gandhi, January 1966–August 1969*. New Delhi: Ministry of Information and Broadcasting.

Gowen, Annie & Lakshmi, Rama (2014) 'Modi Promises a "Shining India" in Victory Speech'. *The Washington Post*, 16 May. Available at *https://www.washingtonpost.com/world/hindu-nationalist-narendra-modis-party-heads-to-victory-in-indian-polls/2014/05/16/c6eccaea-4b20-46db-8ca9-af4ddb286ce7_story.html*.

Gramsci, Antonio (1971) *Selections from the Prison Notebooks of Antonio Gramsci*. New York: International Publishers.

Gray, Colin S. (1999) 'Strategic Culture as Context: The First Generation of Theory Strikes Back'. *Review of International Studies* 25(1): 49–69.

Gupta, Amit Kumar (2006) 'An Exciting Second Innings: Bush and India', in Amit Gupta & Cherian Samuel (eds), *The Second Bush Presidency: Global Perspectives*. New Delhi: Dorling Kindersley, pp. 65–78.

Gupta, Amit Kumar (2008) 'Commentary on India's Soft Power and Diaspora'. *International Journal on World Peace* 25(3): 61–8.

Gupta, Anirudha (1990) 'A Brahmanic Framework of Power in South Asia?' *Economic and Political Weekly* 25(14): 711–14.

Gupta, K.R. & Shukla, Vatsala (2009) *Foreign Policy of India*. New Delhi: Atlantic Publisher and Distributors.

Hagerty, Devin T. (1991) 'India's Regional Security Doctrine'. *Asian Survey* 31(4): 351–63.

Hardgrave, Robert L., Jr & Kochanek, Stanley A. (2008) *India, Government and Politics in a Developing Nation*. Boston: Thomson Learning.

Hawksworth, John & Cookson, Gordon (2008) *The World in 2050*. London: PricewaterhouseCoopers. Available at *https://www.pwc.ch/user_content/editor/files/publ_tls/pwc_the_world_in_2050_e.pdf*.

He, Kai (2009) 'Dynamic Balancing: China's Balancing Strategies towards the United States, 1949–2005'. *Journal of Contemporary China* 18(58): 113–36.

Held, David & McGrew, Anthony (2003) *Global Transformations Reader: An Introduction to the Globalization Debate*. Cambridge: Polity.

Hemmer, Christopher & Katzenstein, Peter (2002) 'Why is There No NATO in Asia? Collective Identity, Regionalism, and the Origins of Multilateralism'. *International Organization* 56(3): 575–607.

Hempson-Jones, J.S. (2005) 'The Evolution of China's Engagement with International Governmental Organizations: Toward a Liberal Foreign Policy?' *Asian Survey* 45(5): 702–21.

Hill, Christopher R. (2007) *Remarks at 'North Korea: The February 13th Agreement'*. Washington, DC: US Government Printing Office.

The Hindu (2014) 'India's Staggering Wealth Gap in Five Charts', *The Hindu*, 8 December. Available at *http://www.thehindu.com/data/indias-staggering-wealth-gap-in-five-charts/article6672115.ece*.

Hobsbawm, Eric (1991) *The Age Of Empire: 1875–1914*. London: Abacus.

Holloway, David & Lei, Cui (2014) 'US–China Relations in the Shadow of the Future'. *Dynamics of Asymmetric Conflict* 7(2–3): 137–49.

Hook, Steven W. & Pu, Xiaoyu (2006) 'Framing Sino-American Relations under Stress: A Reexamination of News Coverage of the 2001 Spy Plane Crisis'. *Asian Affairs* 33(3): 167–83.

Hopf, Ted (1998) 'The Promise of Constructivism in International Relations Theory'. *International Security* 23(1): 171–200.

Horner, Charles (2009) *Rising China and Its Postmodern Fate: Memories of Empire in a New Global Context*. Athens: University of Georgia Press.

Hoshiyama, Takashi (2008) 'New Japan–China Relations and the Corresponding Positioning of the United States: History, Values, Realism in a Changing World'. *Asia-Pacific Review* 15(2): 68–101.

Huang, Yanzhong (2011) 'The Sick Man of Asia: China's Health Crisis'. *Foreign Affairs*, November: 119–36.

Hurrell, Andrew (2006) 'Hegemony, Liberalism and Global Order: What Space for Would-Be Great Powers?' *International Affairs* 82(1): 1–19.

ICCR (2015) 'Constitution', Indian Council for Cultural Relations. Available at *http://iccr.gov.in/content/constitution*.

Ikenberry, G. John (2000) *After Victory: Institutions, Strategic Restraint, and the Rebuilding of Order after Major Wars*. Princeton: Princeton University Press.

Ikenberry, G. John & Kupchan, Charles A. (1990) 'Socialization and Hegemonic Power'. *International Organization* 44(3): 283–315.

Illmer, Andreas (2016) 'China's Growth Data – Can You Trust It?' BBC News Online, 19 January. Available at *http://www.bbc.co.uk/news/business-35341869*.

IMF (2015) 'GDP Based on PPP Share of World Total (%)'. International Monetary Fund, Google Public Data. Available at *http://www.google.com/publicdata/explore?ds=k3s92bru78li6_&ctype=l&met_y=pppsh*.

IMF (2016) 'IMF Members' Quotas and Voting Power, and IMF Board of Governors'. International Monetary Fund, 16 February. Available at *https://www.imf.org/external/np/sec/memdir/members.aspx*.

India Strategic (2015) 'Text of Indo-US Defense Framework Agreement 2015'. *India Strategic*, June. Available at *http://www.indiastrategic.in/topstories 3823_Text_of_Indo_US_Defense_Framework_Agreement_2015.htm*.

Indian Express (2014) 'India, 20 Others Set up Asian Infrastructure Investment Bank'. *Indian Express*, 24 October. Available at *http://indianexpress.com/article/business/economy/india-20-others-set-up-asian-infrastructure-investment-bank/*.

IOSC (2009) 'China's National Defense in 2008'. Information Office of the State Council, Beijing, January. Available at *http://carnegieendowment.org/files/2008DefenseWhitePaper_Jan2009.pdf*.

IOSC (2013) *The Diversified Employment of China's Armed Forces*. Beijing: Information Office of the State Council. Available at *http://news.xinhuanet.com/english/china/2013-04/16/c_132312681.htm*.

Iriye, Akira (1979) 'Culture and Power: International Relations as Intercultural Relations'. *Diplomatic History* 3(2): 115–28.

Jabeen, Mussarat (2010) 'Indian Aspiration of Permanent Membership in the UN Security Council and American Stance'. *South Asian Studies* 25(2): 237–53.

Jacques, Martin (2009) *When China Rules the World: The Rise of the Middle Kingdom and the End of the Western World*. London: Penguin Books.

Jain, B.M. (2009) *Global Power: India's Foreign Policy, 1947–2006*. Lanham, MD: Lexington Books.

Jayakar, Pupul (1992) *Indira Gandhi: A Biography*. New Delhi: Viking.

Jenkins, Rob (2000) *Democratic Politics and Economic Reform in India*. Cambridge: Cambridge University Press.

Jervis, Robert (1969) 'Hypotheses on Misperception'. *World Politics* 20(3): 454–79.

Johnston, Alastair Iain (1995) 'Thinking about Strategic Culture'. *International Security* 19(4): 32–64.

Johnston, Alastair Iain (1996) 'Cultural Realism and Strategy in Maoist China', in Peter Katzenstein (ed.), *The Culture of National Security: Norms and Identity in World Politics*. New York: Columbia University Press, pp. 216–68.

Johnston, Alastair Iain (2008) *Social States: China in International Institutions, 1980–2000*. Princeton: Princeton University Press.

Johnston, Alastair Iain & Evans, Paul (1999) 'China's Engagement with Multilateral Security Institutions', in Alastair Iain Johnston & Robert S. Ross (eds), *Engaging China: The Management of an Emerging Power*. New York: Routledge, pp. 235–72.

Johnston, Alastair Iain & Ross, Robert S. (2006) *New Directions in the Study of China's Foreign Policy*. Stanford: Stanford University Press.

Johri, Devika & Miller, Mark (2002) 'Devaluation of the Rupee: Tale of Two Years, 1966 and 1991'. *Centre for Civil Society Working Paper*, 28.

Jones, Catherine (2014) 'Constructing Great Powers: China's Status in a Socially Constructed Plurality'. *International Politics* 51: 597–618.

Jones, Rodney W. (2006) *India's Strategic Culture*. Washington, DC: Defense Threat Reduction Agency.

Kamphausen, Roy D. & Liang, Justin (2007) 'PLA Power Projection: Current Realities and Emerging Trends', in Michael D. Swaine, Andrew N.D. Yang, Evan D. Medeiros & Oriana Skylar Mastro (eds), *Assessing the Threat: China's Military and Taiwan's Security*. Washington, DC: Carnegie, pp. 111–50.

Kang, David C. (2007) *China Rising: Power and Order in East Asia*. New York: Columbia University Press.

Kapur, Devesh (2009) 'Public Opinion in Indian Foreign Policy'. *India Review* 8(3): 286–305.

Katzenstein, Peter J. (1996) *Cultural Norms and National Security: Police and Military in Post-War Japan*. Ithaca, NY: Cornell University Press.

Kennedy, Paul (1988) *The Rise and Fall of the Great Powers*. London: Unwin Hyman.

Kennedy, Scott (2010) 'The Myth of the Beijing Consensus'. *Journal of Contemporary China* 19(65): 461–77.

Keohane, Robert O. & Nye, Joseph (1977) *Power and Interdependence: World Politics in Transition*. Boston: Little, Brown.

Keohane, Robert O. & Nye, Joseph S. (2008) 'Power and Interdependence in the Information Age'. *Foreign Affairs* 77(5): 81–94.

Khilnani, Sunil (1997) *The Idea of India*. London: Hamish Hamilton.

Khilnani, Sunil et al. (2012) *Nonalignment 2.0: A Foreign and Strategic Policy for India in the 21st Century*. New Delhi: Centre for Policy Research.

Kim, Samuel S. (1999) 'Introduction: China Joins the World', in Elizabeth Economy, Michael Oksenberg & Lawrence J. Korb (eds), *China Joins the World: Progress and Prospects*. New York: Council on Foreign Relations Press, pp. 42–53.

Kim, Samuel S. & Lee, T.H. (2002) 'Chinese–North Korean Relations: Managing Asymmetrical Independence', in Samuel S. Kim and T.H. Lee (eds), *North Korea and Northeast Asia*. Oxford: Rowman & Littlefield Publishers, pp. 130–45.

Kinnvall, Catarina (2002) 'Nationalism, Religion and the Search for Chosen Traumas: Comparing Sikh and Hindu Identity Constructions'. *Ethnicities* 2(1): 79–106.

Kirby, William C. (1998) 'Traditions of Centrality, Authority and Management in Modern China's Foreign Relations', in Thomas W. Robinson & David Shambaugh (eds), *Chinese Foreign Policy: Theory and Practice*. Oxford: Clarendon Press, pp. 13–29.

Kirshner, Jonathan (2010) 'The Tragedy of Offensive Realism: Classical Realism and the Rise of China'. *European Journal of International Relations* 18(1): 53–75.

Kissinger, Henry (2012) *On China*. New York: Penguin.

Kornberg, Judith F. (1996) 'Comprehensive Engagement: New Frameworks for Sino-American Relations'. *The Journal of East Asian Affairs* 10(1): 13–44.

Krasner, Stephen D. (1992) 'Realism, Imperialism and Democracy'. *Political Theory* 20(1): 38–52.

Krishna, S. (1994) 'Cartographic Anxiety: Mapping the Body Politic in India'. *Alternatives: Global, Local, Political* 19(4): 507–21.

Krishnappa, V. & George, Princy (2012) *Grand Strategy for India: 2020 and Beyond*. New Delhi: Institute for Defence Studies & Analyses.

Kristensen, Hans M. & Robert S. Norris (2015a) 'China's Nuclear Forces, 2015'. *Bulletin of the Atomic Scientists* 71(4): 77–84.

Kristensen, Hans M. & Robert S. Norris (2015b) 'Indian Nuclear Forces, 2015'. *Bulletin of the Atomic Scientists* 71(5): 77–83.

Kronstadt, K.A., Kerr, P.K., Martin, M.F. & Vaughn, B. (2011) *India: Domestic Issues, Strategic Dynamics, and US Relations*. Washington, DC: Congressional Research Service.

Kugiel, Patryk (2012) 'India's Soft Power in South Asia'. *International Studies* 49(3–4): 351–76.

Kuik, Cheng-Chwee (2005) 'Multilateralism in China's ASEAN Policy: Its Evolution, Characteristics and Aspirations'. *Contemporary Southeast Asia* 27(1): 102–22.

Ladwig, Walter C. (2009) 'Delhi's Pacific Ambition: Naval Power, "Look East" and India's Emerging Influence in the Asia-Pacific'. *Asian Security* 5(2): 87–113.

Ladwig, Walter C. (2015) 'Indian Military Modernization and Conventional Deterrence in South Asia'. *Journal of Strategic Studies* 38(5): 1–44.

Lampton, David M. (2001) *The Making of Chinese Foreign and Security Policy in the Era of Reform*. Stanford: Stanford University Press.

Lampton, David M. (2008) *The Three Faces of Chinese Power: Might, Money and Minds*. Berkeley: University of California Press.

Lansdown, Helen & Wu, Guoguang (2008) *China Turns to Multilateralism: Foreign Policy and Regional Security*. New York: Routledge.

Lanteigne, Marc (2005) *China and International Institutions: Alternate Paths to Global Power*. New York: Routledge.

Lanteigne, Marc (2007) 'The Developmentalism/Globalization Conundrum in Chinese Governance', in André Laliberté & Marc Lanteigne (eds), *The Chinese Party-State in the 21st Century: Adaptation and the Reinvention of Legitimacy*. London: Routledge, pp. 162–84.

Lanteigne, Marc (2008) 'China's Maritime Security and the "Malacca Dilemma"'. *Asian Security* 4(2): 143–61.

Lanteigne, Marc (2013) *Chinese Foreign Policy: An Introduction*. London: Routledge.

Lary, Diana (2007) 'The Uses of the Past: History and Legitimacy', in André Laliberté & Marc Lanteigne (eds), *The Chinese Party-State in the 21st Century*. London: Routledge, pp. 129–39.

Lasmar, Jorge (2012) 'Managing Great Powers in the Post-Cold War World: Old Rules New Game? The Case of the Global War on Terror'. *Cambridge Review of International Affairs* 28(3): 396–423.

Lee, Lavina Rajendram (2010) *US Hegemony and International Legitimacy: Norms, Power and Followership in the Wars on Iraq*. London: Routledge.

Lee, Pal K., Chan, Gerald & Chan, Lai-Ha (2010) 'China in Darfur: Humanitarian Rule-Maker or Rule-Taker?' *Review of International Studies* 38(2): 1–22.

Legro, Jeffrey W. (2009) 'The Plasticity of Identity under Anarchy'. *European Journal of International Relations* 15(1): 37–65.

Legro, Jeffrey W. & Moravcsik, Andrew (1999) 'Is Anybody Still a Realist?' *International Security* 24(2): 5–55.

L'Etang, Jacquie (2009) 'Public Relations and Diplomacy in a Globalized World: An Issue of Public Communication'. *American Behavioral Scientist* 53(4): 607–26.

Levy, Jack S. (1983) *War in the Modern Great Power System, 1495–1975*. Lexington: University Press of Kentucky.

Levy, Jack S. (1994) 'Learning and Foreign Policy: Sweeping a Conceptual Minefield'. *International Organization* 48(2): 279–312.

Lewis, John Wilson (1963) *Leadership in Communist China*. Ithaca, NY: Cornell University Press.

Li, Xiaoting (2013) 'The Taming of The Red Dragon: The Militarized Worldview and China's Use of Force, 1949–2001'. *Foreign Policy Analysis* 9(4): 387–407.

Lieberthal, Kenneth (2004) *Governing China: Revolution through Reform*. London: W.W. Norton & Co.

Lieberthal, Kenneth & Wang Jisi (2012) 'Addressing US–China Strategic Distrust'. *John L. Thornton China Center Monograph Series* 4, March.

Lindsay, Jon (2014/15) 'The Impact of China on Cybersecurity: Fiction and Friction'. *International Security* 39(3): 7–47.

Luttwak, Edward N. (1996) 'Where Are the Great Powers? At Home with the Kids'. *Foreign Affairs* (July/August): 23–8.

McKirdy, Euan (2015) 'China's Online Users More Than Double Entire US Population'. CNN, 4 February. Available at *http://edition.cnn.com/2015/02/03/world/china-internet-growth-2014/index.html*.

McSpadden, Kevin (2015) 'China Has Become the World's Biggest Crude Oil Importer for the First Time,' *Time*, 11 May. Available at *http://time.com/3853451/china-crude-oil-top-importer/*.

Maddison Project (2013). Available at *http://www.ggdc.net/maddison/maddison-project/home.htm*.

Maddison, Angus (2003) *The World Economy: Historical Statistics*. Paris: OECD Publishing.

Mahnken, Thomas G. (2011) *Secrecy and Stratagem: Understanding Chinese Strategic Culture*. Sydney: Lowy Institute for International Peace.

Malone, David M. (2012) *Does the Elephant Dance? Contemporary Indian Foreign Policy*. Oxford: Oxford University Press.

Mao Zedong (1998) *On Diplomacy*. Beijing: Foreign Language Press.

MarEx (2014) 'India's Oil Supply and Demand Gap Widening'. Maritime Executive, 1 July. Available at *http://www.maritime-executive.com/article/Indias-Oil-Supply-and-Demand-Gap-Widening-2014-07-01*.

Markey, Daniel (2009) 'Developing India's Foreign Policy "Software"'. *Asia Policy* 8: 73–96.

MEA (2012) 'Fourth BRICS Summit – Delhi Declaration'. Ministry of External Affairs, 29 March. Available at *http://mea.gov.in/bilateral-documents.htm?dtl/19158/Fourth+BRICS+Summit++Delhi+Declaration*.

Mearsheimer, John J. (2001) *The Tragedy of Great Power Politics*. New York: W.W. Norton & Co.

Menon, Raja & Kumar, Rajiv (2010) *The Long View from Delhi: To Define the Indian Grand Strategy for Foreign Policy*. New Delhi: Academic Foundation.

Meredith, Robyn (2007) *The Elephant and the Dragon: The Rise of India and China*. London: Norton & Co.

Military Balance (2016) 'Chapter Two: Comparative Defence Statistics'. *The Military Balance* 116(1): 19–26.

Miller, Manjari Chatterjee (2013) 'India's Feeble Foreign Policy: A Would-Be Great Power Resists Its Own Rise'. *Foreign Affairs* 92(3): 14–19.

Mishra, Bhabani (2005) 'India–US Relations: A Paradigm Shift'. *Strategic Analysis* 29(1): 79–100.

Mishra, Vivek (2014) 'Indo-US Relations: After Narendra Modi's Visit'. *Institute of Peace and Conflict Studies Issue Brief* 257 (November).

Mochizuki, Mike M. (2007) 'Japan's Shifting Strategy toward the Rise of China'. *Journal of Strategic Studies* 30(4–5): 739–76.

Modelski, George (1972) *Principles of World Politics*. New York: Free Press.

Modelski, George (1974) *World Power Concentrations: Typology, Data, Explanatory Framework*. Morristown, NJ: General Learning Press.

MoHA (2016) 'Banned Organisations'. Ministry of Home Affairs, Government of India. Available at *http://mha.nic.in/BO*.

Mohan, C. Raja (2004) *Crossing the Rubicon: The Shaping of India's New Foreign Policy*. New York: Palgrave Macmillan.

Mohan, C. Raja (2006) 'India and the Balance of Power'. *Foreign Affairs* 85(4): 17–32.

Mohan, C. Raja (2008) 'India's Quest for Continuity in the Face of Change'. *The Washington Quarterly* 31(4): 143–53.

Mohan, C. Raja (2013) 'Uncertain Trumpet? India's Role in Southeast Asian Security'. *India Review* 12(3): 134–50.

Moore, Gregory J. (2010) 'Less Beautiful, Still Somewhat Imperialist: Beijing Eyes Sino-US Relations', in Shaun Breslin (ed.), *Handbook of China's International Relations*. London: Routledge, pp. 129–37.

Morgenthau, Hans (1973) *Politics among Nations: The Struggles for Power and Peace*. Boston: McGraw-Hill.

Morrison, Michael (2012) 'China's Foreign Policy Research Institutes: Influence on Decision-Making and the Fifth Generation Communist Party Leadership'. *Yale Journal of International Affairs* 7(2): 77–86.

Morrison, Wayne M. (2015) *China's Economic Rise: History, Trends, Challenges, and Implications for the United States*. Washington, DC: Congressional Research Service.

Mukherjee, Pranab (2007) 'Aerospace Power in Tomorrow's World'. Embassy of India, Washington. Available at *https://www.indianembassy.org/archives_ details.php?nid=928*.

Muni, S.D. & Mohan, C. Raja (2004) 'Emerging Asia: India's Options'. *International Studies* 41(3): 313–33.

Narang, Vipin & Staniland, Paul (2012) 'Institutions and Worldviews in Indian Foreign Security Policy'. *India Review* 11(2): 76–94.

Narlikar, Amrita (2006) 'Peculiar Chauvinism or Strategic Calculation? Explaining the Negotiating Strategy of a Rising India'. *International Affairs* 82(1): 59–76.

Narlikar, Amrita (2007) 'All That Glitters Is Not Gold: India's Rise to Power'. *Third World Quarterly* 28(5): 983–96.

Nathan, Andrew & Ross, Robert J. (1997) *The Great Wall and the Empty Fortress: China's Search for Security*. London: W.W. Norton.

Nayar, Baldev Raj & Paul, T.V. (2003) *India in the World Order: Searching for Major-Power Status*. Cambridge: Cambridge University Press.

Nehru, Jawaharlal (1946) *The Discovery of India*. New York: John Day.

Nehru, Jawaharlal (1961) *'We Lead Ourselves': India's Foreign Policy, Selected Speeches of Jawaharlal Nehru, September 1946–April 1961*. Delhi: Publications Division, Ministry of Information and Broadcasting.

Nehru, Jawaharlal (1963) 'Changing India'. *Foreign Affairs* 41(3): 453–65.

Nehru, Jawaharlal (2007) 'A Tryst with Destiny – Great Speeches of the 20th Century'. *Guardian*, 1 May. Available at *http://www.theguardian.com/ theguardian/2007/may/01/greatspeeches*.

Nixon, Richard (1967) 'Asia after Viet Nam'. *Foreign Affairs* 46(1): 111–25.

Noronha, Ligia & Sudarshan, Anant (2011) 'Contextualizing India's Energy Security', in Ligia Noronha & Anant Sudarshan (eds), *India's Energy Security*. London: Routledge, pp. 3–18.

Nye, Joseph S. (1990) 'Soft Power'. *Foreign Policy* 80: 153–71.

Nye, Joseph S. (2004) *Soft Power: The Means to Success in World Politics*. New York: Public Affairs.

Ogden, Chris (2013) 'A Normalized Dragon: Constructing China's Security Identity'. *Pacific Focus* 28(2): 243–68.

Ogden, Chris (2014a) *Hindu Nationalism and the Evolution of Contemporary Indian Security: Portents of Power*. New Delhi: Oxford University Press.

Ogden, Chris (2014b) *Indian Foreign Policy: Ambition and Transition*. Cambridge: Polity.

Ollapally, Deepa & Rajagopalan, Rajesh (2013) 'India: Foreign Policy Perspectives of an Ambiguous Power', in Henry R. Nau & Deepa Ollapally (eds), *Worldviews of Aspiring Powers: Domestic Foreign Policy Debates in China, India, Iran, Japan and Russia*. Oxford: Oxford University Press, pp. 73–113.

Onuf, Nicholas (1998) 'Constructivism: A User's Manual', in Vendulka Kubálková, Nicholas Onuf & Paul Kowert (eds), *International Relations in a Constructed World*. London: M.E. Sharpe, pp. 58–78.

Organski, Abramo F.K. & Kugler, Jack (1980) *The War Ledger*. Chicago: University of Chicago Press.

OUSTP (2016a) 'US–China Bilateral Trade and Investment'. Office of the United States Trade Representative. Available at *http://ustr.gov/countries-regions/china-mongolia-taiwan/peoples-republic-china*.

OUSTP (2016b) 'US–India Bilateral Trade and Investment'. Office of the United States Trade Representative. Available at *http://www.ustr.gov/countries-regions/south-central-asia/india*.

Pan, Zhenqiang (2010) 'China's Nuclear Strategy in a Changing World Strategic Situation', in Barry M. Blechman and Alex K. Bollfrass (eds), *National Perspectives on Nuclear Disarmament: Unblocking the Road to Zero*. Washington, DC: The Stimson Center, pp. 121–45.

Panagariya, Arvind (2004) 'India in the 1980s and 1990s: A Triumph of Reforms'. *IMF Working Papers* 4(43): 1–37.

Panagariya, Arvind (2008) *India: The Emerging Giant*. New York: Oxford University Press.

Panda, Rajaram (2012) 'Japan and China: Negotiating a Perilous Course'. *India Quarterly: A Journal of International Affairs* 68(2): 135–54.

Pant, Harsh V. (2009a) 'Indian Foreign Policy Challenges: Substantive Uncertainties and Institutional Infirmities'. *Asian Affairs* 40(1): 90–101.

Pant, Harsh V. (2009b) 'The US–India Nuclear Pact: Policy, Process, and Great Power Politics'. *Asian Security* 5(3): 273–95.

Pant, Harsh V. (2011a) 'India's Relations with China', in David Scott (ed.), *Handbook of India's International Relations*. London: Routledge, pp. 233–42.

Pant, Harsh V. (2011b) 'India's Strategic Culture: The Debate and Its Consequences', in David Scott (ed.), *Handbook of India's International Relations*. London: Routledge, pp. 14–22.

Pant, Harsh V. (2012) 'Great Power Politics in East Asia: The US and China Competition'. *China Report* 48(3): 237–51.

Pant, Harsh V. (2013) 'India–Russia Ties and India's Strategic Culture: Dominance of a Realist Worldview'. *India Review* 12(1): 1–19.

Payne, Anthony (1994) 'Hegemony and the Reconfiguration of the Caribbean'. *Review of International Studies* 20(2): 149–68.

Peng Guangqian & Yao Youzhi (2005) 'Determinants of Strategy', in Peng Guangqian & Yao Youzhi (eds), *The Science of Military Strategy*. Beijing: Military Science Publishing House, pp. 29–45.

Perkovich, George (2004) 'Is India a Major Power?' *The Washington Quarterly* 27(1): 129–44.

Pham, J. Peter (2007) 'India's Expanding Relations with Africa and Their Implications for US Interests'. *American Foreign Policy Interests* 29: 341–52.

Phillips, Tom (2015) '"Old-School Tub-Thumping": 12,000 Chinese Troops Prepare for WW2 Parade'. *Guardian*, 15 August. Available at *http://www.thegu ardian.com/world/2015/aug/21/chinese-second-world-war-parade-xi-jinping,*.

Phukan, Sandeep (2015) 'Here's How Manmohan Singh Will Renew His Congress Membership Today'. NDTV, 30 March. Available at *http://www. ndtv.com/india-news/heres-how-manmohan-singh-will-renew-his-congress- membership-tomorrow-750585*.

Piao, Lin (2005) *Quotations from Chairman Mao Tse-Tung*. Sacramento: University Press of the Pacific.

Pillai, Mohanan B. & Premashekhara, L. (2010) *Foreign Policy of India: Continuity and Change*. New Delhi: New Century Publications.

Pocha, Jehangir (2003) 'The Rising "Soft Power" of India and China'. *NPQ*, Winter. Available at *http://www.digitalnpq.org/archive/2003_winter/pocha. html*.

Power, Paul F. (1964) 'Indian Foreign Policy: The Age of Nehru'. *The Review of Politics* 26(2): 257–86.

Prys, Miriam (2008) 'Developing a Contextually Relevant Concept of Regional Hegemony: The Case of South Africa, Zimbabwe and "Quiet Diplomacy"'. *GIGA Research Programme* 77.

Prys, Miriam (2013) 'India and South Asia in the World: On Embeddedness of Regions in the International System and Its Consequences for Regional Powers'. *International Relations of the Asia-Pacific* 13(2): 267–99.

Qiao, Guangyu (2014) 'Competition Gives Way to Cooperation: Rethinking Sino-Indian Relations in Climate Change Negotiations'. *Chinese Journal of Population Resources and Environment* 12(4): 324–29.

Qin, Y. (2007) 'Why is There No Chinese International Relations Theory?' *International Relations of the Asia-Pacific* 7(3): 313–40.

Ralhan, O.P. (1983) *Jawaharlal Nehru Abroad: A Chronological Study*. Delhi: S.S. Publishers.

Ramachandran, Sudha (2013) 'The Indian Foreign Service: Worthy of an Emerging Power?' *The Diplomat*, July: 1–3.

Rao, Nirupama (2010) 'Address by Foreign Secretary on Inaugural Session of Conference on Public Diplomacy in the Information Age'. Ministry of External Affairs, 10 December. Available at *http://www.mea.gov.in/Speeches- Statements.htm?dtl/844/*.

Reed, Ananya Mukherjee (1997) 'Regionalization in South Asia: Theory and Praxis'. *Pacific Affairs* 70(2): 235–51.

Reny, Marie-Eve & William Hurst (2013) 'Social Unrest', in Chris Ogden (ed.), *Handbook of China's Governance and Domestic Politics*. London: Routledge, pp. 210–20.

Ringmar, Erik (2002) 'The Recognition Game: Soviet Russia Against the West'. *Cooperation and Conflict* 37(2): 115–36.

Roberts, Brad, Manning, Robert A. & Montaperto, Ronald N. (2000) 'China: The Forgotten Nuclear Power'. *Foreign Affairs* 79(4): 53–63.

Roberts, Dexter (2013) 'China's State Press Calls for "Building a De- Americanized World"'. *Bloomberg BusinessWeek*, October. Available at *http:// www.businessweek.com/articles/2013-10-14/chinas-state-press-calls-for-buil ding-a-de-americanized-world*.

Robinson, Thomas W. & Shambaugh, David (eds) (2004) *Chinese Foreign Policy: Theory and Practice*. Oxford: Clarendon Press.

Rose, Charlie (2006) 'Charlie Rose Interviews Indian PM Manmohan Singh'. Council on Foreign Relations, 16 February.

Ross, Madelyn C. (1998) 'China's International Economic Behaviour', in Thomas W. Robinson & David Shambaugh (eds), *Chinese Foreign Policy: Theory and Practice*. Oxford: Clarendon Press, pp. 435–52.

Rothstein, Robert (1968) *Alliances and Small Powers*. New York: Columbia University Press.

Roy, Denny (1996) 'The "China Threat" Issue: Major Arguments'. *Asian Survey* 36(8): 758–71.

Roy, Denny (1998) *China's Foreign Relations*. London: Macmillan.

Ruggie, John Gerard (1993) 'Multilateralism: The Anatomy of an Institution', in John Gerard Ruggie (ed.), *Multilateralism Matters: The Theory and Praxis of an Institutional Form*. New York: Columbia University Press, pp. 3–47.

Ruggie, John Gerard (1998) 'What Makes the World Hang Together? Neo-Utilitarianism, and the Social Constructivist Challenge'. *International Organization* 52(4): 855–86.

Sahni, Varun (2007) 'India's Foreign Policy: Key Drivers'. *South African Journal of International Affairs* 14(2): 21–35.

Saksena, K.P. (1996) 'India's Foreign Policy: The Decisionmaking Process'. *International Studies* 33(4): 391–405.

Sarkees, M.R. & Wayman, Frank (2010) *Resort to War: 1816–2007*. Washington, DC: CQ Press.

SATP (2016a) 'Fatalities in Left-Wing Extremism: 2005–2016'. South Asia Terrorism Portal. Available at *http://www.satp.org/satporgtp/countries/india/maoist/data_sheets/fatalitiesnaxal05-11.htm*.

SATP (2016b) 'Indian Fatalities 1994–2016'. South Asia Terrorism Portal. Available at *http://www.satp.org/satporgtp/countries/india/database/indiafatalities.htm*.

SATP (2016c) 'India – Terrorist, Insurgent and Extremist Groups'. South Asia Terrorism Portal. Available at *http://www.satp.org/satporgtp/countries/india/terroristoutfits/index.html*.

Schoeman, M. (2007) 'China in Africa: The Rise of Hegemony?' *Strategic Review for Southern Africa* 29(2): 74–97.

Scott, David (2007) *China Stands Up: The PRC and the International System*. New York: Routledge.

Scott, David (2008) 'The Great Power "Great Game" between India and China: The "Logic of Geography"'. *Geopolitics* 13(1): 1–26.

Scott, David (2011) 'India and Regional Integration', in David Scott (ed.), *Handbook of India's International Relations*. London: Routledge, pp. 118–27.

Scott, James & Wilkinson, Rorden (2011) 'China and the WTO.' *Indiana University Research Center for Chinese Politics and Business Working Paper* 5: 1–26.

Shah, M.A. Zafar (1983) *India and the Superpowers: India's Political Relations with the Superpowers in the 1970s*. Dhaka: Dhaka University Press.

Shambaugh, David (2002) *Modernizing China's Military: Progress, Problems and Prospects*. Berkeley: University of California Press.

Shambaugh, David (2004) 'China Engages Asia: Reshaping the Regional Order'. *International Security* 29(3): 64–99.

Shambaugh, David (2009) 'The Evolving Security Order in Asia: Implications for US–India Relations', in Alyssa Ayres & C. Raja Mohan (eds), *Power Realignments in Asia: China, India, and the United States*. London: Sage Publications, pp. 137–47.

Shen, Simon (2004) 'Nationalism or Nationalist Foreign Policy? Chinese Nationalism and Its Role in Shaping Chinese Foreign Policy in Response to the Belgrade Embassy Bombing'. *Politics* 24(2): 122–30.

Shen, Wei (2008) 'In The Mood For Multilateralism? China's Evolving Worldview'. Centre Asie IFRI, Working Paper.

Shepperd, Taryn (2013) *Sino-US Relations and the Role of Emotion in State Action*. London: Palgrave Macmillan.

Shih, Chih-yu (2005) 'Breeding a Reluctant Dragon: Can China Rise into Partnership and Away from Antagonism?' *Review of International Studies* 31(4): 755–74.

Shirk, Susan (1993) *The Political Logic of Economic Reform in China*. Berkeley: University of California Press.

Shirk, Susan (2007) *China: Fragile Superpower*. Oxford: Oxford University Press.

Shukla, Saurabh (2006) 'Soft Power'. *India Today*, 30 October: 24–5.

Singer, J. David & Small, Melvin (1972) *The Wages of War, 1816–1965: A Statistical Handbook*. New York: John Wiley & Sons.

Singh, Jaswant (2000) 'Interview: Diplomat Minister'. *The Times of India*, 24 July.

Singh, Manmohan (1991) 'Budget 1991–92 Speech of Shri Manmohan Singh, Minister of Finance'. Ministry of Finance (Union Budget), 24 July. Available at *http://indiabudget.nic.in/bspeech/bs199192.pdf*.

Singh, Neha (2015) 'India, US Announce Civil Nuclear Deal during Joint Press Conference by Obama, Modi'. *International Business Times*, 25 January.

Singh, Sandeep (2014) 'From a Sub-Continental Power to an Asia-Pacific Player: India's Changing Identity'. *India Review* 13(3): 187–211.

Sinha, Radha (2003) *Sino-American Relations: Mutual Paranoia*. New York: Palgrave Macmillan.

SIPRI (2016a) 'SIPRI Arms Transfers Database'. Stockholm International Peace Research Institute. Available at *http://www.sipri.org/databases/armstransfers*.

SIPRI (2016b) 'SIPRI Military Expenditure Database'. Stockholm International Peace Research Institute. Available at *http://www.sipri.org/research/armaments/milex/milex_database*.

Snyder, Jack (1977) *The Soviet Strategic Culture: Implications for Limited Nuclear Operations*. Washington, DC: Defense Technical Information Center.

Sohn, Injoo (2012) 'After Renaissance: China's Multilateral Offensive in the Developing World'. *European Journal of International Relations* 18(1): 77–101.

Srinivasan, T.N. & Tendulkar, Suresh D. (2003) *Reintegrating India with the World Economy*. Washington, DC: Institute for International Economics.

Srivastava, Moulishree (2015) 'Mobile Internet Users in India to Double by 2017, Says Study'. *Live Mint*, 20 July. Available at *http://www.livemint.com/Industry/VThUq5I4BivpTDZdQb5sNN/Mobile-Internet-users-in-India-to-double-by-2017-says-study.html*.

Srivastava, Renu (1995) *India and the Nonaligned Summits: Belgrade to Jakarta*. New Delhi: Northern Rock Centre.

Steans, Jill & Pettiford, Lloyd (2001) *International Relations: Perspectives and Themes*. Harlow: Pearson Education.

Strange, Susan (1987) 'The Persistent Myth of Lost Hegemony'. *International Organization* 41(4): 551–74.

Sun, Jiazheng (2004) 'Culture Minister on China's Foreign Exchange'. *People's Daily*, 21 December. Available at *http://en.people.cn/200412/21/print20041221_168135.html*.

Suzuki, Shogo (2008) 'Seeking "Legitimate" Great Power Status in Post-Cold War International Society: China's and Japan's Participation in UNPKO'. *International Relations* 22(45): 45–63.

Suzuki, Shogo (2014) 'Journey to the West: China Debates Its "Great Power" Identity'. *Millennium – Journal of International Studies* 42: 632–50.

Swaine, Michael D. (2005) 'China's Regional Military Posture', in David Shambaugh (ed.), *Power Shift: China and Asia's New Dynamics*. Berkeley: University of California Press, pp. 23–47.

Swaine, Michael D. & Tellis, Ashley J. (2000) *Interpreting China's Grand Strategy: Past, Present, and Future*. Santa Monica: RAND.

Tanham, George K. (1992) 'Indian Strategic Culture'. *The Washington Quarterly* 15(1): 129–42.

Tanner, Murray Scot (2013) 'Internal Security', in Chris Ogden (ed.), *Handbook of China's Governance and Domestic Politics*. London: Routledge, pp. 88–96.

Taylor, A.J.P. (1952) *Rumours of Wars*. London: Hamish Hamilton.

Taylor, Ian (2012) 'India's Rise in Africa'. *International Affairs* 88(4): 779–98.

Thakur, Ramesh (1997) 'India in the World: Neither Rich, Powerful, nor Principled'. *Foreign Affairs* 76(4): 15–22.

Tharoor, Shashi (2012) *Pax Indica: India and the World of the 21st Century*. New Delhi: Allen Lane.

Thottam, Jyoti (2010) 'India's Scourge'. *TIME Magazine*, 24 October.

TI (2014) '2014 Corruption Perceptions Index'. Transparency International. Available at *http://www.transparency.org/cpi2014*.

Times of India (2015) 'India Has Right to Demand Permanent Seat in UN Security Council: Narendra Modi'. *Times of India*, 11 April. Available at *http://timesofindia.indiatimes.com/india/India-has-right-to-demand-permanent-seat-in-UN-security-council-Narendra-Modi/articleshow/46891874.cms*.

TPF (1978) 'Treaty of Peace and Friendship between Japan and the People's Republic of China, Article 2'. Taiwan Documents. Available at *http://www.taiwandocuments.org/beijing.htm*.

TRAI (2014) 'Highlights of Telecom Subscription Data'. Telecom Regulatory Authority of India, 30 September. Available at *http://www.trai.gov.in/WriteReadData/WhatsNew/Documents/PR-TSD-Sep-14.pdf*.

Twomey, Christopher (2008) 'Explaining Chinese Foreign Policy toward North Korea: Navigating between the Scylla and Charybdis of Proliferation and Instability'. *Journal of Contemporary China* 17(56): 401–23.

UN (2015) '2015 Revision of World Population Prospects'. United Nations Department of Economic and Social Affairs Working Paper ESA/P/WP.241. Available at *http://esa.un.org/unpd/wpp/Publications/Files/Key_Findings_WPP_2015.pdf*.

UN (2016a) 'Fatalities by Nationality and Mission'. United Nations Peacekeeping, 31 May. Available at *http://www.un.org/en/peacekeeping/fatalities/documents/stats_2.pdf*.

UN (2016b) 'Ranking of Military and Police Contributions to UN Operations'. United Nations, 30 June. Available at *http://www.un.org/en/peacekeeping/contributors/2016/jun16_1.pdf.*

UN (2016c) 'Security Council – Veto List'. United Nations Dag Hammarskjöld Library. Available at *http://research.un.org/en/docs/sc/quick/veto.*

UNCTAD (2016) 'Inward and Outward Foreign Direct Investment Flows, Annual, 1970–2014'. United Nations Conference on Trade and Development. Available at *http://unctadstat.unctad.org/wds/.*

US Census Board (2016a) 'Trade in Goods with China'. US Census Board. Available at *https://www.census.gov/foreign-trade/balance/c5700.html.*

US Census Board (2016b) 'Trade in Goods with India'. US Census Board. Available at *http://www.census.gov/foreign-trade/balance/c5330.html.*

USDT (2016) 'Major Foreign Holders of Treasury Securities'. United States Department of the Treasury. Available at *http://ticdata.treasury.gov/Publish/mfh.txt.*

USEIA (2013) 'Country Analysis: China'. US Energy Information Administration, Washington, DC. Available at *http://www.eia.gov/countries/country-data.cfm?fips=ch#pet.*

USEIA (2016a) 'China – International Energy Data and Analysis'. US Energy Information Administration, Washington, DC. Available at *http://www.eia.gov/beta/international/analysis.cfm?iso=CHN.*

USEIA (2016b) 'India – International Energy Data and Analysis'. US Energy Information Administration, Washington, DC. Available at *http://www.eia.gov/beta/international/analysis.cfm?iso=IND.*

Uz Zaman, R. (2006) 'Kautilya: The Indian Strategic Thinker and Indian Strategic Culture'. *Comparative Strategy* 25(3): 231–47.

Varkey, K.T. (2002) *Krishna Menon and India's Foreign Policy.* New Delhi: Indian Publishers Distributors.

Vezirgiannidou, Sevasti-Eleni (2013) 'The United States and Rising Powers in a Post-Hegemonic Global Order'. *International Affairs* 89(3): 635–51.

Volodzko, David (2015) 'China's Confucius Institutes and the Soft War'. *The Diplomat*, 8 July. Available at *http://thediplomat.com/2015/07/chinas-confucius-institutes-and-the-soft-war/.*

Wadha, Anil (2015) 'Keynote address by Secretary (East) on "ASEAN-India Cultural Links: Historical and Contemporary Dimensions"'. Ministry of External Affairs, 23 July. Available at *http://mea.gov.in/aseanindia/Speeches-Statements.htm?dtl/22588/.*

Wagner, Christian (2005) 'From Hard Power to Soft Power? Ideas, Interactions, Institutions, and Images in India's South Asia Policy'. *Heidelberg Papers in South Asian and Comparative Politics Working Paper* 26: 1–16.

Walker, William (1998) 'International Nuclear Relations after Indian and Pakistani Test Explosions'. *International Affairs* 74(3): 505–28.

Walt, Stephen M. (1990) *The Origins of Alliances.* Ithaca, NY: Cornell University Press.

Walton, C. Dale (2012) *Grand Strategy and the Presidency: Foreign Policy, War and the American Role in the World.* London: Routledge.

Waltz, Kenneth (1959) *Man, the State and War: A Theoretical Analysis.* New York: Columbia University Press.

Waltz, Kenneth (1979) *Theories of International Politics.* Reading, MA: Addison-Wesley Publishing Company.

Waltz, Kenneth (1981) 'The Spread of Nuclear Weapons: More May Be Better'. *Adelphi Papers* 171.

Waltz, Kenneth (2000) 'Structural Realism after the Cold War'. *International Security* 25(1): 5–41.

Wang, Hongying (2000) 'Multilateralism in Chinese Foreign Policy: The Limits of Socialization'. *Asian Survey* 40(3): 475–91.

Wang, Hongying (2015) 'The Asian Infrastructure Investment Bank: A New Bretton Woods Moment? A Total Chinese Triumph?' *Centre for International Governance Innovation Policy Brief 59.*

Wang, Jianwei (2005) 'China's Multilateral Diplomacy in the New Millennium', in Yong Deng & Fei-Ling Wang (eds), *China Rising: Power and Motivation in Chinese Foreign Policy*. Lanham, MD: Rowman & Littlefield Publishers, pp. 159–200.

Wang Jisi (2011) 'China's Search for a Grand Strategy – A Rising Great Power Finds Its Way'. *Foreign Affairs* 90(2): 68–79.

Wang, Yi (2013) 'Embark on a New Journey of China's Diplomacy'. Foreign Ministry of the PRC, 16 December. Available at *http://www.fmprc.gov.cn/mfa_eng/wjb_663304/wjbz_663308/2461_663310/t1109943.shtml.*

Wendt, Alexander (1992) 'Anarchy is What States Make of It: The Social Construction of Power Politics'. *International Organisation* 46(2): 391–425.

Wendt, Alexander (1995) 'Constructing International Politics'. *International Security* 20(1): 71–81.

Wendt, Alexander (1999) *Social Theory of International Politics*. Cambridge: Cambridge University Press.

White House (2010) 'Remarks by the President to the Joint Session of the Indian Parliament in New Delhi, India'. The White House Office of the Press Secretary, 8 November. Available at *http://www.whitehouse.gov/the-press-office/2010/11/08/remarks-president-joint-session-indian-parliament-new-delhi-india.*

White House (2013) 'Remarks by President Obama and President Xi Jinping of the People's Republic of China before Bilateral Meeting'. The White House. Available at *http://www.whitehouse.gov/the-press-office/2013/06/07/remarks-president-obama-and-president-xi-jinping-peoples-republic-china-.*

Whiting, Allen S. (1995) 'Chinese Nationalism and Foreign Policy after Deng'. *The China Quarterly* 142: 295–316.

Wight, Martin (1979) *Power Politics*. London: Pelican Books.

Williams, Michael (2005) *The Realist Tradition and the Limits of International Relations*. Cambridge: Cambridge University Press.

Wolpert, Stanley (1996) *Nehru: A Tryst with Destiny*. Oxford: Oxford University Press.

Womack, Brantley (2013) 'Beyond Win-Win: Rethinking China's International Relationships in an Era of Economic Uncertainty'. *International Affairs* 89(4): 911–28.

World Bank (2016a) 'Foreign Direct Investment, Net Inflows (BoP, current US$)'. World Bank Data. Available at *http://databank.worldbank.org/data/.*

World Bank (2016b) 'GDP (Current US$)'. World Bank Data. Available at http://databank.worldbank.org/data/.

World Bank (2016c) 'GDP Growth (Annual %)'. World Bank Data. Available at *http://databank.worldbank.org/data/.*

World Bank (2016d) 'GDP Per Capita (Current US$)'. World Bank Data. Available at *http://databank.worldbank.org/data/.*

World Bank (2016e) 'IBRD Voting Shares'. The World Bank, 16 February. Available at *https://finances.worldbank.org/Shareholder-Equity/IBRD-Voting-Shares-Column-Chart/wf2k-zkn9*.

World Bank (2016f) 'Life Expectancy at Birth, Total (Years)'. World Bank Data. Available at *http://databank.worldbank.org/data/*.

World Bank (2016g) 'Poverty Headcount Ratio at $1.90 a Day (2011 PPP) (% of Population)'. World Bank Data. Available at *http://databank.worldbank.org/data/*.

WTO (2001) 'WTO Successfully Concludes Negotiations on China's Entry'. World Trade Organization, 17 September. Available at *https://www.wto.org/english/news_e/pres01_e/pr243_e.htm*.

WTO (2003) *World Trade Report 2003: Trade and Development*. Washington, DC: World Trade Organization.

Wu, Baiyi (2001) 'The Chinese Security Concept and its Historical Evolution'. *Journal of Contemporary China* 10(27): 275–83.

Wu, Xinbo (1998) 'China: Security Practice of a Modernizing and Ascending Power', in Muthiah Alagappa (ed.), *Asian Security Practice: Material and Ideational Influences*. Stanford: Stanford University Press, pp. 115–56.

Wu, Xinbo (2010) 'Understanding the Geopolitical Implications of the Global Financial Crisis'. *The Washington Quarterly* 33(4): 155–63.

Wulbers, Shazia Aziz (2011) *The Paradox of EU–India Relations: Missed Opportunities in Politics, Economics, Development Cooperation and Culture*. Lanham, MD: Lexington Books.

Wyatt, Andrew (2005) '(Re)imagining the Indian (Inter)national Economy'. *New Political Economy* 10(2): 163–79.

Xi Jinping (2012) 'Transcript: Xi Jinping's Speech at the Unveiling of the New Chinese Leadership'. *South China Morning Post*, 15 December. Available at *http://www.scmp.com/news/18th-party-congress/article/1083153/transcript-xi-jinpings-speech-unveiling-new-chinese*.

Xi Jinping (2014a) 'Address (Central Conference on Work Relating to Foreign Affairs)'. Foreign Ministry of the PRC, 29 November. Available at *http://www.fmprc.gov.cn/mfa_eng/zxxx_662805/t1215680.shtml*.

Xi Jinping (2014b) 'Carry Forward the Five Principles of Peaceful Coexistence to Build a Better World through Win-Win Cooperation'. Meeting Marking the 60th Anniversary of the Initiation of the Five Principles of Peaceful Coexistence, 28 June. Beijing: Foreign Ministry of PRC. Available at *http://www.fmprc.gov.cn/mfa_eng/zxxx_662805/t1170143.shtml*.

Xiang, Lanxin (2012) 'The Bo Xilai Affair and China's Future', *Survival* 54(3): 59–68.

Xinhua (2009) 'China, US to Build Positive, Cooperative and Comprehensive Relationship in 21st Century'. *Xinhua*, 2 April. Available at *http://news.xinhuanet.com/english/2009-04/02/content_11116139.htm*.

Xinhua (2013) 'Public Diplomacy Adds Soft Touch for China'. *Xinhua*, 29 March. Available at *http://news.xinhuanet.com/english/china/2013-03/29/c_132272053.htm*.

Yee, Herbert & Feng, Zhu (2002) 'Chinese Perspectives of the China Threat: Myth or Reality?' in Herbert Yee & Ian Storey (eds), *The China Threat: Perceptions, Myths, and Reality*. London: RoutledgeCurzon, pp. 21–42.

Yong, Deng (2008) *China's Struggle for Status: The Realignment of International Relations*. New York: Cambridge University Press.

Yu, Bin (1999) 'China and Its Asian Neighbours: Implications for Sino-US Relations', in Yong Deng & Fei-Ling Wang (eds), *In the Eyes of the Dragon: China Views the World*. Lanham, MD: Rowman & Littlefield Publishers, pp. 183–210.

Yuan, Jing-Dong (2010) 'China's Role in Establishing and Building the Shanghai Cooperation Organization (SCO)'. *Journal of Contemporary China*, 19(67): 855–69.

Yuan, Jing-Dong (2013) 'Defence and Foreign Policy', in Chris Ogden (ed.), *Handbook of China's Governance and Domestic Politics*. London: Routledge, pp. 97–106.

Yunling, Zhang & Tang Shiping (2005) 'China's Regional Strategy', in David Shambaugh (ed.), *Power Shift: China and Asia's New Dynamics*. Berkeley: University of California Press, pp. 48–70.

Zakaria, Fareed (2009) 'Interview with Manmohan Singh'. CNN Transcripts, 22 November.

Zhao, Hong (2007) 'India and China: Rivals or Partners in Southeast Asia?' *Contemporary Southeast Asia* 29(1): 121–42.

Zhao, Hong (2012) *China and India: The Quest for Energy Resources in the Twenty-First Century*. London: Routledge.

Zhao, Suisheng (2004) *Chinese Foreign Policy: Pragmatism and Strategic Behavior*. Armonk, NY: M.E. Sharpe.

Zheng Bijian (2004) 'China's Peaceful Rise and Opportunities for the Asia-Pacific Region'. Roundtable Meeting between the Bo'ao Forum for Asia and the China Reform Forum, 18 April.

Zoellick, Robert B. (2005) 'Whither China: From Membership to Responsibility? Remarks to the National Committee on US–China Relations'. *NBR Analysis* 16(4): 5–14.

INDEX